T0305148

Who Runs Japanese Business?

Who Runs Japanese Business?

Management and Motivation in the Firm

Edited by
Toshiaki Tachibanaki

Professor of Economics, Kyoto Institute of Economic
Research, Kyoto University, Japan

IN ASSOCIATION WITH THE RESEARCH INSTITUTE FOR
ADVANCEMENT FOR LIVING STANDARDS (RIALS)

Edward Elgar
Cheltenham, UK • Northampton, MA, USA

Published by
Edward Elgar Publishing Limited
Glensanda House
Montpellier Parade
Cheltenham
Glos GL5O 1UA
UK

Edward Elgar Publishing, Inc.
6 Market Street
Northampton
Massachusetts 01060
USA

A catalogue record for this book
is available from the British Library

Library of Congress Cataloguing-in-Publication Data

Who runs Japanese business? : management and motivation in the firm/
    edited by Toshiaki Tachibanaki.
        'In association with the Research Institute for Advancement for
    Living Standards (RIALS).'
        Includes bibliographical references.
        1. Industrial management — Japan. 2. Employee motivation — Japan.
    3. Executives — Japan — Attitudes. 4. Executive ability.
    I. Tachibanaki, Toshiaki, 1943– .
    HD70.J3W53 1998
    658.4'00952 — dc21
                                                                        97-35437
                                                                            CIP

ISBN 1 85898 511 0

Printed and bound in Great Britain by Bookcraft (Bath) Ltd.

Contents

Figures

Tables

Contributors

Hideshi Itoh is Associate Professor of Economics, Institute of Social and Economic Research, Osaka University

Yoshinobu Kobayashi is the Principal Research Officer, Denki Rengo Research and Information Center

Hisakazu Matsushige is Associate Professor of Economics, Osaka School of International Public Policy, Osaka University

Naoki Mitani is Professor of Economics, Faculty of Economics, Kobe University

Tomohiko Noda is a Lecturer, Faculty of Economics, St. Andrew's (Momoyama Gakuin) University

Isao Ohashi is Professor of Economics, Faculty of Economics, Nagoya University

Fujikazu Suzuki is a Research Officer, Research Institute for Advancement of Living Standards

Toshiaki Tachibanaki is Professor of Economics, Kyoto Institute of Economic Research, Kyoto University

Hiroshi Teruyama is Associate Professor of Economics, Kyoto Institute of Economic Research, Kyoto University

Yasunobu Tomita is Professor of Economics, Faculty of Economics, Osaka Prefecture University

Preface and acknowledgements

The aim of this book is to investigate the issues of promotion, corporate governance and related subjects in Japanese firms. Questions are raised concerning who becomes department heads (middle management) and chief executives (top managers); who governs the company; and in what ways business is managed.

In order to examine these issues we conducted two comprehensive surveys: the first was a survey of white-collar employees in several large enterprises, and the second was a survey of executives/board members, in large listed corporate firms. These surveys are explained in more detail in the introduction.

We believe that we have obtained some very interesting results, demonstrating the essence of Japanese business, which will help readers to reach a better understanding of the ways in which Japanese business is conducted.

In Japan, the issues of promotion, corporate governance and business management can be summarized in a few words, which have been adopted as the title of this book: *Who Runs Japanese Business?*

The editor would like to express his gratitude to all the contributors, who have been enthusiastic and cooperative participants since the beginning of this project, and to Professor Sei Kuribayashi, Director of RIALS, who has given his full support to this enterprise.

TOSHIAKI TACHIBANAKI

Introduction

Toshiaki Tachibanaki

---

1   MOTIVATIONS FOR THIS BOOK

Many business people desire promotion, preferably to the most important position in the firm. The advantages of a higher rung on the
hierarchical ladder are not only a better salary but also greater responsibility and leadership. Since individuals often prefer a position where they
can supervise other people rather than one in which they are supervised,
the degree of satisfaction is higher if they occupy a higher position.
There are, however, various levels of high-status position in the firm.
The most capable and ambitious person aspires to become the president
(that is, Chief Executive Officer, or CEO) of the company. Most people
do not want the job of top executive (that is, to be a board member), but
would prefer one which is more suited to their capabilities and lifestyle.
A significant number of people do not enjoy fierce competition, which is
one of the necessary conditions for being promoted, and they may
simply say that they work to ensure a decent standard of living, without
wishing for any promotion.

The purpose of this book is to examine various issues related to promotion in the firm, such as the reasons and motivations for it, and the
characteristics and lifestyles of the people who are promoted. Although
the principal tool used here is based on economic analysis, some tools
from the disciplines of psychology, sociology and education are also
employed, to reflect broader factors associated with promotion.

In this book, the two main targets for promotion are top executives (or
board members) such as presidents, vice-presidents, chief and managing
executives, ordinary executives and auditors, and department heads (a
description which encompasses a wide range of positions). These two
ranks can be regarded as symbols of promotion, namely the highest position and middle management. It is not an exaggeration to say that people
aspire to these two symbolic positions when they desire promotion. The
ultimate winners in the promotion race, whose numbers are extremely
small, are the top executives. In other words, most people are unable to
attain such a position regardless of their wishes. The position of depart-

ment head includes various elements. For some people it is the final goal in their career, while for others it is merely the intermediate rung on the ladder. We should also not forget those who are unable to attain middle management, whether they want to or not.

We shall investigate in depth the question of who are promoted to these two positions. The following related issues will also be investigated: the degree of desire for promotion; working style, lifestyle and expectations; and the reward of promotion among the winners in the promotion competition. The effects of a university education, including the name of the university and the speciality studied, the assessment of individual performance by managers, opinions concerning competition, and related issues will also be examined. We shall also investigate the economic incentives behind the fierce competition for promotion, both theoretically and empirically, and study what kind of effort incentives are offered by the firm. Accordingly, we shall evaluate whether or not the seniority and/or the merit system has worked well for the determination of both wages and promotion.

Finally, in Japan, these issues of promotion, corporate governance and business management can be summarized in the few words which have been adopted as the title of this book. Questions such as 'Who is promoted to department head and top executive?', 'Who governs the company?', and 'In what way is business managed?', are all related to the question 'Who runs Japanese business?'.

2   TOP EXECUTIVES

First, we shall consider the promotion of top executives (that is, board members). They were obviously the winners in the cut-throat competition for promotion. The following questions will be addressed: 'Who are the winners?', 'Does the name of the university matter?', 'Did they study humanities or sciences at university?', 'What kind of career pattern did they have?' and 'Have they frequently changed their job and position in the firm, or did they have a broad or narrow career?'

It is useful to know the conditions under which top executives achieved their promotion in spite of stiff competition. Was it achieved because of the merit system, or through the influence of superiors, or simply as a consequence of luck? At the same time, we shall investigate what kind of working style and lifestyle top executives had before achieving such a position. In other words, whether they worked conscientiously for the firm and whether they were involved exclusively in company life became central issues.

The managerial principle relating to top executives, that is, their role in the firm, is vital in determining the future of the firm because the highest decisions are made by top executives. Therefore it is important to understand the role of top executives. This role is closely related to the following questions: 'Who owns the firm?', 'Who governs the firm?', 'Why does the firm exist?' and 'What is the relationship among share-holders, top executives and employees?'. These issues are simply called 'corporate governance'. Corporate governance is still an open question in Japan, and therefore its understanding will be enriched by the results obtained in this book.

One controversy in this field in Japan, is whether firms are owned by share-holders or by workers (that is, labour-managed firms). The labour-managed firm hypothesis, is more popular in Japan than the shareholder hypothesis, at least for Japanese firms, although it is true that corporate firms are legally owned by shareholders. Some specialists emphasize the intermediary role of top executives between shareholders and employees. This book intends to examine these issues carefully, and to give an answer to these questions.

One novel feature in this book is that we are concerned with the differences among various levels of top executives, such as presidents, vice-presidents, chief and managing executives, ordinary executives and auditors. It will be possible to identify the different level and range of responsibilities which they undertake, and such differences will reflect different managerial principles, lifestyles, and naturally, salaries. Also, we shall be concerned with the influence that the name of a particular university may have on the possibility of achieving the position of top executive.

Another interesting concern in this book will be to investigate the effect of both internal and external experience in the development of the managerial role of top executives. Although many of the top executives surveyed here were promoted internally, several executives were appointed by financial institutions, or parent companies in the case of subsidiary firms. Consequently, they have had longer external experience in other firms. This difference between internal and external experience may provide a new insight into our understanding of corporate governance in Japan.

3 WHITE-COLLAR EMPLOYEES INCLUDING MANAGERS

The next subject to investigate will be the promotion process to middle management, that is, department head. More broadly, the work incentive, and treatment of white-collar employees in general, will be examined.

The following comments reveal attitudes towards the middle manager position as a symbol of promotion in Japanese firms: 'I would like to be promoted at least to department head during my career', 'I desire to be promoted to a higher position than a department head', 'The position of department head does not suit my personal taste', 'I do not want to be promoted because supervising subordinates is worrying and uncongenial', 'There is no chance of promotion for me because of my qualifications', and so on. Impressions from managers that business people regard middle management as a symbol are complex and mixed. It will be interesting and valuable to investigate who are promoted to department heads, and in what way.

The investigation on promotion probabilities to department head will enable us to collect useful information, such as wage determination and promotion in general, for the understanding of the treatment of white-collar workers. In other words, we shall be able to find out how employers evaluate the ability and performance of individual employees, and in what way they utilize such information for the determination of wages and promotion. The most crucial policy goal of human resource management for firms is to provide the highest incentive for employees, and to design the most efficient human resource allocation. It will be interesting to examine whether or not such a goal has been achieved in Japanese firms.

We shall investigate the firm's system of assessment of its workers' ability and performance. In other words, we shall investigate when the firm starts to differentiate promotion possibilities among employees who entered the firm in the same year. Also, we shall investigate the extent of the maximum range in wage rates between the most and the least productive employee. This differentiation in promotion and wages implies that the firm will respond positively to the high contribution of productive employees, or will raise their incentive levels. This is a rational assessment system because it is important to maintain strong incentives for productive employees. A difficult and controversial subject will be to evaluate the degree of work incentive for less productive workers, when favourable treatment of productive workers seems excessive. It is said that Japanese firms do not have a very wide wage differential between productive and less productive workers, or an early promotion policy (which implies that promotion is determined at a relatively young age) because they are afraid that this would be a poor incentive for less productive workers and would lead to shirking and uncooperative behaviour. For three recent international comparisons on this subject, see Tachibanaki (1994), Ohashi and Tachibanaki (1998) and Tachibanaki (1998). This book will investigate the relationship between work incentives and the assessment system in several large firms, both theoretically and empirically.

One of the common systems in Japan is called the seniority system, in which both wages and promotion are determined mainly on the basis of the workers' period of employment in the firm. This system has worked fairly well, maintaining a strong work incentive for all employees, and deterring them from shirking. Three of the economic interpretations of the seniority system are called the insurance, human capital and the non-shirking hypotheses. We would like to find out which hypothesis is appropriate for the Japanese system. In other words, we shall be concerned with the economic rationality of the seniority system. The Japanese system also sets a high premium on the role of education and age in the determination of wages and promotion, in addition to seniority (that is, length of employment) in the firm. An overall economic interpretation will be made, taking into account variables such as age, seniority and education.

Although we have talked about assessment of individual performance in business activity, it will not be easy to implement such an assessment in reality. Employees who are engaged in sales activity are easily assessed because their performance can be quantified without much difficulty. Take the example of a car dealer who is engaged in selling cars. Assessment of this kind of activity is easy, and invites no severe criticism. Other types of jobs, however, such as planning, accounting, personnel, general administration, and so on, cannot be so easily assessed. Several types of engineering jobs and jobs in team production are also difficult to assess. If an assessment is judged as unfair by employees, then the degree of dissatisfaction, which is likely to undermine work incentives, may grow. In particular, an assessment which is made largely on the basis of subjective judgement is a risky undertaking.

Although firms try to prepare an assessment system which will minimize such risks, there is no ideal system. A fruitful area of investigation will be to assess how fairness is evaluated by workers. We shall consider the opinion of workers on the concept of fairness, which plays an important role in the actual implementation of assessments of individual performance.

Another worthwhile approach in this book will be to investigate the importance of each individual worker's own assessment of his or her performance. Normally, an assessment is made by other people such as managers, or those who occupy superior positions. If the discrepancy between self-assessment and that made by the manager is large, then trouble will arise. Alternatively, it is possible to understand that self-assessment is more reliable than that made by other people because a person normally knows him- or herself best. Therefore, we shall use the information of individual workers' self-assessment to evaluate the

economic implication of performance on work incentive. The idea is to
estimate a possible discrepancy between the current wage, and the potential wage which corresponds to the individual's self-assessed contribution
to the firm. The sign and the degree of such a possible discrepancy will
enable us to derive the economic implication of work incentives.

This will complete the section associated with the promotion to managers. The information will enable us to discuss the economic
interpretation of the relationship between work incentives and promotion
for white-collar workers. There are three methods which can be employed
for the empirical investigation of promotion in the firm. The first is to
conduct statistical analyses from a survey (that is, a questionnaire) completed by workers, and to derive some conclusions. The second is to trace
the individual careers of workers from entry into the firm to their current
position, and to assess the implications. The third is to conduct frequent
interviews of many employees, and to collate the results. Although we use
the first method principally, we shall also supplement our examination
with the other two.

4 PRESTIGIOUS VERSUS OTHER UNIVERSITIES, AND SCIENCE VERSUS HUMANITIES GRADUATES

A socially controversial and popular concern in Japan is the effect that
the name of a university has on promotion in the firm, or more broadly
on the success of an individual career. Another interesting subject is the
difference between graduates in science and technology, and those in
humanities and social science. These factors are relevant only to university graduates, so white-collar graduates will be studied in greater detail.

It is not only in Japan where meritocracy or preferential treatment for
the graduates of prestigious universities is observed. Meritocracy here
implies that those people will reap the benefits throughout their career in
both firms and public institutions. We can cite several examples of these
universities: Tokyo and Kyoto in Japan, Harvard and Yale in the United
States, Oxford and Cambridge in the United Kingdom, and Ecole
Polytechnique and ENA in France. Germany is the only exception among
the G–5 countries, as it does not have any comparable universities. We
shall investigate whether the graduates of prestigious universities have a
higher probability of being promoted to higher office in Japanese firms,
and, if this is the case, we shall look for explanations.

The words 'examination hell' are common in Japan, implying that
very fierce competition is observed among candidates for university
entrance, in particular for prestigious universities. Not only higher intel-

lectual capability but also significant effort are required to be able to pass the difficult entrance examinations. Those who graduate from prestigious universities have higher qualifications for their business and professional careers. This success, however, only indicates academic achievements. There should be particular reasons or qualifications other than academic capability, if these graduates are to have a higher chance of promotion. We shall search for such particular reasons and qualifications and, at the same time, discuss whether or not such favourable treatment is socially justifiable.

The next subject will be an investigation into the difference between science and technology, and humanities and social science graduates. There are three common assumptions in Japan about university graduates who have studied science and technology subjects such as mathematics, physics, chemistry, biology, engineering and agriculture. First, the probability of their being promoted to a higher position in the firm is lower than that for humanities and social science graduates. Second, employees who have studied science and technology wish to be specialists rather than managers in the firm for various reasons. Third, there are many people who have completed postgraduate degrees in science and technology, who are in many respects very different from graduates with degrees in the humanities or social sciences. We shall examine whether or not the above three assumptions are true, and provide reasons. In sum, we shall analyse the differences between science and technology, and humanities and social science graduates regarding promotion likelihood, career patterns, lifestyles, and other related factors.

5 SIGNIFICANCE OF WORKING ACTIVITY AND TRADE UNIONS

To conclude this study, we shall discuss a final but very important subject – the significance of work activity in human life. It is natural that employees who have been promoted to a higher position should work hard. There should be no serious problem regarding the motivation of these people. Most workers, however, even white-collar employees, do not achieve the desired promotion because competition is so fierce and, of course, a large proportion of workers do not even seek promotion.

If the degree of work satisfaction among those workers who fail to achieve promotion were higher, it would not be necessary to take any action. It is, however, possible that they are dissatisfied. Therefore, we shall study the important subject: 'Why do white-collar workers work?'. Is it only for wages (that is, to ensure a basic standard of living), or for promotion, for job satisfaction, or for other reasons? Finally, the role of the trade unions in achieving the highest satisfaction level for workers will be discussed.

6 SUMMARY

It is useful to present here a brief survey of selected topics which have been discussed in this introduction, and which will be investigated in depth in this book.

1. Who is promoted to the two symbolic positions in the firm, namely top executive (board members) and middle management (department heads)? The mechanism for the determination of promotion, that is, when it is decided, who determines it, and on what ground it is selected, will be carefully evaluated.

2. What is the economic rationality of the seniority system which is a common determinant for both wages and promotion in Japan? There are also other economic theories which can explain the relationship between work incentive and wages or promotion. We shall discuss these theories in the Japanese context.

3. Is it preferable to prepare for broader or narrower careers for white-collar workers? At the same time, the role of professional or specialized, rather than managerial, careers will be discussed.

4. The role or the management principles of top executives will be thoroughly investigated. This is likely to shed light on the understanding of corporate governance in Japanese firms.

5. We shall investigate the role played by 'prestige' universities in the determination of promotion in the firm, and clarify the difference in career, lifestyle, and so on between science and humanities graduates.

6. There are many workers who have no possibility of promotion, whether through choice or not, and therefore it is important to increase their degree of job satisfaction. There will be a full discussion on this issue, including the role played by trade unions.

The overall summary of these subjects is expressed in the title of this book, *Who Runs Japanese Business?*, and we hope that the book will provide readers with some answers.

7 SURVEY DATA USED IN THIS BOOK

Survey of White-collar Employees

This survey was conducted in 1993 for white-collar employees in five significantly large firms. These five firms are, of course, anonymous, but it is possible, nevertheless, to specify the different kinds of business, namely, automotive, electronics, chemical and electric power companies, and a department store. The employees surveyed included both those who had been promoted and those who had not – including section heads, department heads and directors but excluding top executives. The number of questionnaires distributed was 2,100, and the response rate was an impressive 86.5 per cent. Thus, the total number of completed questionnaires was 1,816.

Survey of Top Executives

This survey was also conducted in 1993. We posted questionnaires to 8,000 top executives and auditors, described as board members in a total of 2,128 listed corporate firms which were randomly selected from the data base *Toyokeizai Top Executive Survey*. The survey included 40,800 top executives, who were all appointed at the firms' shareholders' meeting. The selection rate from the original survey was 19.6 per cent, and the response rate was 28.1 per cent. The total number of completed questionnaires was 2,246.

REFERENCES

Ohashi, I. and T. Tachibanaki (eds) (1998), *Internal Labour Markets, Incentives, and Employment*, London: Macmillan.

Tachibanaki, T. (ed.) (1994), *Labour Market and Economic Performance: Europe, Japan and the U.S.A.*, London: Macmillan.

Tachibanaki, T. (ed.) (1998), *Wage Differentials: An International Comparison*, London: Macmillan.

1. Road to the top and executive management goals

Toshiaki Tachibanaki*

1.1 INTRODUCTION

Top executives (that is, board members) are the winners in the fierce competition regarding promotion in a firm. Because most top executives in Japanese firms have had their status determined through internal promotion, it will be interesting and useful to examine who are the final winners, that is, who are the top executives in Japanese firms. Before examining this issue, it is important to understand that a large number of employees are excluded from the internal promotion ladder to top executive status, for example, nearly all blue-collar employees. Also, we recognize that a significant number of employees do not seek promotion even if they were eligible and that most female employees may discontinue their career in a firm for various reasons. More than half the employees belong to these groups in Japanese firms. In other words, only a small proportion of employees should be regarded as candidates for top executive positions. Fierce competition ensures that only an extremely small number of employees can attain the position of a top executive. Therefore, in this chapter we are concerned only with a very small minority who are called 'top executives'. In particular, their native ability, career in the firm, reasons for success, lifestyle, management policy, formal education (that is, whether they graduated from famous and prestigious universities), salaries, and so on, will be investigated. A very small sample number of top executives does not necessarily imply that the implications of this study are minor. Since these top executives determine the highest level of management policy in the firm, it is crucially important to know their characteristics, management goals, and so on, in order

* The members of the research group on top executives provided me with various useful comments on earlier versions of this study, and these comments changed the content of this chapter substantially. Comments by Ryutaro Komiya were also stimulating. I am very grateful for useful suggestions and research assistance given by Hiroshi Futamura and Tomohiko Nakajima. All remaining errors and responsibility for opinions, however, are entirely mine.

1

to understand the Japanese firm. In other words, knowing top executives enables us to understand the management style of the Japanese firm, and more broadly, to evaluate the corporate governance structure in Japan.

The study in this chapter relates to our own survey of top executives, and is based on the analysis of the information collected from this survey. The respondents are all top executives who were selected randomly. Therefore, the empirical results are based on top executives' own responses, and do not include any other assessments. Thus we shall have to make a distinction between surveys answered by a particular group of people, top executives in this book, and surveys answered by people in general.

Let us briefly explain the data. We distributed questionnaires to about 8,000 top executives (both board members and standing auditors of large firms in Japan which were selected randomly from the *Toyokeizai Top Executive Survey of Listed and Non-listed Firms in Japan*. It includes both corporate firms and mutual companies. The response rate was 28.1 per cent, and in total, we analysed 2,246 questionnaires.

1.2   TOP EXECUTIVE POSITIONS AND PROFESSIONAL CAREERS

The questionnaire posed many questions about the job nature, classification or position (that is, directorates such as sales, accounting, production and engineering) at six different career stages. Indeed, each respondent answered questions about the nature of his or her job at these different stages, namely (1) entry point, (2) non-managerial position, (3) section head, (4) department head, (5) director, and (6) top executive. In other words, the vertical promotion proceeds in the following way: entry – non-managerial – section head – department head – director top executive.

We prepared the following 15 job classifications or job descriptions (1) accounting and finance, (2) personnel and labour welfare, (3) general affairs and public relations, (4) managerial planning, (5) information analysis, (6) sales, (7) purchase and outside order, (8) distribution, (9) production, (10) engineering, (11) research, (12) international and import–export, (13) temporary transfer to another (mainly subsidiary) firm, (14) working abroad, and (15) other. Since the 15 job classifications are too numerous for a clear understanding of career patterns, we aggregated into the following seven classifications: (1)' Indirect managerial = (1) + (2) + (3), (2)' planning = (4) + (5), (3)' sales and trade = (6) + (7) + (8), (4)' production = (9), (5)' engineering and research = (10) + (11), (6)' international and temporary transfer = (12) + (13) + (14), (7)' other = (15). Basically, we use both classifications (that is, 15 and seven), although we use the latter more frequently than the former, because it is easier to understand.

We conducted two different analyses based on these job classifications. The first method is fairly primitive, namely, we prepared graphs of career changes for the six different stages, and simply calculated the number of occupants of each job classification at each career stage. The second is more sophisticated, that is, we estimated the transition probability from each career stage to the next. Since we have the six career stages in this data source, we can obtain five different transition matrices, namely (1) from entry to non-managerial position (that is, no promotion but only transfer), (2) from non-managerial to section head, (3) from section head to department head, (4) from department head to director and (5) from director to top executive.

There is one technical problem in this data set. Several individuals occupy more than two positions even in the common job rank. For example, one individual may be the head of two different departments, say accounting and sales, at different times. In other words, such people experienced a horizontal transfer at the departmental head level. The question arose whether we should count this person as being in accounting or sales at the departmental head level. We selected the department which was occupied by the largest number of people. In other words, we searched for the most popular department (that is, frequency is high) which was occupied by the largest number of people. Going back to the above example, we chose accounting if the number of accounting department heads is larger than that of sales department heads. Since there is no best way to solve this technical problem, we had to adopt the above method. The risk of errors, however, was slight, because we did not find many cases where this problem arose.

Let us examine the first method. Figures 1.1 and 1.2 show the change in position at the six different career stages (using 15 and seven different job classifications, respectively). The horizontal line shows the career stages, and the vertical line shows the number of occupants. Two relevant comments should be made. First, the sample for this figure consists only of current top executives. In other words, the careers of employees who were not promoted to top executive positions are entirely ignored, and thus we are concerned only with the professional careers of top executives. Second, the graph does not indicate the career path or history of any individual top executive. It merely indicates the total number of occupants at each position for all samples. It should be noted that these figures include all past experience of positions, that is, we count two or more positions even at one hierarchical rank. Therefore, the graphs in Figures 1.1 and 1.2 tend to be upward sloping because the number of positions which are occupied within the common rank (that is, department head, or director) increases as one person is promoted to a higher position.

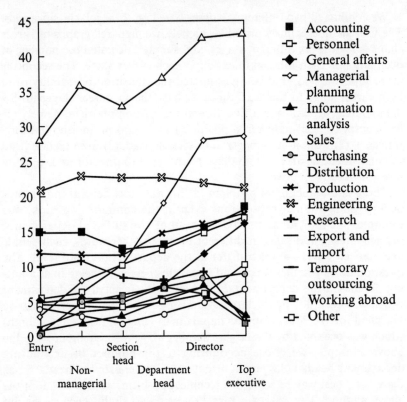

Figure 1.1 Career patterns of top executives (15 different job classifications)

Several noteworthy observations based on the results in Figures 1.1 and 1.2 are as follows. First, the growth rate of both sales (or sales and trade) and management planning is very high. In particular, employees who were engaged in these positions at a young age, represented by a first-entry or non-managerial position, have a higher probability of promotion to a top executive position. In other words, the promotion prospects of employees who are engaged in a sales job at a young age are quite promising. Management planning jobs have slightly different features compared to sales jobs because these positions are prominent at the middle management stage or with ranks such as department head or director. In other words, top executives held management planning jobs at some time during the middle management, departmental head or director stages. Since it is possible to learn a broad range of management problems peculiar to the firm when one occupies a job at management planning, departmental or directorate level, this experience should be

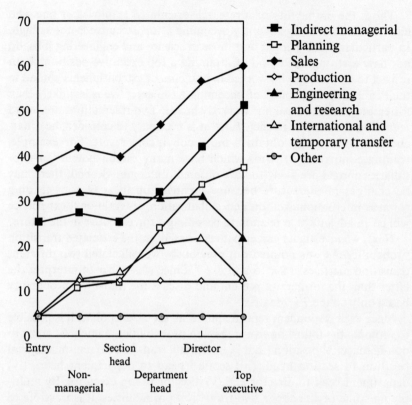

*Figure 1.2 Career patterns of top executives (seven different job
        classifications)*

very useful in relation to various top-level management issues when such
a person becomes a top executive. In other words, the firm is likely to
choose outstanding and successful employees, who showed superior performance in various activities such as sales, production and indirect
management early in their careers, for the job of management planning
in their middle career.

Second, a significant number of employees who were engaged in sales
and production at a younger age are promoted and transferred to general
management and/or the personnel department. Employees who were
engaged in engineering, accounting and finance tended to keep their job
status as engineers or accountants. This consistent pattern is for them
quite understandable in view of their higher professional proficiency,
which is required to perform these tasks successfully. The probability of
an engineer or accountant becoming a top executive is not impressively
high, but not much lower compared with other professions.

Third, the probability of a research-orientated employee or one who has worked in a foreign country becoming a top executive is not as high. In particular, R&D people, and those in science and engineering jobs, do not have a strong likelihood of attaining a top executive position. With respect to employees who worked in branches or establishments abroad in their career, the possibility of becoming a top executive is less likely than for employees who have not worked abroad. Two reservations are noted regarding the above tendency. First, it is necessary to consider the differences in industry to obtain a more convincing result. For example, trading companies or firms which have many establishments or subsidiaries abroad are likely to have different outcomes. Second, there may be changes in the future because Japanese business is now heading towards internationalization and globalization. International experience will be an advantage in relation to becoming a top executive in the future.

Next, we investigate career patterns based on the estimated transition probability. As was pointed out previously, we calculated two different transition matrices: 15 × 15 and 7 × 7. Since it is easier to interpret the latter than the former, we present and discuss the transition probability based only on the 7 × 7 matrix.

Since each respondent reported, in total, six career points, it is possible to estimate the following five transition probabilities, namely (i) entry to non-managerial position (that is, horizontal transfer), (ii) non-managerial position to section head, (iii) section head to department head, (iv) department head to director and (v) director to top executive. By multiplying some of the above five transition probabilities, it is possible to estimate the transition probability from one particular point to another such as from entry point to top executive, or from department head to top executive.

By applying Bayes theorem, it is in turn possible to estimate past positions held, given the particular top executive position, with the following conditional probability,

$$P\,(j/i) = \frac{P\,(i/j)}{\sum\limits_{k=1}^{n} P(i/k)}$$

where $P(i/j)$ is the estimated transition probability.

Tables 1.1–4 show the estimated transition probability based on the above two methods. Tables 1.1 and 1.3 show the matrix A_{ij} which indicates the probability of attaining the jth job at the top executive level, for a person who was at the ith job in the past, while Tables 1.2 and 1.4 show the matrix A_{ij} which indicates the probability of experiencing the ith job

Table 1.1 *Estimated transition probability, entry to top executive (a)*

	Indirect managerial	Planning	Sales	Production	Engineering and research	International and temporary transfer	Other
Indirect managerial	0.1787	0.1442	0.1440	0.1192	0.1076	0.1395	0.1296
Planning	0.1555	0.1588	0.1337	0.1242	0.1179	0.1497	0.1272
Sales	0.1386	0.1512	0.1759	0.1329	0.1169	0.1347	0.1315
Production	0.1278	0.1468	0.1546	0.1989	0.1682	0.1300	0.1184
Engineering and research	0.1157	0.1220	0.1199	0.1838	0.2577	0.1356	0.1411
International and temporary transfer	0.1305	0.1441	0.1310	0.1151	0.1091	0.1673	0.1713
Other	0.1532	0.1333	0.1411	0.1258	0.1226	0.1433	0.1810

Note: The element of the matrix A_{ij} signifies the probability of attaining jth job at the top executive level for a person who was at the ith job at the entry point.

7

Table 1.2 Estimated transition probability, entry to top executive (b)

	Indirect managerial	Planning	Sales	Production	Engineering and research	International and temporary transfer	Other
Indirect managerial	0.2213	0.1263	0.1842	0.0424	0.0774	0.2885	0.0599
Planning	0.1926	0.1388	0.1710	0.0442	0.0848	0.3098	0.0588
Sales	0.1716	0.1324	0.2251	0.0473	0.0842	0.2786	0.0608
Production	0.1582	0.1286	0.1978	0.0708	0.1210	0.2689	0.0547
Engineering and research	0.1433	0.1068	0.1534	0.0654	0.1854	0.2805	0.0652
International and temporary transfer	0.1615	0.1262	0.1676	0.0410	0.0785	0.3461	0.0791
Other	0.1897	0.1167	0.1805	0.0448	0.0882	0.2964	0.0836

Note: The element of the matrix A_{ij} signifies the probability of experiencing ith job at the entry point for a person who is now at the jth job at the top executive level.

Table 1.3 *Estimated transition probability, department head to top executive (a)*

	Indirect managerial	Planning	Sales	Production	Engineering and research	International and temporary transfer	Other
Indirect managerial	0.3802	0.1183	0.1099	0.0494	0.0433	0.1169	0.0827
Planning	0.1909	0.2319	0.1162	0.0848	0.0813	0.1562	0.0696
Sales	0.0779	0.2038	0.3514	0.0906	0.0504	0.0913	0.0762
Production	0.1198	0.1137	0.1314	0.5060	0.2365	0.0533	0.0505
Engineering and research	0.0559	0.1036	0.0975	0.1593	0.4311	0.1245	0.0612
International and temporary transfer	0.0522	0.1332	0.0738	0.0401	0.0791	0.2879	0.2342
Other	0.1231	0.0955	0.1197	0.0698	0.0784	0.1699	0.4257

Note: The element of the matrix A_{ij} signifies the probability of attaining jth job at the top executive level for a person who was at the ith job at the department head level.

Table 1.4 Estimated transition probability, department head to top executive (b)

	Indirect managerial	Planning	Sales	Production	Engineering and research	International and temporary transfer	Other
Indirect managerial	0.4435	0.0982	0.1382	0.0262	0.0384	0.2153	0.0402
Planning	0.2227	0.1927	0.1462	0.0449	0.0721	0.2877	0.0338
Sales	0.0909	0.1693	0.4419	0.0480	0.0447	0.1682	0.0371
Production	0.1397	0.0945	0.1653	0.2679	0.2099	0.0982	0.0245
Engineering and research	0.6520	0.0860	0.1226	0.0844	0.3827	0.2294	0.0297
International and temporary transfer	0.0608	0.1107	0.0928	0.0212	0.0702	0.5304	0.1139
Other	0.1436	0.0793	0.1506	0.0370	0.0695	0.3130	0.2070

Note: The element of the matrix A_{ij} signifies the probability of experiencing ith job at the department head level for a person who is now at the jth job at the department head level.

in the past, for a person who is now at the *j*th job at the top executive level. We show only two points of career for the past post, that is, entry point, and department head which is a symbol of middle management. Tables 1.1 and 1.2 are concerned with the transition between entry point and top executive, and Tables 1.3 and 1.4 are concerned with the transition between department head and top executive.

We can observe the following results based on these tables. First, in both Tables 1.1 and 1.2, figures are not high but rather are very low. Most of them are about 0.1–0.2, and even the highest value, namely 0.34, is less than 0.5. These results imply that the correlation between entry points and top executive positions with respect to present jobs is very low, and thus that there are very few people who occupied the same jobs both at entry point and at top executive level. In other words, people who have become top executives had considerably different kinds of jobs during their career in the firm. It is interesting to note, nevertheless, that the probability at the diagonal elements is normally higher than that at the off-diagonal elements. This implies that there are many people who had the same jobs both at entry point and at top executive level.

Second, there are few figures which are close to zero in these tables. This implies that careers are relatively broad, indicating that top executives had many relatively different job experiences in the course of their career. It is important to point out, however, that the probability at the diagonal elements in Tables 1.3 and 1.4 (that is, the transition between department head and top executive) is considerably higher than that at the off-diagonal elements. At the same time, the probability at the diagonal elements in Tables 1.3 and 1.4 is higher than that at the diagonal elements in Tables 1.1 and 1.2. These two results suggest that promotion from the middle management level, such as department head, to top executive, in many cases does not accompany a change in jobs. In other words, it accompanies only vertical transfer (that is, vertical promotion) within the same job classification, and does not accompany horizontal transfer among different job classifications. One exception to this rule is 'planning', because this type of job and position comes from many other different positions, and similarly goes to many other different positions.

Third, there is not much mobility between workers in business administration, such as indirect management, planning and sales, and those in technical administration such as production, engineering and research. In particular, the transfer from business administration to technical administration is nearly zero, although the transfer from the latter to the former is higher than the inverse transfer. This implies that workers in technical administration (that is, mainly science and technology graduates) can engage in both business and technical administration, while workers in business administration (that is, mainly non-science and non-technology graduates) cannot engage in technical administration.

It would be useful to summarize the empirical findings regarding the career pattern of top executives. First, the position or kind of job that a worker was engaged in at his or her entry point into the firm does not matter at all for future prospects as to whether or not such a worker will be promoted to a top executive position, and for what field or job he or she will be responsible if he or she becomes a top executive. Second, workers who engaged in sales, production and general (that is, indirect) administration at their non-managerial and section head positions have a higher probability of becoming a top executive than those in other fields. Workers in research and development, and those who were in foreign countries at these career points have a lower probability of promotion to a top executive position. Third, workers who were involved in management planning at their middle management level (that is, departmental head or director level) have a higher probability of becoming a top executive than those who never experienced management planning jobs during their mid-career. Fourth, the probability of occupying the same job or field responsibility as a top executive, as the job or field responsibility in middle management, is higher than that of occupying a different job or field responsibility as a top executive compared to that in middle management. Fifth, the career pattern of top executives is broader than that of workers who were not promoted to a top executive position. In other words, top executives have greater job variety and field experience than other workers. This result, however, should not be regarded as a necessary condition for becoming a top executive.

1.3 REASONS FOR BECOMING A TOP EXECUTIVE: ABILITY AND BACKGROUND

This section investigates the reasons for achieving the position of top executive, based on each respondent's self-assessment. What kind of ability and background is important for achieving the highest management position? Another important subject is to investigate the lifestyle of top executives prior to their attaining a top position. In other words, it will be interesting to examine whether or not they worked hard in their professional life, possibly at the expense of their family and private life.

The principal method for investigation is *factor analysis*. It is useful to explain briefly the essence of factor analysis in order to understand the empirical results of this section. The explanation is not so technical, but intuitive in terms of revealing and consolidating the implication of the empirical results.

Factor analysis begins with the following equation,

$$X_j = a_{j1}f_1 + a_{j2}f_2 + \dots + a_{jm}f_m + d_j u_j$$

where f_j $(j = 1, \dots, m)$ is the common factor, a_{ji} $(j = 1, \dots, m, i = 1, \dots, p)$ is the factor loading of kth common factor for ith characteristic, and u_j is the specific factor which has no correlation with f_j. X_j $(j = 1, \dots, m)$ is the standardized variable with average zero and variance unity. Factor analysis estimates first m, and then a_{jm}. Next, we interpret the factor and rotate it. The choice of the number of the common factor (that is, m) is based on the characteristic value greater than unity. The characteristic value is equal to the variance of its factor, and shows the relative contribution (or weight) to the variable. The common factor symbolizes the power of several similar and closely related explanatory variables, as one factor. The factor loading a_{ji} indicates the weight of common factor to each variable. We adopt the varimax method as a rotation strategy because it is simple and easy to understand. This description is somewhat technical, and therefore I shall provide some intuitive interpretation of factor analysis, using Table 1.5 as an example.

Table 1.5 shows the reasons for achieving the position of top executive based on each respondent's own assessment. The table indicates, in total, nine variables (that is, A, B, C, ..., I) which are supposed to be significant for becoming a top executive. Since a total of nine variables is too many and too complicated, the number of variables will be reduced to a smaller number of common factors (three in Table 1.5) where each common factor is unobservable, in principle, but intuitively understood. I provide such an intuitive interpretation for each factor. The italics indicates the maximum value of the factor loading among the three factors, which implies the highest contribution of such a variable to each factor. For example, the four variables A, C, D and H, have high correlations for factor 1, and can be assembled into one factor. The intuitive interpretation of these variables regarding factor 1 is as follows: raising individual performance, experiencing a broader career, and the firm having high expectations for the respondent. It is very important to point out the fact that the relative contribution decreases from factor 1 to factor 2, and from factor 2 to factor 3 with respect to the likelihood of becoming a top executive. Thus Table 1.5 is an example of how an intuitive interpretation can be derived from factor analysis. Detailed examinations and interpretations are given below.

Table 1.5 Reasons for achieving the position of top executive (factor loading after varimax rotation, characteristic value greater than one)

	Factor 1	Factor 2	Factor 3
A. Individual performance in own profession	*0.485*	0.162	-0.226
B. No major faults and steady effort	0.186	*0.542*	0.097
C. Broader career experience and perspective based on the entire company level	*0.519*	0.092	-0.214
D. Fulfilling expectations after entering the firm and making good progress	*0.672*	0.135	0.177
E. Better superior managers	0.073	*0.737*	-0.184
F. Trusted and supported by subordinates	0.438	*0.44*	-0.436
G. No suitable competitors	0.059	0.18	*0.854*
H. The firm needed me	*0.724*	-0.206	0.198
I. Good luck	-0.131	*0.726*	0.239

Notes
Factor 1: Raising individual performance, experiencing a wider career, and being expected to do well.
Factor 2: Steady effort and better superior managers (that is, good luck).
Factor 3: No major competition.

Proportion which explains the variance
Factor 1: 1.734
Factor 2: 1.686
Factor 3: 1.187.

The italics indicates the case where the factor loading has the maximum value.

14

Table 1.5 shows top executives' own assessment on why they attained their high-status position. The most important reasons (represented by factor 1) are that they achieved better individual performance in their business activity, had various and broad career experiences, and during their career they were expected by the firm to become future top executives. The second most important reasons (represented by factor 2) are making steady efforts, and having good luck in encountering excellent managers. The third most important reason is the lack of serious competition, although its relative contribution is considerably minor, in view of its lower characteristic value. Summarizing the above, it is possible to conclude that the crucially important criterion for achieving the position of top executive is a combination of excellent performance in business activity and broad experience (or career) in the firm. The next most important are effort and luck, respectively.

Table 1.6 presents the estimated results regarding the required ability and personality for becoming a top executive. The most important factor is associated with cooperativeness, fairness, credibility, leadership and popularity. All are related to individual personality. It is interesting to observe that individual personality is the most important. Japanese firms put a lot of emphasis on the evaluation of personality in determining who is promoted to top executive positions. Loyalty to the firm may be added to this category. The next important factor is related to a strong determination, originality, and risk-taking. The third most important factor is associated with sound knowledge, and skilful planning, although its relative importance is considerably weaker in view of its lower characteristic value. Summarizing the above, it is possible to conclude that the crucially important element for the successful career of top executives is individual personality, followed by leadership and willingness to take risks. Knowledge and planning ability are not so important.

It is useful here to present an overall evaluation based on both Tables 1.5 and 1.6. While the former suggested the importance of individual performance in business activity, a broad career and experience in becoming a top executive, the latter suggested the importance of a reliable and modest personality (which excludes those of a combative and competitive disposition) as a desirable qualification for top executives. Superior positions are normally obtained through fierce competition among many workers who desire promotion. Fierce competition requires a strong determination and sometimes even ruthlessness, if one wants to be a winner, and this is normally incompatible with a reliable and modest personality. This would imply that employees should be less reliable and less modest before becoming top executives, and be more so after achieving

Table 1.6 Ability and background of top executives (factor loading after varimax rotation, characteristic value greater than one)

	Factor 1	Factor 2	Factor 3
A. Sound professional knowledge of specific field	−0.044	0.003	*0.870*
B. Broad knowledge of the business of the firm	0.189	0.263	*0.512*
C. Novel ideas and can implement them	0.016	*0.628*	0.197
D. Strong ideology and philosophy	0.163	*0.692*	−0.080
E. Sense of adventure and willing to take risks	−0.085	*0.704*	0.122
F. Skilful planning	0.305	0.297	*0.311*
G. Good organization and strong leadership	*0.495*	0.351	0.026
H. Loyalty to the firm	*0.652*	−0.090	0.115
I. Cooperation with other top executives	*0.677*	−0.131	0.132
J. Fairness	*0.558*	0.177	−0.025
K. Ability to process various information	0.322	*0.354*	0.144
L. Reputation among shareholders and financial firms	*0.604*	0.065	0.091
M. Popularity in the firm	*0.570*	0.131	−0.054

Notes
Factor 1: Cooperation, fairness and credibility.
Factor 2: Strong determination, novelty and risk-taking.
Factor 3: Sound knowledge and planning ability.

Proportion which explains the variance
Factor 1: 2.439
Factor 2: 1.853
Factor 3: 1.240.

The italics indicates the case where the factor loading has the maximum value.

top executive status. In other words, it is expected that one will abandon any strong fighting spirit, once one is promoted to a top executive position. One question remains, namely, is it possible to change one's character so easily after a person is promoted to the top? Since these people will already be middle-aged (say 40 or 50 years old) at this stage of their career, it is likely that their individual character and personality have already been consolidated, and therefore it will not be easy to change their personality. Alternatively, it may even require a hypocritical change in personal character. Or double-standards may be required. Anyway, such a change is necessary for top executives in order that they may be promoted and be successful in their job.

Another interesting and important finding is that luck is considerably important as one reason for achieving a top position. If the degree of competition among workers is so fierce, it is possible that the final deciding factor may be luck, such as a senior manager who pushes strongly for his subordinate to be selected for promotion. This is particularly true among ambitious and qualified workers whose potential competitors are numerous in larger firms. Although I do not deny but rather emphasize the importance of luck, this result may include a possible bias, caused by the fact that the survey is based on top executives' self-assessment. The justification for this statement is that some of those questioned may have preferred to give more modest reasons for their success, such as luck, instead of providing the real answers such as a strong determination or their own superior qualifications. It is also conceivable that top executives wanted to show their good nature deliberately in view of the previous result, namely that the most important qualification for top executives was revealed to be a reliable and modest personality. In the other extreme case, some arrogant top executives may openly draw attention to their superior ability and effort. Since it is difficult to judge which opinion is more plausible among the various interpretations described above, I cannot provide any decisive interpretations. It is, nevertheless, possible to conclude that 'luck' is important as one of the crucial causes for the determination of top executives. This is particularly true for larger listed firms where many qualified and ambitious workers are employed.

It is interesting to examine what kind of private and company lifestyles top executives experienced, because this may help to explain the success of top executives. Table 1.7 shows the result of top executives' own assessment of their lifestyle. The most impressive result is given by the fact that factor 1, which is the most important, indicates a strong desire for promotion and an emphasis on company loyalty. The priority given to company life signifies some sacrifice of personal and

Table 1.7 Lifestyle of top executives (factor loading after varimax rotation, characteristic value greater than one)

	Factor 1	Factor 2	Factor 3
A. Did not want to be delayed in promotion competition among the employees who entered in the firm in the same year	*0.810*	−0.091	−0.031
B. The most important weight was given to company life	*0.251*	−0.648	−0.021
C. Did not care about promotion but wanted to use own ability	−0.789	0.068	−0.032
D. Hobbies, study and social activities were the main interests	0.110	*0.837*	−0.086
E. Emphasized own speciality in the profession rather than managerial position	−0.139	0.376	0.342
F. Regarded job as a source of income	0.073	−0.077	*0.939*

Notes
Factor 1: Desiring higher positions and sacrificing private life.
Factor 2: Emphasizing own speciality in the firm and life outside the firm.
Factor 3: Regarding job as a source of income.

Proportion which explains variance
Factor 1: 1.377
Factor 2: 1.281
Factor 3: 1.008.

The italics indicates the case where the factor loading has the maximum value.

18

private life, because all their efforts are focused on working hard for the firm. It is fairly straightforward to accept the necessity of fierce competition in order not to delay the speed of promotion, and therefore to work hard in the firm. I feel that the top executives responded frankly, and moreover would suspect them of being less than honest had they provided the opposite answers to these questions. The empirical result based on the previous tables suggested the importance of a strong determination, ideology and philosophy in the face of very fierce competition regarding promotion. Emphasizing company life and sacrificing private life, which was found here for top executives, increases the probability of achieving the position of top executive. Winning in an atmosphere of fierce competition requires such a lifestyle for top executives, and it is easy to criticize it as inhuman. However, we have to accept the fact that it is difficult to accomplish the following simultaneously: winning against fierce competition among employees, and not neglecting private and personal life. Competition in both business and promotion can be cruel and heartless.

Although many top executives admitted that their life was dominated by company life and business activity at the expense of their private life, they expressed the opinion that the second most important lifestyle was to be able to specialize in their chosen profession; they claimed not to care about promotion because of this preference. This is inconsistent with the first and most important lifestyle evaluation. Why did we obtain such a contradiction? There are several reasons. First, some top executives wanted to avoid giving a true evaluation concerning their lifestyle, because of a guilty conscience. Second, some top executives merely wanted to express their own desire (that is, dream) regarding their way of life, although they did, in reality, accept the importance of fierce competition and emphasis on company life. This inconsistent result can be regarded as a limitation stemming from the fact that the survey was based on self-assessment, and this suggests to us a psychological complexity of human nature. One positive aspect, which would lessen the effect of the inconsistency, is that only a small number of top executives who graduated in science and technology could enjoy their personal life and engage in a specialized profession.

Finally, some top executives mentioned a third lifestyle – they regarded the job merely as a source of income, and said that they worked in order to maintain a decent standard of living. Since this factor is relatively minor in comparison with the other two factors, I shall not provide any serious interpretation of it.

1.4   THE ROLE OF TOP EXECUTIVES (OR MANAGEMENT PRINCIPLES)

Who owns the corporate firm, who governs it and who manages it? These questions are important to interpret the nature of the firm, or more broadly, the corporate governance structure. This section sheds light on one aspect of Japanese firms, by investigating the role and management principles of top executives.

Table 1.8 shows the estimated results of factor analysis for this. The most impressive observation based on the table is that top executives point out that the stability of the firm, the safeguarding of jobs, and coordination with directorates are the most important goals for top executives. It is interesting to note that the following two variables, namely consolidating the firm's financial position and making a contribution to society, have higher correlations with the previous three variables. In addition, the variable, raising overall performance of the firm's group, also aims to improve the stability of the group. These observations suggest to us the following general hypothesis: the most important goals of top executives are to maintain the stability of the firm and to safeguard jobs. This provides us with a crucial clue in interpreting the nature of the Japanese firm. The result supports the view of the Japanese labour-managed firm. In other words, although it appears to be owned by the shareholders and monitored by debtholders, in reality the firm is owned by its employees. Thus, top executives, who are the representatives of the employees, feel responsible for safeguarding the employment of their members (that is, their employees). Representative studies which propose the labour-managed firm as a plausible interpretation of the Japanese firm, include Iwai (1988), Komiya (1989 a and b) and Itami (1989). The current study supports them, although indirectly. The Japanese firm stresses the importance of employment and stability in business activity.

Although the present study supports the view of the labour-managed firm for the Japanese firm, at least on the basis of top executives' management principles, it would be useful to compare it with other interpretations of top executives. In particular, it would be interesting to make a comparison with the popular view in the United States, namely the tournament hypothesis for example, see Rosen (1986, 1990), Jensen and Murphy (1990), Gibbons and Murphy (1992), and Main, O'Reilly and Wade (1993), among others. There are several examples for Japan, namely Kaplan (1994) and Xu (1992, 1996). This hypothesis stresses the importance of very fierce competition in achieving the position of top executive, and gives us a clue towards understanding their extremely high rewards. Winners are entitled to receive very high salaries, which

Table 1.8 Role of top executives (factor loading after varimax rotation, characteristic value greater than one)

	Factor 1	Factor 2	Factor 3
A. Raising the rate of dividends	0.309	*0.567*	-0.011
B. Expansion of business activity	-0.097	*0.512*	0.338
C. Safeguarding employment of employees and their livelihood	*0.454*	0.220	-0.018
D. Increasing the number of managerial positions	-0.017	0.234	*0.653*
E. Raising the share price of the firm	0.214	*0.698*	0.004
F. Raising the relative position of the firm in the industry	0.221	*0.515*	0.193
G. Contribution to the society	*0.444*	0.237	0.096
H. Expansion of both budget and human resource at own directorate	-0.027	0.058	*0.803*
I. Coordination with other directorates	*0.577*	-0.292	0.498
J. Consolidating the firm's financial position	*0.740*	0.057	-0.035
K. Raising overall performance of the firm's group	*0.575*	0.184	-0.098

Notes

Factor 1: Stability of the firm and its employees.

Factor 2: Growth of the firm and raising overall performance of the firm.

Factor 3: Increasing the number of top executives and expansion of own directorate.

Proportion which explains the variance

Factor 1: 1.815

Factor 2: 1.619

Factor 3: 1.492.

The italics indicates the case where the factor loading has the maximum value.

compensate them for the fierce competition they have faced. Since this hypothesis is concerned largely with monetary remuneration for top executives, the interpretation based on the labour-managed firm hypothesis in this study does not constitute a counter hypothesis against the tournament hypothesis.

Moreover, it is possible to argue that these two hypotheses are compatible. In other words, they are concerned with different aspects of top executives in the following way. The labour-managed firm interpretation addresses the subject of management principles of top executives, while the tournament interpretation addresses their monetary compensations. Both admit that there is fierce competition to achieve a top executive position.

I would like to propose my own interpretation of the compatibility between both the labour-managed firm hypothesis and the tournament hypothesis in Japan. The idea is that Japanese top executives receive considerably high non-pecuniary compensations. These non-pecuniary compensations are represented by prestige, a feeling of satisfaction as top executives, and some other non-cash rewards such as the membership to a golf club, a large and luxurious office and a company car. I shall assume that the sum of both pecuniary and non-pecuniary compensation is the total payment to top executives. If this assumption is correct, then the tournament hypothesis would be applied even to Japanese top executives who receive the considerably higher total sum of the two types of compensation. Top executives in Japan want to safeguard employment of employees in the firm, and the stability of the firm in exchange for non-pecuniary payments such as prestige and satisfaction. Mutual understanding between top executives and ordinary employees within the firm enables them to adopt such an arrangement. Top executives wish to respond favourably to subordinates who supported the appointment of top executives, by trying to safeguard their employment. Ordinary employees are happy to accept the extensive range of non-pecuniary compensation which is received by top executives.

Non-pecuniary compensation is not unique to Japan. Hicks (1963) discussed it with regard to Europe and North America. Frank (1984) discussed the discrepancy between marginal productivity and wages. I understand that the cause of the discrepancy is due to non-pecuniary compensations such as prestige, glory, satisfaction and non-cash payments in the case of top executives in Japan.

It is useful to add another important difference between top executives in the United States and Japan: while top executives in the United States have to listen to the opinions and preferences of shareholders because of their powerful position, those in Japan do not care about shareholders because of Japan's intercorporate shareholding. In other words, the management side in Japanese firms has a position superior to that of the shareholders, because the latter are largely quiescent. Therefore, top executives are more able to safeguard the welfare of their employees.

Going back to the role of top executives, it is possible to point out the second most important role and goal, that is, the growth strategy of the firm, such as the growth of the firm and the performance in the firm. Factor 2, for example, is explained by raising the rate of dividend payments, expanding business activity, raising the share price and raising the relative position of the firm within the industry. These variables are highly correlated, and can be regarded as a propensity to grow. One interesting factor is that the relative importance of the growth propensity is inferior to the first priority, that is, safeguarding employment and the stability of the firm. Top executives in Japan prefer stability to growth, if they are asked to choose between them. This result, again, can be explained by the quiescence of Japanese shareholders.

There remains an irony or inconsistency here, too. The previous section presented the empirical result that the most important reason for achieving the position of top executive was to demonstrate excellent individual business performance. This is equivalent to the growth preference in general. Top executives are keen on growth prior to their appointment to a top executive position, but afterwards they prefer stability. It might be said to be a human tragedy that individuals are obliged to alter their preference during their career, but this is an overstatement.

The third important factor is associated with the number of workers and the budget in the directorate, and coordination with other directorates. Since the characteristic value is considerably higher than unity, the effect of factor 3 is not negligible but is in fact fairly strong. It is natural that a top executive attempts to expand or at least maintain the business activity of his or her own directorate or field of responsibility.

Finally, it is necessary to evaluate the proposition made by Aoki (1984, 1988), who suggested the intermediary role of top executives between shareholders and employees. Both sides normally hold various conflicting views, and thus top executives are expected to play an intermediary role between them. This study presented a view that top executives in Japan assess the interests of employees in the firm as the first priority, and that of shareholders as secondary. In other words, top executives are on the side of employees rather than of shareholders, at least according to the top executives themselves. Thus, top executives in Japan are unable to play an intermediary role with rigorous fairness. It is impossible, nevertheless, to conclude that all top executives are on the side of employees, for the following reasons. First, there are some differences in opinion among various classes of top executives, from the CEO to ordinary board members, implying that some of them, in particular the higher classes, are on the side of shareholders, as shown in Chapter 3 of this book (by Itoh and Teruyama). Second, this study has one further limitation, in the sense that top executives may behave differently in the case of an emergency even if they would prefer to be on the side of employees.

1.5   ARE GRADUATES OF PRESTIGIOUS UNIVERSITIES MORE LIKELY TO BECOME TOP EXECUTIVES?

It is said that Japan is a country of meritocracy, implying that people who receive higher education at various prestigious universities have better occupations and a higher probability of promotion in the firm, and finally, receive higher wages. It is not true, however, that the difference in the average wage earnings among various school levels such as junior high school, senior high school and university, is great. In fact, it is much smaller than that in other industrialized countries. Thus, it is not a country of meritocracy in terms of *average* wage earnings. In some other fields, however, education and schooling matter significantly. One example is that the promotion probability for university graduates is influenced strongly by the graduation level, and in particular by the name of the university.

This finding may be a contradiction because a smaller difference in *average* wages according to the level of education and a wider difference in promotion probability in firms according to both graduation level and the name of the university, may be inconsistent. The following example regarding the salary of CEOs in both Japan and the United States may provide an answer. The difference between the CEOs and ordinary employees with respect to their salaries in the United States is much larger than that in Japan, while most of the CEOs in large firms in Japan are graduates of several prestigious Japanese universities. See Tachibanaki (1982,1987,1988,1996) on the effect of education on both wages and promotion.

Meritocracy in Japan, therefore, is associated with the particular university from which a person graduated. In particular, the difference between prestigious universities and ordinary universities is important in many social and economic aspects, and it is said that the graduates from prestigious universities are treated more favourably, regarding, for example, employment, promotion and so on. One of the reasons for the entrance 'examination hell' in Japan is because of a belief in the advantages of attending a prestigious university. This section investigates the effect on the promotion prospects to top executive status, by examining whether or not the graduates from these universities have higher probabilities of promotion, the reasons for it and if any preferential treatment is observed.

First, the probability of promotion to top executive status is examined statistically. Before performing such a task, it is necessary to specify which universities are prestigious since that is rather a vague word. The survey which I use in this chapter, is addressed to top executives who are normally more than 40 years old. It is better to specify the universities from where people have graduated in the past, say 20 or 30 years ago, because the overall evaluation and impression of universities changes from time to time.

We regard the following universities as prestigious universities for this sample: the former seven imperial universities (Hokaido, Tohoku, Tokyo, Nagoya, Kyoto, Osaka and Kyushu), Hitotsubashi, the Tokyo Institute of Technology (TIT), Kobe, Waseda and Keio, that is, a total of twelve universities among the approximately 250 universities of 20–30 years ago. There should be a wide consensus about which universities are prestigious.

The survey includes 2,026 observations from top executives. Among these top executives 1,056 graduated from the above twelve universities. This is a surprisingly high proportion, that is, about 50 per cent of top executives. The graduates of only twelve universities comprise about half of the top executives in listed firms. Incidentally, the number of top executives who had no university education was 220, or about 10 per cent. It is, therefore, possible to conclude that graduating from universities is more or less a necessary condition, and at the same time, being the graduate of a prestigious university is greatly advantageous for achieving the position of top executive. This is a meritocracy.

It is necessary to conduct a more careful analysis to obtain a more solid conclusion on the effect of the name of universities on promotion, by estimating the rate at which various universities produced top executives, that is, the number of top executives compared to the total number of graduates who went into any business occupation, for each university, as was given by, for example, Koike and Watanabe (1979) for department heads. Since such a calculation requires intensive research, we did not repeat this exercise. It is anticipated, nevertheless, that a very similar result would be obtained in the case of top executives.

It is interesting to see the number of top executives from each university. Such a calculation shows the following result: Tokyo (184), Kyoto (179), Waseda (164), Keio (138), Hitotsubashi (67) and TIT (26). The top four universities' share is quite high. In view of the smaller number of total graduates at Hitotsubashi than other universities, 67 is an impressively high number. Instead, the figure for TIT is smaller. This is due largely to the fact that Japanese firms tend to select for promotion graduates who majored in humanities and social science. This is not an appropriate policy because the role of science and technology majors will be crucial in view of the future course of business in Japan. Although the figures were not shown for the other prestigious universities, it is possible to conclude that one of the most important necessary conditions for promotion to top executive status is to be a graduate of one of the prestigious universities.

One important remark about the above conclusion is that being a graduate of a prestigious university is not a sufficient condition to become a top executive, because there are many such graduates who are unable to become top executives, although the exact figures are not provided. Competition even among graduates of prestigious universities is fierce, as was pointed out previously. It is true that being a graduate of a prestigious university is certainly advantageous in the sense that there are higher expectations of them and more attention is paid to them in the firm. The deciding factor, however, is to win at the promotion game, which requires excellent individual performance, effort, luck, and so on.

What kind of people are graduates of prestigious universities? Table 1.9 shows the empirical results which show their characteristics as evaluated by top executives themselves. The most astonishing and interesting observation in Table 1.9 is that the most important qualification of the graduates of prestigious universities is not their high intellectual ability, which enabled them to pass the difficult entrance examinations for these universities, but their skills in forming and managing organizations, their determination and their ability to make an effort. At the same time, the second most important factor (that is, qualification) is sociability, cooperativeness, human networking and the ability for self-expression. Profound professional knowledge and high intellectual ability (factor 3) appear to be relatively unimportant. It is interesting that the graduates of prestigious universities are evaluated as those who are determined and who are prepared make an effort, and that their high intellectual capability, which was required for passing the difficult entrance examinations, is not highly appreciated.

Firms find that these attributes of strong determination and ability to make an effort, which were revealed at the time of the entrance examination, should be useful and applicable in overcoming various difficulties faced in daily business activities. In other words, the graduates of prestigious universities are expected to demonstrate these characteristics in their business life.

Table 1.9 Characteristics of graduates from prestigious universities (factor loading after varimax rotation, characteristic value greater than one)

	Factor 1	Factor 2	Factor 3
A. Sound professional knowledge	0.188	0.077	*0.804*
B. High intellectual ability	0.171	0.187	*0.806*
C. Sociable and cooperative	0.363	*0.540*	0.080
D. Performing all activities with confidence	0.287	*0.567*	0.263
E. Superior abilities to express oneself	0.182	*0.536*	0.344
F. Knowing various and helpful people (human networking)	-0.073	*0.806*	-0.014
G. Skill of forming organization and managing it	*0.530*	0.492	0.141
H. Strong determination and philosophy	*0.835*	0.186	0.166
I. Making effort	*0.795*	0.061	0.237

Notes
Factor 1: Strong determination and making effort.
Factor 2: Cooperativeness, knowing many people, and better ability to express oneself.
Factor 3: Higher intellectual and professional ability.

Proportion which explains the variance
Factor 1: 1.927
Factor 2: 1.871
Factor 3: 1.594.

The italics indicates the case where the factor loading has the maximum value.

Many firms in Japan do not take into account the type of degree obtained by candidates for new jobs, but attempt to hire as many graduates of prestigious universities as they can regardless of the discipline studied. This interpretation is supported by the preceding observation, because strong determination and the ability to make an effort are the most important qualifications of these graduates, at least from Japanese firms' point of view. This does not necessarily imply, however, that Japanese firms entirely ignore their high intellectual ability and sound professional knowledge.

Why and in what way are these graduates favoured for promotion in firms? It is useful to inquire into the reasons for the higher probability of selecting them for top executive positions, or for promotion in general. Table 1.10 presents the empirical results of this investigation. The most important reason is that there is a higher probability of them being assigned to favourable job fields, and encountering excellent managers. At the same time, the firm has higher expectations of them and more attention is paid to them, and their colleagues do not resent the preferential treatment, because the name of the university is not regarded as a subjective judgement. The next important factor is that they perform various business matters with confidence. Finally, the fact that they know many Alma Mater graduates in the government and other firms, that is, a favourable human network has already been established, is considered an advantage. The second and final points are related to the characteristics of the graduates of prestigious universities examined in Table 1.9. Chapter 8 in this book (by Ohashi) investigates the subject further, based on a different motivation and method.

An economic interpretation is provided for the first factor, namely, the reason for the higher probability of both hiring and promotion of the graduates of prestigious universities. The most plausible interpretation is that firms can save hiring and monitoring costs. It also reduces the risk factor because firms can minimize the probability of hiring less productive workers. Therefore, several very large firms in Japan accept job applicants only from a limited number of universities. Hiring the graduates of prestigious universities, and promoting them fairly quickly will reduce the probability of a misjudgement being made in both new hiring and promotion because the graduates are likely to possess the favourable qualifications proposed previously, and the system will be less costly. Another important motivation lies in the fact that it does not seem unfair to hire and promote them quickly because the criterion is not regarded as subjective, and therefore is not seriously criticized.

Now an overall evaluation, and several remarks concerning the preferential treatment of the graduates of prestigious universities, can be made. First, it is too simplistic to conclude that firms regard the name of the

Table 1.10 Reasons for successful career for graduates from prestigious universities (factor loading after varimax rotation, characteristics value greater than one)

	Factor 1	Factor 2	Factor 3
A. Having many friends in the government and other firms	0.128	0.041	*0.749*
B. Higher possibility of being assigned to a better job	*0.770*	0.035	0.131
C. Many graduates from prestigious universities among current managers	*0.572*	-0.031	0.497
D. Attention is paid to these people and so they are more appealing to others	*0.739*	0.274	0.040
E. Other employees do not object to favourable treatment for graduates from prestigious universities	*0.621*	0.315	0.091
F. Since expectation is high, those people make an effort	0.248	*0.804*	0.112
G. Job is performed with confidence	0.111	*0.831*	0.149
H. Having many Alma Mater graduates	0.062	0.276	*0.724*

Notes
Factor 1: Higher possibility of being allocated to favourable jobs without strong resistance from other people.
Factor 2: Having confidence and making effort.
Factor 3: Having many friends.

Proportion which explains the variance
Factor 1: 1.927
Factor 2: 1.871
Factor 3: 1.594.

The italics indicates the case where the factor loading has the maximum value.

university as the only criterion for new hiring and promotion. Selection based on fierce competition is more crucial than that. Second, it is neither academic clique nor favouritism, but rather economic rationality, which was the overriding argument for preferring the graduates of prestigious universities. These two points lead us to conclude that the preferential treatment is rational.

There is, however, a possible shortcoming in this preferential treatment – the opinion of the graduates of non-prestigious universities. They may feel a sense of unfairness when they see a situation where better and more favourable jobs are assigned to the graduates of prestigious universities, with the result that they are more likely to work under qualified and superior managers.

Such feelings may be detrimental, and may induce low work incentives. I understand, nevertheless, that such disincentive effects have not been serious so far for the following reasons. First, since their ambitions and hopes for achieving a top executive position were lower in comparison with the graduates of prestigious universities, the degree of envy is unlikely to be so high. Second, competition for achieving the positions of department head and director is so fierce among them that their incentive must be maintained at a high level, although the prospect for their becoming top executives is not so high. Third, in the past there was nearly always a generally high motivation among employees in Japan. The high propensity for growth in production and sales implied that nearly all workers were willing to work hard for higher incentives. Obviously, this contributed to the high growth of the Japanese economy.

The Japanese socioeconomic situation has changed considerably since the end of the era of rapid growth. Since per-capita income level is very high currently, it is impossible to expect that all workers will be highly motivated to work hard. Also, some criticisms must be made about, and reconsideration given to, the emphasis on working at the expense of personal and private life. If the favourable treatment of the graduates of prestigious universities continues, the work incentive for those workers from non-prestigious universities will be easily lost, because they currently receive a considerably higher wage than the minimum subsistence level. Japanese firms were successful in maintaining high work incentives for nearly all employees in the past, by providing them with various skilful institutional arrangements. It may be desirable, however, to abandon or weaken the preferential treatment given to the graduates of prestigious universities because the costs of retaining such treatment will be greater than the benefits which have been described in this section. Many Japanese firms have started to recognize this.

1.6 SALARIES OF TOP EXECUTIVES

This section briefly examines the remuneration for top executives. The wage structure for non-executives workers in Japan is fairly well known because there is a considerable accumulation of research on the subject, but we lack knowledge on the compensations for top executives because of both a lack of data, and a lack of interest. The present survey includes information on salaries, including the bonus payments, of top executives.

Table 1.11 presents the estimated salary for top executives. Some explanations are provided for the adopted independent variables. 'Senmon' is concerned with the distinction between the humanities and social science graduates, and those in science and technology. Top 1, Top 2 and Top 3 are concerned with the differences in position (say president, managing executives, ordinary executives, auditors, and so on) within the range of top executives. Since the degree of responsibility varies considerably among them, it may be possible to obtain considerably different salary figures. Industry dummy, firm-size variable, and capitalization require no explanation.

The following observations are possible based on Table 1.11. First, the salary for science and technology majors is slightly lower than that for humanities and social science majors, although it is not statistically significant. Second, the salary for presidents and vice-presidents (they may be called CEOs) is much higher than that for ordinary executives. The difference is about 14 million yen. The difference with managing executives is also large, say 4.56 million yen. The salary for auditors is slightly higher than that for ordinary executives. Since the estimated coefficient is not statistically significant, we understand that they receive nearly the same amount. The overall result leads to the conclusion that salary difference between various positions within the class of top executives is important, and that it may contradict the compressed salary hypothesis proposed by Milgrom and Roberts (1988) and Lazear (1989). Also, the result here is likely to support the tournament hypothesis which is compatible with the labour-managed firm hypothesis in our interpretation. We need, nevertheless, more studies to confirm this. Third, the salaries in manufacturing firms are somewhat lower than those in non-manufacturing firms, although the estimated coefficient is not statistically significant. Fourth, the effect of both firm size and capitalization is strongly positive. The salary of top executives in larger firms is much higher than in smaller firms, which is consistent with non-executive wage figures, (see, for example, Tachibanaki, 1996). The same reasons can be proposed to explain the wide difference in the salary of top executives between larger and smaller firms. Another important reason, namely, the more intense competition for promotion in larger firms compared to smaller firms, must also be considered in the case of top executives' salary.

Table 1.11 Estimated salary of top executives

Salary = 871.85 − 38.81 Senmon + 1395.72 Top 1 + 456.53 Top 2 + 37.04 Top 3
            (18.17)   (−1.48)   (29.25)   (16.23)   (0.98)

            −12.214 Industry + 198.17 Employee + 0.0151 Capital
            (−0.48)   (16.92)   (7.49)

$R^2 = 0.434$

Explanatory variables

Salary	Annual income (10,000 yen)
Senmon	Dummy on major at university: science and technology = 1, humanities = 0
Top 1	Dummy on position above vice-president
Top 2	Dummy on managing and executive director
Top 3	Dummy on auditor
Industry	Industrial dummy: manufacturing = 1, non-manufacturing = 0
Employee	Number of employees less than 300 = 1, 300–499 = 2, 500–999 = 3, 1,000–4,999 = 4, 5,000–9,999 = 5, 10,000– = 6
Capital	Capitalization (0.1 billion yen)

Note: Figures in parentheses are the estimated *t*-values.

1.7 CONCLUDING REMARKS

This chapter examined the subject, 'who is promoted to top executive positions in Japanese firms?'. Also, the role and management principles of top executives were investigated. It is necessary to keep in mind that the empirical results were derived from the top executives' own assessment on several questions.

The following subjects were investigated, and results were obtained. The typical career patterns, which enable workers to be promoted to top executive positions, were proposed. At the same time, several jobs and positions, which do not produce a higher probability of becoming a top executive, were presented. The most crucial factor, which allows workers to reach the position of top executive, is to show excellent individual performance in the firm and to make significant effort. Also, luck is another important factor. The examination of lifestyle suggested that top executives placed top priority on company life, sacrificing personal and private life. However, several top executives stressed the importance of their personal life. I provided my own interpretation of this apparent contradiction. The most important role and management principle of top executives is to safeguard the employment of their employees. The importance of the growth of the firm is evaluated only as the secondarily important principle. I presented a mixed and compromising view of the labour-managed firm and the tournament hypotheses in interpreting the relationship between the role of top executives and the corporate governance structure in Japan. One reason for proposing this was that the top executives' goal is not only to seek higher monetary compensations.

Meritocracy, in terms of the importance of the name of a university, was examined to explain the higher probability of promotion for graduates of prestigious universities. It was proposed that a strong determination and work effort rather than high intellectual ability and sound professional knowledge was their main qualification. Firms in Japan regard it as a useful resource for various business activities. Finally, better human networking among the graduates of prestigious universities cannot be ignored.

The final subject was the salary of top executives. The following two observations are noteworthy. First, the salary difference between various positions within the category of top executives is considerably large. Second, the difference in relation to the size of firm is also important.

REFERENCES

Aoki, M. (1984), *Modern Firm: Law and Economy Based on the Game Theory*, Tokyo: Iwanami-shoten (in Japanese).

Aoki, M. (1988), *Information, Incentives, and Bargaining in the Japanese Economy*, Cambridge: Cambridge University Press.

Frank, R. (1984), 'Are Workers Paid Their Marginal Products?', *American Economic Review*, **74**, 549–71.

Gibbons, R. and K.J. Murphy (1992), 'Optimal Incentive Contracts in the Presence of Career Concerns: Theory and Evidence', *Journal of Political Economy*, **100** (3), 468–505.

Hicks, J.R. (1963), *The Theory of Wages*, New York: St. Martin's Press.

Itami, H. (1989), 'Human Capitalism in Japanese Firms', in K. Imai and R. Komiya (eds), *The Japanese Firms*, Tokyo: University of Tokyo Press, Chapter 3 (in Japanese).

Iwai, K. (1988), 'The Japanese Firms as Labour-Managed Firms', in K. Iwata and T. Ishikawa (eds), *Research on the Japanese Economy*, Tokyo: University of Tokyo Press, 295–310 (in Japanese).

Jensen, M. and K.J. Murphy (1990), 'Performance Pay and Top-Management Incentives', *Journal of Political Economy*, **98**, 225–64.

Kaplan, S.N. (1994), 'Top Executive Rewards and Firm Performance: A Comparison of Japan and the U.S.', *Journal of Political Economy*, **102**, 510–46.

Koike, K. and Y. Watanabe (1979), *Virtual Image of School Credentialism*, Tokyo: Tokyokeizai-shimposha (in Japanese).

Komiya, R. (1989a), 'Life Insurance Companies as Firms', in K. Imai and R. Komiya (eds), *The Japanese Firms*, Tokyo: University of Tokyo Press, Chapter 18 (in Japanese).

Komiya, R. (1989b), 'Structural and Behavioral Characteristics of the Japanese Firms', in R. Komiya (ed.), *The Modern Chinese Economy: A Comparison with Japan*, Tokyo: University of Tokyo Press, Chapter 3 (in Japanese).

Lazear, E.P. (1989), 'Pay Equality and Industrial Politics', *Journal of Political Economy*, **97**, 561–80.

Main, B.G.M., C.A. O'Reilly and J. Wade (1993), 'Top Executives Pay: Tournament or Teamwork?', *Journal of Labor Economics*, **11**, 606–28.

Milgrom, P. and J. Roberts (1988), 'An Economic Approach to Influence Activities in Organizations', *American Journal of Sociology*, **94**, S154–179.

Rosen, S. (1986), 'Prizes and Incentives in Elimination Tournaments', *American Economic Review*, **76**, 701–15.

Rosen, S. (1990), 'Contracts and the Market for Executives', *NBER Working Paper*, No. 3542.

Tachibanaki, T. (1982), 'Further Results on Japanese Wage Differentials: Nenko Wages, Hierarchical Positions, Bonuses, and Working Hours', *International Economic Review*, **4**, 43–68.

Tachibanaki, T. (1987), 'The Determination of the Promotion Process in Organization and Earning Differentials', *Journal of Economic Behavior and Organization Review*, **4**, 43–68.

Tachibanaki, T. (1988), 'Education, Occupation, Hierarchy and Earnings', *Economics of Education Review*, **7**, 221–30.

Tachibanaki, T. (1996), *Wage Determination and Distribution in Japan*, Oxford: Clarendon Press.

Xu, P. (1992), 'Is the Japanese Firm Labour Managed?', *Research on the Japanese Economy*, No. 23, 29–46 (in Japanese).

Xu, P. (1993), 'Bonus Payments for Top Executives in the Japanese Economy', *Research on the Japanese Economy*, No. 24, 73–96

Xu, P. (1996), 'Incentives for Managers', in H. Ito (ed.), *The Japanese Firm as a System*, Tokyo: University of Tokyo Press, Chapter 1, pp. 19–49 (in Japanese).

2. Determinants of top executives' promotion and remuneration

Tomohiko Noda

2.1 INTRODUCTION

In this chapter we shall investigate the determinants of top executives' promotion and remuneration in Japanese firms, in order to understand the incentive structure for top executives. There have been a large number of studies on this issue, for example, in the United States, Jensen and Murphy (1990) and Rosen (1990) have developed detailed arguments. Four studies have investigated the incentive structure of top management in Japanese firms – Kato and Roekel (1992), Kaplan (1994) and Xu (1992 and 1993).

Kato and Rockel (1992) provided the first systematic evidence on the determinants of top management remuneration of Japanese and US corporations, with particular emphasis on their personal characteristics. Their most notable finding is that executive remuneration in Japanese corporations is structured so as to penalize managers for job changes, whereas US corporations tend to reward managers for engaging in job hopping.

Kaplan (1994) studied top executive turnover and remuneration, and their relation to firm performance in the largest Japanese and US companies. This study found that Japanese executive turnover and remuneration are related to earnings, stock returns, and, to a lesser extent, sales performance measures.

Xu (1992) and (1993) investigated the determinants of top management remuneration from the viewpoint of agency theory. He examined the appropriateness of employee sovereignty hypothesis by investigating the relationship between top management remuneration and employees' wages, and concluded that the hypothesis was not applicable in large Japanese firms. (Xu 1992). Xu (1993) also discovered that there is a difference in the determinants between bonuses and remuneration of top management.

We shall analyse the incentive structure of top executives from two different aspects. First, we shall focus on the probability of promotion to top management by investigating the effect of personal characteristic variables such as tenure, outside experience and educational qualifications. Second, we shall focus on the relationship between the objectives of top executives and remuneration. This should provide an insight into the incentive structure of top executives in Japanese firms.

2.2 DATA

In order to investigate the determinants of promotion and remuneration in Japanese firms, we used comprehensive new micro data containing personal information on 2,246 top executives, which will be mentioned briefly here. 'The Research Group on Top Executives in Japanese Firms' conducted a survey of company top executives, which was carried out in July–August 1993. The subjects of this research were top executives of listed companies, unlisted non-life insurance companies and life insurance companies, who are registered on the 1994 Toyokeizai Top Executive Survey. We sent surveys to 8,000 top executives randomly selected from this data base, and obtained personal information on 2,246 of them, representing a response rate of 28.1 per cent.[1]

Summary statistics are reported in Table 2.1. We divide the size of firm into two categories. We define small and medium-size firms as firms with less than 1,000 employees and large firms as firms with more than 1,000 employees. Tenure is longer in large firms than in small and medium-size firms, whereas the length of outside experience indicates the opposite pattern. This shows that top executives in large firms tend to have a longer-term relationship and stronger commitment to a particular company compared with top executives in small and medium-size firms.[2]

Top executives have comparable salaries in both firm-size categories. The chairman of the company earned the highest salary.

2.3 DETERMINANTS OF PROMOTION

In this section, we investigate the determinants of promotion to top management. We focus on personal characteristics such as tenure, outside experience and academic background. We also focus on the size of the firm. First, tenure of top executives should be explained. In standard human capital interpretation, tenure measures the amount of firm-specific human capital obtained through experience as a top executive

Who runs Japanese business?

Table 2.1 Summary statistics: mean (standard deviation)

	Large firms			Small and medium-size firms		
	Chair-man	Vice-chairman	President	Chair-man	Vice-chairman	President
Tenure	35.57	29.85	25.50	25.75	15.00	17.22
	(12.78)	(16.54)	(18.00)	(16.58)	(0.000)	(15.92)
Outside experience	8.57	10.14	13.03	14.62	30.00	17.68
	(12.37)	(17.02)	(16.86)	(15.99)	(0.000)	(14.51)
Age	65.57	63.42	61.69	62.87	66.00	58.88
	(4.36)	(2.87)	(5.90)	(5.64)	(0.000)	(6.59)
Salary	4,499	3,142	3,595	2,593	2,499	2,409
in ten thousand yen	(1493)	(801)	(1272)	(934)	(0.000)	(1015)

	Large firms			
	Vice-president	Chief executive	Managing executive	Executive
Tenure	31.57	29.01	27.47	27.97
	(13.34)	(12.51)	(12.67)	(9.54)
Outside experience	6.96	7.26	7.62	3.83
	(12.68)	(12.74)	(12.74)	(9.03)
Age	61.71	57.88	57.88	54.65
	(4.68)	(3.51)	(3.51)	(3.78)
Salary	3,476	2,164	2,164	1,796
in ten thousand yen	(945)	(654)	(654)	(51)

	Small and Medium-size firms			
	Vice-president	Chief executive	Managing executive	Executive
Tenure	25.55	25.43	22.50	24.86
	(16.56)	(14.45)	(14.62)	(11.47)
Outside experience	12.33	11.37	13.08	6.68
	(15.83)	(13.53)	(14.48)	(11.55)
Age	60.83	59.56	57.73	54.39
	(5.70)	(4.71)	(4.46)	(4.72)
Salary	2562	1970	1692	1373
in ten thousand yen	(747)	(440)	(461)	(290)

and an employee of the firm, and its relationship to promotion is expected to be positive. From the viewpoint of incentive, promotion and tenure are also expected to be positively correlated in order to provide an incentive for individuals competing or planning to compete for the top executive positions in the firm.

We were able to calculate the number of years' outside experience that each executive had spent after finishing his or her undergraduate degree and before joining the present company. In the standard human capital interpretation, outside experience measures the amount of general human capital that each executive has acquired through working for other firms.

We were able to construct a number of dummy variables measuring several aspects of academic background of top executives. We created a dummy variable, '*NO UNIVERSITY*' which equals 1 if top executives do not have a university degree and 0 otherwise. It is often argued that alumni of the University of Tokyo form a strong university clique which plays an important role in various aspects of Japanese society. Therefore we created a dummy variable, '*TOKYO*', which equals 1 if executives received their highest degree from the University of Tokyo and 0 otherwise. There are other prestigious universities that play an important role in Japanese society, and we created several similar dummy variables: *KYOTO*, *WASEDA*, *KEIO* and *OSAKA*. We can investigate the effect of academic background on promotion by introducing these educational credential variables.

The educational credential variables are expected to rise with the probability of promotion. In the human capital interpretation, individuals with stronger credentials possess more general human capital. For instance, an individual with a degree from a prestigious university can increase the probability of promotion because of his or her strong ties to influential politicians, bureaucrats and business leaders who are also graduates of the same university (general human capital).

The same prediction can also be derived from the signalling interpretation of credentials. Educational credentials can increase the probability of promotions by signalling innate ability.

Finally, the size of the firm may be an important determinant of promotion to top management. We created firm-size dummies by dividing the size of the firm into six categories.[3] The size of the firm is expected to be negatively correlated with promotion.

We used a probit model in order to investigate the determinants of promotion to top management. We define the president, the vice-president, the chairman and the vice-chairman of the company as top management in this analysis. Thus, the dependent variable is the dummy variable which equals 1 if the top executive is top management and 0 otherwise.[4]

$$y_i = f\,(TENURE,\ OUTSIDE\ EXPERIENCE,\ EDUCATIONAL$$
$$CREDENTIAL\ DUMMY\ VARIABLES,\ FIRM\text{-}SIZE\ DUMMIES)$$
$$(2.1)$$

We estimated this model by dividing the size of firm into two categories and the results are reported in Table 2.2. Column 1 shows the result for large firms. *TENURE* and *OUTSIDE EXPERIENCE* are positive and statistically significant. The magnitude of coefficient of *TENURE* is larger than that of *OUTSIDE EXPERIENCE*. This suggests that the effect of tenure on promotion is larger than that of outside experience.

Table 2.2 Estimated result for determinants of promotion

	Large firms	Small and medium-size firms	All samples
TENURE	0.151	0.035	0.092
	(7.628)	(1.922)	(7.207)
OUTSIDE EXPERIENCE	0.141	0.048	0.100
	(6.545)	(2.649)	(7.757)
FIRM SIZE 2		−0.492	−0.608
		(1.428)	(2.050)
3		−0.234	−0.361
		(0.963)	(1.499)
4			−0.681
			(3.025)
5	−0.303		−0.924
	(1.299)		(3.250)
6	−0.940		−1.580
	(2.571)		(4.145)
TOKYO	0.930	1.189	0.925
	(3.659)	(3.785)	(5.056)
KYOTO	1.208	0.224	0.680
	(5.179)	(0.661)	(2.997)
KEIO	0.776	0.609	0.154
	(2.245)	(2.055)	(0.581)
WASEDA	0.163	−0.022	
	(0.459)	(0.046)	
NO UNIVERSITY	−4.832	1.289	0.187
	(0.000)	(1.464)	(0.309)
Log likelihood	−232.3	−121.2	90.74

Note: Numbers in parentheses are *t*-statistics.

Several educational credential dummies are statistically significant. This suggests that holding a degree from prestigious universities will have a positive effect on promotion.[5] *NO UNIVERSITY* is not statistically significant. This suggests that there is no significant differential of promotion between top executives who do not have a university degree and those who do.

Column 2 shows the results for small and medium-size firms. *TENURE* and *OUTSIDE EXPERIENCE* are both positive and significant. In contrast with the result for larger firms, the magnitude of coefficient of *OUTSIDE EXPERIENCE* is larger than that of *TENURE*. This suggests that the effect of outside experience on promotion is larger than that of tenure. Several educational credential dummies are statistically significant.

Table 2.3 Effect of tenure and outside experience on the probability of promotion to top management (percentages)

	Average tenure 26.72 years; Average outside experience 6.73 years	With a further 5 years' tenure	With a further 5 years' outside experience
Large firms	0.49	3.25	2.90
Small and medium-size firms	4.46	6.37	7.22

In order to investigate the exact effect of tenure and outside experience on promotion, we calculated the probability of promotion to top management (see Table 2.3). The probability for top executives in large firms who have the average tenure and outside experience of all the samples is 0.49 per cent. The average tenure and outside experience of all the samples are 26.72 and 6.73, respectively. The probability of promotion to top management in large firms increases from 0.49 per cent to 3.25 per cent when they have a further 5 years' tenure, whereas it increases from 0.49 per cent to 2.90 per cent when they have a further 5 years' outside experience. We obtained the opposite pattern from small and medium-size firms.

These results show that the effect of tenure on the probability of promotion is larger than that of outside experience in large firms, whereas it is smaller than that of outside experience in small and medium-size firms. Executives who have longer tenure have an advantage in the promotion to top management in large firms. This suggests that an internal promotion system prevails in Japanese large firms. However, the effect of outside experience is not so small in large firms. The result for small and medium-size firms suggests that there are a large number in top management who were transferred from a parent company.

We can interpret these results from the viewpoint of incentive structure. Our results suggest that the promotion system in large firms is structured to provide an incentive for individuals competing or planning to compete for the top management positions in the firm. One can argue that perceived difference in the incentive structure of promotion between the firm-size categories will lead to longer-term relationships and a stronger commitment of top executives in large firms to a particular company compared to top executives in small and medium-size firms.

We can also interpret these results from the viewpoint of human capital theory. Our result for the large firms suggests that the accumulation of firm-specific skills is more essential for promotion to top management in large firms. It is well known that large Japanese firms are eager to invest in firm-specific human resources. In order to manage firm-specific human resources effectively, top management needs to acquire firm-specific skills.

Aoki (1988) emphasized that an important consideration in evaluating managers in the promotional hierarchy of the Japanese firm is their ability to arbitrate. Therefore, managers need to develop an understanding of and insight into the full range of organizational activities in which they are directly or indirectly involved. Managers develop a good inside knowledge of the firm as their period of tenure becomes longer. Our result suggests that top management in large firms must be well acquainted with a full range of organizational activities in order to arbitrate effectively.

We now investigate the effect of academic background on the probability of promotion. Table 2.4 shows the differential of the probability of promotion between prestigious and non-prestigious universities, and it can be seen that there is a large differential of the probability of promotion between prestigious and non-prestigious universities. This result is consistent with the human capital interpretation as well as with the signalling interpretation of credentials.

Last, we investigate the effect of firm size on the probability of promotion. We calculate the probability of promotion of top executives who have same length of tenure and outside experience and belong to firms of a different size. The size of the firm is found to have a highly significant negative relationship to the probability of promotion. This shows that the larger the firm, the lower the probability of promotion. The probability of promotion in firms with more than 10,000 employees is 40 times less than in firms with less than 300 employees.

Table 2.4 *Differential of the probability of promotion between prestigious and non-prestigious universities (percentages)*

	Large firms	Small and medium-size firms
TOKYO	5.55	30.5
KYOTO	7.96	21.7
KEIO	3.91	15.1
NON-PRESTIGIOUS UNIVERSITY	0.59	4.40

Note: We used the coefficient of educational credential dummies in each firm size in order to calculate these probabilities. We also assumed that top executives have the average tenure and outside experience of all the samples.

Table 2.5 *Differential of the probability of promotion according to firm size (percentages)*

less than 300	300–499	500–999	1,000–4,999	5,000–9,999	more than 10,000
8.51	2.30	4.94	2.24	1.15	0.20

Note: We used the coefficient of firm-size dummies in order to calculate these probabilities. We assumed that top executives are graduates of non-prestigious universities and have average tenure and outside experience of all the samples.

2.4 TOP EXECUTIVES' REMUNERATION AND RELEVANT FACTORS

The following analysis concerns the procedures for deciding the remuneration for top executives. Two kinds of incentive mechanism are used when examining the relation between top executives' remuneration and incentives. First, the higher the top executives' positions, and the larger the companies, the less probability there is for the promotion of top executives, making it difficult to win in the promotion competition. Top executives can be motivated by the higher remuneration which they receive when they survive the harsh promotion race. Such an incentive mechanism is similar to tournaments of golf or tennis, which use a mechanism called the rank order tournament.

Second, an incentive mechanism for top executives is necessary to ensure that they keep pursuing objectives after they reach the highest position or cannot be promoted further. In this chapter, top executives' managerial efforts and the issue of incentives will be examined through an analysis of the relationship between top executives' remuneration and their objectives. I shall first review the second incentive mechanism. As was shown earlier, regarding the relationship between management's compensation and incentives, various studies have been made on the relationship between corporate performance index or stock prices and remuneration, from the standpoint of agency theory.[6] The data used here lacks information on corporate performance, so, instead of the corporate performance index, we shall deal with the level of effort which executives make in order to achieve their objectives. This chapter discusses top executives' incentive mechanisms through the analysis of the relationship between top executives' remuneration and the level of effort required to achieve those objectives which are regarded as important.

In the survey conducted for this chapter, respondents were asked: 'What do you regard as the most important objective as a top executive of a company?'. Respondents had to choose from four given answers for each of the eleven objectives. The answers represent levels of concern: (1) regard it as most important, (2) regard it as highly important, (3) regard it as important to some extent and (4) give it little consideration. The answers illustrate the importance that top executives attach to certain given objectives while engaged in their everyday work. In other words, they indicate how much effort they are making, that is, the level of their effort, concerning certain given objectives. Accordingly, by analysing the relationship between these items and remuneration, we can see which managerial efforts of top executives are connected to higher remuneration, in other words, which incentive is the basis for top executives' behaviour.

Table 2.6 shows the importance that top executives attach to each of the objectives.[7] If we combine 'regard it as most important' and 'regard it as highly important' into 'regard it as important', the largest number of respondents, 91.3 per cent, chose the objective of 'safeguarding employees' jobs and livelihood' as important. The result supports the argument that Japanese companies embrace employee sovereignty.[8] This is followed by 'reinforcing the company's financial position' and 'trying to improve the position of the company in the industry'. Regarding the objectives related to the interest of stockholders, 47.6 per cent chose 'raising the company's dividend rates' and 23.9 per cent chose 'raising the company's stock prices', showing that less emphasis is laid on these objectives than on 'safeguarding employees' jobs and livelihood'.

Table 2.6 *Importance that top executives attach to each objective (percentages)*

	Regard it as most important	Regard it as highly important	Regard it as important to some extent	Give it little consideration
Raising the company's stock prices	5.8	41.9	47.2	4.7
Expanding the business	19.5	54.5	24.8	1.0
Safeguarding employees' jobs and livelihood	41.4	49.9	8.1	0.2
Increasing the number of posts in the company	0.3	2.9	29.3	67.1
Raising the company's dividend rates	1.9	22.0	54.1	21.5
Trying to improve the position of the company in the industry	23.4	57.4	17.3	1.6
Doing a social service	11.2	46.1	39.3	3.1
Expanding the budget and the staff of charged section	0.7	8.2	38.3	52.2
Coordinating with other sections	3.3	44.3	47.4	4.6
Reinforcing the company's financial position	30.6	55.8	12.2	1.0
Raising the company group's performance	22.8	51.8	21.4	3.4

We shall now proceed to an analysis of the relationship between the level of top executives' efforts towards these objectives and their salaries. On the basis of the theory presented so far, the following remuneration function is estimated using ordinary least squares. The logarithm of top executives' salary is used as the dependent variable.[9]

Log (*salary*) = *f* (*TENURE, OUTSIDE EXPERIENCE, FIRM-SIZE DUMMIES, EDUCATIONAL CREDENTIAL DUMMY VARI-ABLES, POSITION DUMMIES, LEVEL OF TOP EXECUTIVES' EFFORTS*).   (2.2)

As the independent variables, a position dummy and an objective as a top executive are added to other variables used earlier. There are six position dummies from chairman to managing executive. The objectives are evaluated using four grades which are given corresponding points for analysis as follows: 'regard it as most important' = 3 points, 'regard it as highly important' = 2 points, 'regard it as important to some extent' = 1 point and 'give it little consideration' = 0 points. The objectives are: 'safe-guarding employees' jobs and livelihood', 'raising the company's stock prices', 'trying to improve the position of the company in the industry', 'raising the company's dividend rates' and 'expanding the business', and so on as shown in Table 2.6.

Table 2.7 shows the results derived from the estimation of the remuneration function. In order to examine whether there is any difference in each of the positions concerning the relationship between the remuneration and the level of effort, the positions are divided into two categories. One category includes top management (chairman, vice-chairman, president and vice-president), and the other includes lower management (chief executive, managing executive and the executive). For the top management, two additional estimates are given.[10]

For top management, the variable 'safeguarding employees' jobs and livelihood' is significant, which means that the more effort executives make to improve the interest of employees, the larger the remuneration of the top management will be. This result seems to support the argument that Japanese companies embrace the idea of 'employee sovereignty', in other words, Japanese management look on job security and livelihood of employees as management basics. However, the purpose of this chapter is not to examine the appropriateness of the idea of 'employee sovereignty'. We can only deduce that the top management who emphasize employees' job security and livelihood as their own objective receive higher remuneration. In other words, the top management's efforts to improve the interests of employees are reflected in their salary. From this, we can conclude that remuneration forms an incentive for top management to improve their employees' job security and standard of living. This indicates that the payments made to top management are not decided without taking these factors into account. Since employees in Japanese firms acquire more firm-specific human resources, top management need to consider the job security and welfare of their employees, in order to maintain the stock of firm-specific human resources. However, we must bear in mind that the objectives dealt with here are abstract. The task for the future is to examine them in a more tangible way.[11]

'Raising the company's dividend rates' is not significant. In other words, efforts to improve stockholders' interests do not lead to higher remuneration. From this result, we can conclude that compensation does not work as an incentive to improve stockholders' interests. However, as was mentioned earlier, concerning the objective of raising the dividend rate, about 50 per cent of the respondents regard it as most important or as highly important, so we cannot conclude that they do not emphasize this factor. They do not dismiss the objective of raising dividend rates, but their remuneration does not reflect their efforts to do so.

'Raising the company's stock prices' is statistically significant. Top management's efforts to raise dividend rates do not lead to higher remuneration, while those to raise stock prices do. This indicates that top management try to improve stockholders' interests through increased capital gains rather than through dividends.[12]

'Expanding the business' and 'trying to improve the position of the company in the industry' are not statistically significant. Efforts to improve the company's position or to expand business do not lead to higher remuneration. When top management develop innovative products in an attempt to improve the position of the company, and when their efforts are fruitful and the company grows, profits will increase and the stock prices will go up. Furthermore, the growth of the company not only attracts the interest of stockholders and leads to higher wages, but also results in better promotion chances and more stable employment. In other words, it leads to job security and ensures a good standard of living. In order to pursue stockholders' interests and those of employees, it is essential to ensure the growth of the company. That products of their company sell well on the market is the most important condition for guaranteeing the interests of stockholders' and employees. Accordingly, top management will pursue these objectives and their efforts will be reflected in their remuneration. (These are not, however, statistically significant.)

Table 2.7 Determinants of top executives' remuneration

	Top management 1	Top management 2	Lower management	All samples
TENURE	-0.001	-0.002	0.004	0.004
	(0.070)	(0.767)	(3.977)	(4.333)
OUTSIDE EXPERIENCE	0.016	-0.005	0.021	0.002
	(1.064)	(0.179)	(1.957)	(2.466)
FIRM SIZE 2	0.389	0.554	0.015	0.058
	(2.885)	(3.959)	(0.456)	(1.753)
3	0.466	0.469	0.112	0.151
	(4.055)	(3.969)	(3.381)	(5.322)
4	0.657	0.708	0.243	0.287
	(6.162)	(6.162)	(8.949)	(10.93)
5	0.857	0.826	0.392	0.435
	(6.944)	(6.085)	(12.76)	(14.54)
6	0.895	0.896	0.484	0.521
	(7.069)	(6.493)	(15.24)	(16.86)
MANAGEMENT EXECUTIVE			0.173	0.173
			(12.73)	(12.42)
CHIEF EXECUTIVE			0.351	0.348
			(19.06)	(18.56)

48

	(1)	(2)	(3)	(4)
VICE-PRESIDENT	0.011 (0.083)			0.593 (20.19)
PRESIDENT		0.200 (0.317)		0.600 (17.22)
VICE-CHAIRMAN	-0.092 (0.839)			0.514 (5.957)
CHAIRMAN	0.233 (3.019)			0.811 (14.58)
Safeguarding employees' jobs and livelihood	0.085 (1.945)	0.122 (2.618)	-0.115 (1.221)	
Raising the company's stock prices	0.289 (1.770)	0.237 (2.017)	0.068 (2.083)	
Trying to improve the position of the company in the industry	0.063 (0.927)	0.114 (1.607)	0.034 (2.551)	
Raising the company's dividend rates	0.034 (0.397)	-0.001 (0.020)	0.048 (0.335)	
Expanding the business	-0.456 (0.675)	-0.004 (0.009)	-0.002 (0.290)	
Adj. R^2	0.369	0.429	0.414	0.521
F-value	7.569	6.436	74.01	142.0

Note: Numbers in parentheses are *t*-statistics.

According to the analysis made so far, top management have the incentive of higher remuneration to pursue the interests of both stockholders and employees. However, according to Aoki (1984b) and (1988), Japanese companies' top management act as arbitrators of interests of both the stockholders and the employees. According to his theory, the results of this chapter's research can be explained as follows. In the pursuit of the interests of stockholders and employees it is easily assumed that these interests conflict with each other. To pursue two objectives requires arbitration when the two are in conflict. In such cases, top management work as mediators who can reconcile both sets of interests in a way that both sides will be satisfied. Therefore, the objective related to the growth of the companies is not reflected in their salary, because arbitration rather than growth is the factor most related to remuneration. It is not enough for top management to bring about the growth of the company. They can fulfil their role as top management only when they deliver the fruits of this growth to both sides in a well-balanced way. In the case of top management, higher remuneration can be attained only when an equitable distribution is achieved. Furthermore, by skilfully playing the role of arbitrator in the interests of both sides, they not only receive higher remuneration but also more secure positions for themselves. The results of the analysis presented in this chapter may support Aoki's theory, although in an indirect way.[13] We cannot conclude that 'expanding the business' and 'trying to improve the position of the company' have nothing to do with higher remuneration merely because these efforts are not statistically significant, or that top management do not have incentives to pursue the growth of their companies. On the contrary, in order to improve the interests of employees and stockholders in a wellbalanced way, it is necessary for top management to facilitate the growth of their companies.[14]

Next, let us look at the results concerning lower management, that is, chief executive, managing executive and executive positions. The first noticeable point is that the objective of 'safeguarding employees' jobs and livelihood' is not significant, although it is significant in the case of top management. In other words, except in the case of top management, efforts to secure the livelihood and employment of employees have nothing to do with higher remuneration. It can be concluded that executives other than top management are not given salary incentives to try to improve the interests of employees. This is a decisive point which distinguishes top management from other executives. The objective of 'raising the company's dividend rates' is not significant, but that of 'raising the company's stock prices' is, which is the same result as for top management. Lower management executives have incentives to conduct management with the aim of increasing stock prices. The objective of 'trying to improve the position of the company in the industry' is significant. This variable is not significant in the case of top management. Lower management executives have incentives to foster the growth of their company in their own departments, irrespective of objectives such as job security and welfare of employees or raising stock prices. Also, if stock prices rise while they are encouraging the growth of their company, they can get even higher rewards. Lower management executives may only have to foster the growth of the company, without paying much attention to the distribution of the fruit of that growth. Thus, they get salary incentives to perform better in each of their departments leading to a higher status in their company, regardless of the interests of employees and stockholders. If they have the chance of promotion to higher ranks, then the incentive to perform well could be especially strong.

Lastly, let us look at the effect of other variables, taking into consideration the results of the estimation using all the samples. As was mentioned earlier, according to the theory of the rank order tournament, by setting salary scales according to position, competition between executives is activated by giving them the incentive to seek promotion. A position dummy is significant for the whole sample. The higher the post, the larger the salary. The higher the post, the lower the probability of promotion, making promotion competition even more intense. Top executives who are successful in the fiercest competition will gain the highest rewards.

With regard to the size of the firms, all the firm-size dummies are significant. Therefore it can be concluded that top executives' remuneration is related to firm size.

As for the differential of remuneration according to the size of firm, top executives' salary in firms with less than 300 employees is 59 per cent of that in firms with more than 10,000 employees. The larger the firm, the more complicated the top executives' job becomes and the heavier the responsibility they shoulder. Accordingly, the capability required of top executives increases in proportion to the firm size. From this, we can deduce that the salary differential according to firm size actually reflects the difference in managerial capability of top executives.

As was mentioned before, there is a differential of between 1 and 40 in promotion possibilities between firms with less than 300 employees and those with more than 10,000. The fact that there is a remuneration gap – smaller firms get only 59 per cent of that of larger ones – reflects the differential in promotion chances. As was examined in the case of top management, even when the position is the same, if the company size is larger, the probability of reaching the same position becomes smaller. The less possible it is to attain a certain post, the higher the remuneration is set. The fact that there is a differential in top executives' salary according to the firm size can be explained by the rank order tournament theory.[15]

Furthermore, when we look at the differential in firm size according to top executives' posts, the firm-size differential is larger than that for other executives. For example, in the case of top management, executives of firms with less than 300 employees get 41 per cent of the salary paid to those in firms with more than 10,000 employees. For executives in lower management, the figure is 62 per cent. Giving the same interpretation as before, we can deduce that the executives' capability gap as well as the promotion probability gap are wider for top management than for other executives.

Length of tenure and length of outside experience are not significant in the case of top management. For executives at lower positions, both are significant, but do not strongly influence remuneration. In the case of executives, rather than indicators which show an accumulation of human resources, such as length of tenure or length of outside experience, managerial efforts or position are the deciding factors.

From the results presented so far, we can conclude that there are two kinds of incentive mechanism: the first links salary to position in the firm, while the second links it to top management's and top executives' objectives. In concluding this section, let us look at the points to note concerning the analysis. The problem of which managerial efforts are related to increased remuneration has been dealt with in this chapter. This does not automatically lead to the argument that top management do not have any incentives to raise dividend rates, for example, merely because the level of effort to raise these rates is not statistically significant. Some incentive mechanism other than remuneration could work here. The objectives which top executives emphasize includes abstract ones such as 'safeguarding employees' jobs and livelihood'. With regard to this limitation, it will be necessary to investigate more quantifiable factors in the future.

2.5 CONCLUSION

This chapter gives an analysis of the decision mechanism for top executives' promotion and remuneration. The conclusions derived from the analysis made so far are as follows.

1. The analysis of promotion to top management shows that there is a difference in the promotion mechanism between large firms and small and medium-size firms. In both these categories, the length of tenure and length of outside experience influence promotion to top manage-

ment, length of tenure has more effect in large firms, and length of outside experience has more effect in small and medium-size firms. Length of tenure and length of outside experience have much more effect on the probability of promotion in large firms than they do in small and medium-size firms. This difference in promotion decisions is the reason why top executives' tenure is longer in large companies and their length of outside experience is longer in small and medium-size firms. In large firms, top executives who have been promoted to their current position from within the company have a more advantageous position for further promotion.

Concerning academic background, there is no promotion differential between those who are university graduates and those who are not. Next, there is a promotion differential between prestigious and non-prestigious university graduates.

As a result of the analysis of the relation between firm size and the probability of promotion, it emerged that the larger the size of the firm, the smaller the probability of promotion, even when the length of tenure, the length of outside experience and academic background are comparable.

2. The analysis of top management remuneration indicates that the level of effort made in 'safeguarding employees' jobs and livelihood' and 'raising the company's stock prices' are related to higher rewards. The efforts concerning the growth of companies, such as 'trying to improve the position of the company in the industry' and 'expanding the business' do not lead to higher remuneration.

As for executives other than top management, the effort made in 'raising the company's stock prices' is significant. But that of 'safeguarding employees' jobs and livelihood' is not significant. On the other hand, 'trying to improve the position of the company in the industry' is significant. It is concluded that lower management executives are given incentives for objectives which foster the growth of the company rather than objectives whereby they would mediate to make an equitable distribution of the fruit of that growth.

NOTES

1. In this chapter, the term 'top executives' means executives and auditors selected at a general meeting of stockholders, excluding advisers and consultants who are not on the board of directors.
2. Length of outside experience can be obtained by subtracting years of service at the current company from the total working years after graduation. In other words, the number of years spent working in other firms.

3. There are six categories of firm size: less than 300 employees, 300–499, 500–999, 1,000–4,999, 5,000–9,999 and more than 10,000.
4. The positions include the following: chairman, vice-chairman, president (governor), vice-president, chief executive, managing executive, executive, auditor and others. Auditors and others are excluded from the analysis. Even if top management includes the chairman, the vice-chairman, the president and the vice-president, the results are almost the same. If top management is limited to the chairman and the president or to only the president, the results are the same.
5. With regard to Tokyo University, the Tokyo University Law Department dummy is considered, but there are no significant results.
6. Agency theory regards the relationship between stockholders and top management as the agency relation, that is, the relation between principal and agent. In this theory, top management are supposed to act to maximize stock prices. In such a case, it is impossible for stockholders to observe the level of effort made by directors to raise stock prices. A contract is entered into, depending on the results of their managerial efforts. Stockholders give top management incentives according to the contract to maximize their interests. However, since in Japanese companies most of the top management have been promoted from inside and there is no threat of a takeover, it is unreasonable for top management to be the agent of stockholders.
7. The objectives of executives are further elaborated in other chapters of this book.
8. The definition of 'employee sovereignty' is an employee group which decides the basics of corporate actions. It is the employees who have the right to receive a share of the results of the actions (Itami, 1989). In this chapter, we do not go into the problem of 'whose company it is' before making observations.
9. There are seven salary scales as follows: less than 10 million yen, 10 million–14.99 million, 15 million–19.99 million, 20 million–29.99 million, 30 million–49.99 million, 50 million–69.99 million and more than 70 million. To estimate remuneration functions, medians of each scale are used. The minimum is 9.99 million, and the maximum is 79.99 million yen.
10. If by excluding vice-presidents, the number of samples is too small, then vice-presidents should be included in top management.
11. Xu (1992) denies the appropriateness of employee sovereignty because the average wage of employees has no connection to directors' salary. In this chapter, there is no in-depth examination of whether it is employee sovereignty or not. But the results of the analysis in this chapter are contrary to those given by Xu. We can only conclude that an abstract element such as 'safeguarding employees' jobs and livelihood' is related to remuneration. Further research using more tangible factors will be conducted in the future.
12. According to Aoki (1984a), between 1966 and 1977, the average return of stock investments after tax was 17.0 per cent, while the interest rate of deferred time deposits of banks was 5.95 per cent.
13. A full-scale study will be carried out in the future on the hypothesis that the management of Japanese companies work as mediators to balance the interests of employees and stockholders.
14. According to Aoki (1988), in order for management to play the role of arbitrator efficiently, the growth of the company needs to be fostered.
15. According to Xu (1993), top executives' remuneration is strongly linked to sales (a variable representing the size of the company), but Xu explains this result from the viewpoint of the rank order tournament theory. The effect of the size of the company on remuneration reflects both the differential of executives' capabilities and that of promotion probability, but an assessment of the distinction between the two effects is a subject for future study.

REFERENCES

Aoki, M. (1984a), 'Shareholders' Non-Unanimity on Investment Financing: Banks vs. Individual Investors', in Masahiko Aoki (ed.), *The Economic Analysis of Japanese Firms,* Amsterdam: North-Holland, pp. 23–45.

Aoki, M. (1984b), *The Cooperative Game Theory of the Firm*, Oxford: Clarendon Press.

Aoki, M. (1988), *Information, Incentives, and Bargaining in the Japanese Economy*, New York and Cambridge: Cambridge University Press.

Dekop, J.R. (1988), 'Determinants of Chief Executive Officer Compensation', *Industrial and Labor Relations Review*, **41**, 215–26.

Gibbons, R. and K.J. Murphy (1990), 'Relative Performance Evaluation for Chief Executive Officers', *Industrial and Labor Relations Review*, **43**, 30s–51s.

Itami, N. (1989), 'Human Based System at the Japanese Firm', in K. Imai, and R. Komomiya (eds), *The Japanese Firm*, Tokyo: Tokyo University Press, pp. 49–72.

Jensen, M. and K.J. Murphy (1990), 'Performance Pay and Top-Management Incentives', *Journal of Political Economy* **98**, 225–64.

Kaplan, S.N. (1994), 'Top Executive Rewards and Firm Performance: A Comparison of Japan and the US', *Journal of Political Economy*, **102**, 510–46.

Kato, T and M. Rockel (1992), 'Experience, Credentials, and Compensation in Japanese and U.S. Managerial Labor Markets: Evidence from New Micro Data', *Journal of Japanese and International Economies*, **6**, 30–51.

Rosen, S. (1982), 'Authority, Control, and the Distribution of Earnings', *Bell Journal of Economics,* **13**, 311–23.

Rosen, S. (1990), 'Contracts and the Market for Executives', *NBER Working Paper*, No. 3542.

Xu, P. (1992), 'Is the Japanese Firm the Employee Sovereignty Type?', *Nihon Keizai Kenkyu*, No. 23, 29–46.

Xu, P. (1993), 'Executives' Bonus and Top Management's Incentives in Japanese Firms', *Nihon Keizai Kenkyu*, No. 24, 73–96.

3. Do positions and tenure of top executives affect their attitude?

Hideshi Itoh and Hiroshi Teruyama

3.1 INTRODUCTION

Since the amendment of the Commercial Law was implemented in October 1993, which made it easier for a group of shareholders to bring a lawsuit against top executives (board members), the corporate governance of the Japanese firm has been extensively discussed in the press. On the other hand, researchers in economics and business in Japan have been seriously addressing the question: 'To whom does the firm belong?' for a long time. A representative view is that it is unrealistic to see the Japanese firm as a shareholder–sovereign firm as in the theory of the firm in standard microeconomics: the firm does and should belong to its employees even though it is legally owned by the shareholders.[1] The typical argument goes as follows: the firm belongs to its employees because the corporate governance of the Japanese firm does not function to serve the interests of the shareholders (for example, absence of outside directors, difficulty of takeover due to cross-shareholdings, and so on), and because most of the board members are selected, through internal promotion, from those employees who have long tenure; the firm should belong to the employees because in the Japanese firm they have a greater stake in the performance of the firm than do the shareholders, and their investment in firm-specific human capital is essential. However, some argue that the interests of the shareholders are not ignored in the Japanese firm and that they do have important influence on managerial decision-making. Examples are the bargaining theoretic model of the firm (see Aoki, 1984), in which managers serve as arbitrators between shareholders and employees, and the model of the main bank that works as a mechanism to reflect the interests of the shareholders (see, for example, Miyazaki, 1993).

In this chapter we shall investigate abilities, qualifications and goals of top executives which they think are important, using the survey results based on questionnaires. Opinion surveys of executives and managers are often referred to as evidence of employee-sovereignty in the Japanese firm. However, the literature that studies the connection between executives' rewards and various firm performance measures using Japanese data, in the framework of agency theory, reports that their rewards vary accordingly to the amount of profit made by the firm and hence the interests of the shareholders have not been ignored.[2] None of these studies takes hierarchy across executives into consideration. Executives have different positions such as president, executive director, managing director, auditor and so on, which will have some influence on their behaviour. Furthermore, in the Japanese firm, board members appointed from outside banks or parent companies are likely to have distinctive roles.

We do not intend to answer whether the Japanese firm belongs to shareholders or employees. Our objective is to assert that the directors' positions and experiences can be important determinants of their behaviour: we want to open the black box of top management, and our analysis of the opinion survey results is a step in this direction.

The organization of the rest of the chapter is as follows. In Section 3.2, we shall explain data and summary statistics. In Section 3.3, we shall explain our estimation method, and report the results in Section 3.4. A brief summary is offered in Section 3.5.

3.2 DATA

The data set is based on the questionnaires distributed to approximately 48,000 directors on the board listed in *Toyokeizai Top Executive Survey*, 1994 Edition, of which 2,246 (28.1 per cent) responded. We further restricted the data set so that it contains 2,062 directors who answered all the relevant questions correctly.

The distribution of positions is as follows: chairman or vice-chairman (1.21 per cent), president (2.33 per cent), vice-president (3.78 per cent), executive director (10.52 per cent), managing director (22.74 per cent), nontitled director (46.31 per cent) and auditor (13.09 per cent). Those who are not members of the board are excluded. Comparing firms with less than 1,000 employees (hereafter called 'small firms') and those with 1,000 or more employees ('large firms'), we find that in the former the percentage of president is smaller and that of the vice-president is larger, while the percentage of president and vice-president is about 6 per cent irrespective of firm size.[3]

Table 3.1 summarizes age and tenure distributions in terms of positions and firm sizes. First, the president has a shorter tenure than any other rank. The age and tenure of the president may tend to be lower and shorter, respectively, if the president is the final winner of the promotion

Table 3.1 Age and tenure distribution

Position	Small firms (observations = 613)		Large firms (observations = 1,449)		t-value
	Observation	Mean (standard deviation)	Observation	Mean (standard deviation)	(mean comparison)
Age					
Chairman	7	61.43 (4.43)	18	65.83 (4.31)	-2.28[5]
President	24	58.83 (6.75)	24	61.37 (5.91)	-1.39
Vice-president	12	60.92 (5.74)	66	61.42 (4.95)	-0.32
Executive director	55	59.13 (4.84)	162	59.12 (4.13)	0.01
Managing director	132	57.61 (4.42)	337	57.86 (3.45)	-0.67
Nontitled director	290	54.43 (4.77)	665	54.65 (3.75)	-0.77
Auditor	93	60.33 (4.39)	177	60.46 (3.58)	-0.26
Tenure					
Chairman	7	26.29 (16.93)	18	35.67 (12.84)	-1.50
President	24	20.42 (15.55)	24	25.62 (18.01)	-1.07
Vice-president	12	29.58 (16.23)	66	33.74 (12.89)	-0.99
Executive director	55	27.25 (14.37)	162	30.80 (12.09)	-1.79[10]
Managing director	132	24.47 (14.36)	337	29.42 (12.29)	-3.73[1]
Nontitled director	290	26.58 (11.12)	665	29.39 (9.38)	-4.02[1]
Auditor	93	23.73 (14.32)	177	32.20 (11.92)	-5.17[1]

Notes: [10] = Significant at the 10 per cent level. [5] = Significant at the 5 per cent level. [1] = Significant at the 1 per cent level. These figures also apply in Tables 3.2 and 3.4–8.

competition. Actually the average age of the president in small firms is lower than that of the executive director. However, the difference is larger in tenure than in age. These findings may suggest that many presidents joined the firms in mid-career.[4] For example, although there are very few founder-presidents in the data set, a relative may have joined the firm in mid-career and become president. The observation that the president in small firms has on average shorter tenure is also consistent with the possibility that those sent on loan or transferred from the core firm of the business group take the president's post in the member firms.[5] On the other hand, in large firms the standard deviation of tenure and age of the president is larger than those of the other positions. It suggests that some presidents may be very old and/or have long tenure in large firms.

Second, comparing small firms with large firms, we find that the average age does not differ significantly while the average tenure of executive directors or lower positions is significantly shorter in small firms. This observation cannot be explained by the possibility that in small firms hierarchy is less pronounced or that a great deal was expected of the employees when they joined the firm after graduation, and they were promoted quickly. Again, it appears to be more likely in small firms that those who joined the firms in mid-career become board members.

Third, the data on auditors reveal interesting features. The auditor is on average the oldest after top executives such as chairman, president and vice-president, irrespective of firm size. However, the average tenure of the auditor is significantly different between small firms and large firms. These observations suggest that the determinants of appointment to the auditor position are distinctive across firm sizes. In particular, they are consistent with the typical pattern that in small firms those transferred from large shareholders or the firms which have strong business relationships become auditors, while in large firms, ex-employees or those who cannot become directors tend to take the position.[6]

Our main interest is in the relationship of the executives' positions and tenure with their abilities, qualifications and goals which they think important. As control variables, we also utilize the question concerning the reasons why executives think they were appointed as board members. Table 3.2 shows summary statistics for the question: 'Why do you think you became a board member?'. For each statement, a larger score implies that the respondent agrees with the statement more strongly. The following three statements have the highest average scores in both firm-size categories: 'C. Experiencing a wide range of tasks, enabled me to acquire a company-wide viewpoint'; 'F. I won subordinates' confidence and support'; and 'H. The company badly needed a well-qualified person like me'. Focusing on differences across firm size, we first find that the executives in large firms agree significantly more on 'A. I performed

Table 3.2 *Reasons for appointment (firm size)*

Reason	Small firms	Large firms	t-value
A. I performed brilliantly in my field of specialization	3.68 (1.03)	3.83 (0.97)	-3.11[1]
B. I worked hard without making serious mistakes	3.62 (1.07)	3.53 (1.07)	1.67[10]
C. Experiencing a wide range of tasks enabled me to acquire a company-wide viewpoint	3.86 (0.98)	3.88 (0.94)	-0.29
D. The company expected a great deal from me when I was employed	3.18 (1.08)	3.06 (1.06)	2.17[5]
E. I was fortunate to work with good bosses	3.57 (1.15)	3.80 (1.07)	-4.48[1]
F. I won subordinates' confidence and support	3.79 (0.80)	3.94 (0.74)	-4.12[1]
G. There was no other well-qualified person for the post	3.07 (1.12)	2.87 (1.08)	3.75[1]
H. The company badly needed a well-qualified person like me	3.82 (0.80)	3.85 (0.75)	-0.56
I. I was just lucky	3.62 (0.99)	3.78 (0.97)	-3.39[1]

Notes
Question: Why do you think you became a board member?
Score: 5 = Definitely true. 4 = Somewhat true. 3 = Cannot say one way or the other. 2 = Somewhat incorrect.
1 Definitely incorrect.
The figures represent means, with standard deviations in the parentheses.

brilliantly in my field of specialization'. A reason may be that the degree of task specialization is higher in large firms because specialization tends to be easier. Furthermore, the average scores of the reasons related to personal relations ('E. I was fortunate to work with good bosses' and reason F) and 'I. I was just lucky' are higher for executives in large firms. On the other hand, executives in small firms agree significantly more on two reasons: 'D. The company expected a great deal from me when I was employed, and promoted me on a fast track' and 'G. There was no other well-qualified person for the post'. Small firms may suffer from the lack of high-quality human resources, and hence determine future executive candidates soon after the time of employment (fast promotion pattern).

Table 3.3 compares the reasons for appointments in terms of tenure. The average scores of reasons A, E, F, I and 'B. I worked hard without making serious mistakes', tend to be higher for executives with longer tenure. Among them, the trend of the average score for reason A may be counterintuitive: the executives with less than 20 years of tenure agree on reason C (experience in a wide range of tasks) more than reason A (successful performance in the field of specialization). We thus do not observe the pattern that those who were employed in mid-career became board members because of their specialized knowledge. It appears more likely that those with short tenure attained the posts due to their experience with previous employers.

Table 3.3 Reasons for appointment (tenure)

Reason	Years of tenure (observations)				
	<5 (135)	5–19 (300)	20–29 (228)	30–39 (1,168)	≥40 (231)
A	3.56 (1.16)	3.66 (1.18)	3.87 (0.90)	3.81 (0.94)	3.90 (0.94)
B	3.30 (1.19)	3.36 (1.18)	3.51 (1.06)	3.62 (1.03)	3.71 (1.02)
C	4.04 (1.02)	3.88 (0.98)	3.80 (0.90)	3.85 (0.96)	3.98 (0.85)
D	2.90 (1.21)	3.26 (1.13)	3.22 (1.03)	3.03 (1.03)	3.19 (1.04)
E	3.53 (1.22)	3.46 (1.18)	3.67 (1.15)	3.83 (1.03)	3.79 (1.14)
F	3.69 (1.07)	3.71 (0.98)	3.86 (0.66)	3.95 (0.68)	4.03 (0.66)
G	2.90 (1.15)	3.12 (1.24)	3.05 (1.10)	2.86 (1.04)	2.92 (1.06)
H	4.07 (0.95)	4.22 (0.77)	3.81 (0.75)	3.73 (0.72)	3.79 (0.72)
I	3.49 (1.13)	3.49 (1.13)	3.84 (0.92)	3.81 (0.91)	3.70 (1.01)

Note: The question and measures are the same as those in Table 3.2. The figures represent means, with standard deviations in parentheses.

Tables 3.4 and 3.5 show summary statistics for those responses to the questions which we will later use as dependent variables. Table 3.4 shows the abilities and qualifications that board members think are important for directors. The average scores of the following four categories are high (higher than 4 points), irrespective of firm size: 'J. Sense of equity and fairness'; 'G. Ability to organize and lead'; 'K. Ability to integrate diverse information'; and 'B. General knowledge of the company and its business'. The next high scores (3.9's) are found, for small firms, in 'M. Popularity and credibility with subordinates' and 'C. Ability to produce and accept new and creative ideas', and for large firms, one more category 'D. Sound and consistent value and belief' is added to the list. Since 'A. Depth of professional knowledge in a specific field' achieves an average score of 3.6 in either firm-size category, it appears the generalist trait is regarded as more important than the specialist. Directors in large firms select significantly higher scores on average in abilities D, J, M and 'E. Willingness to take a risk' than those in small firms: it can be understood that a personal network is important in large firms and hence qualifications in personal relations and value are emphasized more. The willingness to take a risk attains the lowest average score in either firm-size category, while it is significantly higher for large firms. We do not know whether the main reason is that risk-taking is absent within large firms or that large firms are more tolerant to risk. The average score of 'F. Ability to formulate detailed plans' is significantly higher in small firms: executives in small firms may have to undertake leadership and formulate business plans by themselves, while those in large firms may delegate actual formulation of plans to subordinates.

Table 3.5 shows executives' objectives. Irrespective of firm size, 'C. Protect employees in terms of their employment and welfare' attains the highest average score (3.3). Other high scoring categories are 'J. Strengthen the company's financial base', 'F. Improve the company's status in its business field', 'B. Expand the company's businesses', and 'K. Improve the performance of the business group as a whole'. The score representing growth orientation is high, as expected, while the categories for stability orientation, such as the group performance and financial base, also achieve high scores. On the other hand, the average score of 'A. Increase the company's dividend ratio' is about 2.5, and that of 'E. Raise the company's stock price' is about 2.0: consistent with other opinion survey results, directors in our data set clearly think that the company is 'for employees rather than for shareholders'. The comparison in terms of firm size reveals that the average scores of goals B, E, F, K and 'G. Promote corporate philanthropy' are higher in large firms, while those of 'H. Increase budgets and personnel of the managing unit' and 'I. Coordination across business units' are higher in small firms. This implies that directors in small firms must be involved in the management of business units.

Table 3.4 Important abilities and qualifications (firm size)

Ability	Small firms	Large firms	t-value
A. Depth of professional knowledge in a specific field	3.63 (0.71)	3.66 (0.67)	−0.83
B. General knowledge of the company and its business	4.07 (0.63)	4.10 (0.62)	−0.92
C. Ability to produce and accept new and creative ideas	3.90 (0.63)	3.94 (0.63)	−1.38
D. Sound and consistent value and belief	3.86 (0.89)	3.93 (0.88)	−1.74[10]
E. Willingness to take a risk	3.05 (0.96)	3.19 (0.99)	−2.78[1]
F. Ability to formulate detailed plans	3.88 (0.66)	3.83 (0.65)	1.67[10]
G. Ability to organize and lead	4.32 (0.63)	4.32 (0.63)	−0.05
H. Commitment to and identification with the company	3.83 (0.81)	3.89 (0.82)	−1.53
I. Ability to promote harmony and collaboration among executives	3.52 (0.66)	3.55 (0.67)	−1.12
J. Sense of equity and fairness	4.25 (0.71)	4.33 (0.68)	−2.54[5]
K. Ability to integrate diverse information	4.09 (0.61)	4.11 (0.64)	−0.48
L. Credibility with stockholders and financial institutions	3.51 (0.79)	3.48 (0.79)	0.70
M. Popularity and credibility with subordinates	3.93 (0.64)	3.98 (0.60)	−1.84[10]

Notes
Question: What abilities and qualifications do you think are important for directors?
Score: 5 = Indispensable. 4 = Important. 3 = Important. 2 = Not important. 1 = Undesirable.

Table 3.5 Executive objectives (firm size)

Goal	Small firms	Large firms	*t*-value
A. Increase the company's dividend ratio	2.52 (0.66)	2.47 (0.68)	1.50
B. Expand the company's business	2.86 (0.69)	2.95 (0.70)	−2.72[1]
C. Protect employees in terms of their employment and welfare	3.36 (0.64)	3.32 (0.63)	1.31
D. Increase the number of managerial positions	1.37 (0.57)	1.35 (0.55)	0.70
E. Raise the company's stock price	1.98 (0.68)	2.07 (0.72)	−2.81[1]
F. Improve the company's status in its business units	2.90 (0.67)	3.09 (0.68)	−5.76[1]
G. Promote corporate philanthropy	2.56 (0.72)	2.71 (0.71)	−4.20[1]
H. Increase budgets and personnel of the managing unit	1.63 (0.69)	1.54 (0.66)	2.83[1]
I. Coordination across business units	2.53 (0.66)	2.44 (0.62)	3.00[1]
J. Strengthen the company's financial base	3.19 (0.66)	3.15 (0.67)	1.13
K. Improve the performance of the business group as a whole	2.84 (0.81)	2.99 (0.73)	−4.28[1]

Notes
Question: What are your important goals as executives?
Score: 4 = Most important. 3 = Very important. 2 = Somewhat important. 1 = Not important.

3.3 ESTIMATION PROCEDURES

Since the values of the dependent variables are discrete and ordered, we use the ordered logit analysis for estimation. It is a generalization of the logit analysis which is concerned with two values in a dependent variable, and the equation is given as follows:

$$\Pr(Y_j = i) = \Pr(\kappa_{i-1} < \beta_1 X_{1j} + \beta_2 X_{2j} + \dots + \beta_n X_{nj} + \varepsilon_j \leq \kappa_i)$$

where Pr(.) means probability. Y_j is a dependent variable whose value i takes either 1, 2, ..., I. For ability variables $I = 5$, and for goal variables $I = 4$. For each variable, a higher value implies the statement is more appropriate for the respondent. $X_{1j}, \dots, X_{nj}$ are independent, explanatory variables. ε_j is a noise term, which is assumed to be logistically distributed. We estimate the coefficients $\beta_1, \dots, \beta_n$ and the cut points $\kappa_1, \dots, \kappa_{I-1}$. Note $\kappa_0 = -\infty$ and $\kappa_I = +\infty$ are given.

We use the following explanatory variables.

TOPEXEC	Top executive dummy (=1 if vice-president or higher).
MANAGE	Executive/managing director dummy (=1 if executive or managing director).
NOMANAGE	Nontitled director dummy (=1 if nontitled director).
SHORT5	Tenure less than five years = 1.
SHORT20	Tenure five years or more and less than twenty years = 1.
COLLEGE	College or higher education graduate = 1 (527 or 85.97 per cent in small firms and 1,324 or 91.37 per cent in large firms have college or higher degrees).
PROMOTE	Careerist dummy (=1 if yes for the statement 'worked hard so as to keep up with others in the same cohort in terms of promotion'; 232 or 37.85 per cent in small firms and 542 or 37.41 per cent in large firms answered yes).
PRIVATE	Privacy dummy (=1 if yes for the statement 'spent a lot of time on personal matters other than his/her job at the company, such as hobbies, study, social activities, and so on'; 277 or 45.19 per cent in small firms, and 619 or 42.72 per cent in large firms answered yes).
REASON$_k$	Reason k dummy (=1 if the response to the kth statement in Table 3.2 was 'definitely true' or 'somewhat true') for $k = A, \dots, I$.

The estimation was conducted separately for the directors in small firms and those in large firms. Table 3.6 provides the results for the

Table 3.6 Estimation result (a): auditors excluded

	Ability L		Goal E		Ability M		Goal C	
Small firm								
TOP EXEC	0.549[10]	0.325	0.537	0.588[10]	1.212[1]	1.014[1]	0.670[5]	0.403
	[1.695]	[0.970]	[1.630]	[1.729]	[3.473]	[2.832]	[1.977]	[1.153]
MANAGE	0.224		−0.051		0.198		0.267	
	[1.231]		[−0.272]		[1.006]		[1.423]	
Pseudo-R^2	0.0286		0.0308		0.0741		0.0187	
χ^2	34.61		32.66		73.10		18.27	
Large firm								
TOP EXEC	0.602[1]	0.319	0.354[10]	0.372[10]	0.304	0.254	0.520[5]	0.367[10]
	[3.081]	[1.601]	[1.848]	[1.902]	[1.400]	[1.148]	[2.519]	[1.757]
MANAGE	0.283[5]		−0.018		0.050		0.152	
	[2.501]		[−0.156]		[0.401]		[1.295]	
Pseudo-R^2	0.0186		0.0154		0.0405		0.0227	
χ^2	55.18		42.55		93.67		53.54	

	Ability D		Ability H		Ability I		Ability J	
Small firm								
TOP EXEC	0.285	−0.290	0.151	0.222	0.077	−0.069	0.946[1]	0.878[5]
	[0.884]	[−0.873]	[0.458]	[0.651]	[0.235]	[−0.203]	[2.775]	[2.356]
MANAGE	0.575[1]		−0.071		0.146		0.118	
	[3.191]		[−0.392]		[0.767]		[0.641]	
Pseudo-R^2	0.0333		0.0371		0.0370		0.0300	
χ^2	43.95		45.71		37.78		32.58	

Large firm

	Goal K		Ability A		Ability E		Goal H	
TOP EXEC	0.420[5] [2.151]	0.344[5] [1.727]	0.553[1] [2.802]	0.491[5] [2.439]	0.246 [1.222]	0.003 [0.017]	0.200 [0.983]	−0.005 [−0.022]
MANAGE		0.076 [0.681]		0.062 [0.551]		0.242[5] [2.071]		0.204[10] [1.744]
Pseudo-R^2	0.0107		0.0391		0.0269		0.0279	
χ^2	33.95		119.32		70.20		69.89	

Small firm

	Goal K		Ability A		Ability E		Goal H	
TOP EXEC	0.530[10] [1.717]	0.208 [0.652]	−0.584[10] [−1.751]	−0.667[10] [−1.932]	0.329 [1.059]	0.191 [0.594]	−0.423 [−1.257]	−0.046 [−0.133]
MANAGE		0.322[10] [1.763]		0.083 [0.444]		0.138 [0.781]		−0.376[5] [−2.002]
Pseudo-R^2	0.0292		0.0576		0.0224		0.0354	
χ^2	35.93		62.87		31.21		36.22	

Large firm

	Goal K		Ability A		Ability E		Goal H	
TOP EXEC	0.451[1] [2.284]	0.283 [1.406]	−0.300 [−1.467]	0.055 [0.264]	−0.265 [−1.361]	−0.057 [−0.288]	−0.606[1] [−2.824]	−0.135 [−0.613]
MANAGE		0.168 [1.456]		−0.355[1] [−3.001]		−0.208[10] [−1.883]		−0.471[1] [−3.935]
Pseudo-R^2	0.0123		0.0463		0.0177		0.0266	
χ^2	34.11		119.14		60.86		63.46	

Note: The figures in square parentheses are *t*-values.

estimation which excluded auditors from the data, in order to make comparison across different positions. For the analysis whose results are reported in Tables 3.7 and 3.8, all the data were used. However, not all coefficients are reported as is explained in the next section: Table 3.6 reports the coefficients and *t*-values for position dummies, and Tables 3.7 and 3.8 report those for position and tenure dummies.

3.4 RESULTS

3.4.1 Role of Directors

For the purpose of focusing on the effects of the executives' position, we first conducted the estimation by excluding auditors from the data. Table 3.6 reports the coefficients for the position dummies (*t*-values are in the square parentheses). In a row corresponding each dependent variable, the left-hand side shows the coefficients for *TOPEXEC* and *MANAGE* from the estimation results when these are included as position dummies, while the right-hand side shows those for *TOPEXEC* when *NOMANAGE* is included instead of *MANAGE*. In other words, the left-hand side is the position effects of top executives and executive/managing directors compared to nontitled directors, while the right-hand side presents the effects of top executives and nontitled directors compared with executive/managing directors. The coefficient (as well as the *t*-value) for *NON-MANAGE* in the latter analysis is different from that for *MANAGE* only in terms of the sign, and hence omitted.

The first part of Table 3.6 examines how directors emphasize the shareholders' and employees' interests. Although which constituent members' interests the Japanese firm respects most is a frequently discussed issue, we find no research that investigates the effects of positions on the balance between the shareholders' interests and the employees'. The top part of Table 3.6 shows that irrespective of firm size, top executives emphasize the interests of both the shareholders and the employees more than nontitled directors. Compared with executive/managing directors, top executives also put more emphasis on increases in the share price (goal E). Furthermore, there is partial evidence that top executives emphasize the interests of employees more than executive/managing directors, following the significance of *TOPEXEC* in ability M in small firms and in goal C in large firms. On the other hand, the executive/managing director dummy (*MANAGE*) is not significant except for ability L in large firms. The difference between executive/managing directors and nontitled directors, if any, appears to be smaller than the difference from top executives.

The middle part of Table 3.6 provides the results concerning value orientation and personal relations. In large firms, the top executive effects are significant for those related to value orientation (abilities D and H). There is also significant difference between executive/managing directors and nontitled directors with respect to interpersonal skills (abilities I and J). These observations imply that top executives in large firms have distinct roles of leading the company by value and belief with the help of loyalty, while personal relations are emphasized by executive/managing directors.[7] We may expect that coordination among directors is a role of executive/managing directors in large firms (ability I). On the other hand, we do not find clear results for directors in small firms. We only find that executive/managing directors emphasize value and belief more than nontitled directors (ability D), and top executives put emphasis on equity and fairness more than other directors (ability J).

The bottom part of Table 3.6 reports the estimation results for specialization and segmentation. Irrespective of firm size, top executives emphasize the performance of the business group significantly more than nontitled directors (goal K), while specialized knowledge and the managing units of their responsibility are emphasized more by nontitled directors than by others (ability A and goal H). The difference between top executives and executive/managing directors is significant only for those in small firms in ability A, and hence the main distinction in terms of scope exists between executive/managing directors and nontitled directors. It is a clear finding that nontitled directors focus on the management of those units they are responsible for, in particular in large firms.

3.4.2 Role of Auditors

While the legal role of the auditor is to monitor accounting and management, a common view is that the auditor does not work as a monitoring device of management in Japan. It is often heard that the auditor is a position for those who cannot reach directors, and that there is little auditor independence from management because of the appointment of former executives of the same company, and so on. Here we study auditor independence by examining whether auditors have opinions different from directors in terms of important abilities, qualifications and objectives.

All the data were used for estimation with position dummies *TOPEXEC*, *MANAGE*, and *NOMANAGE*, and hence the position effects are measured compared with auditors. Tables 3.7 and 3.8 report the estimation results (the coefficients and *t*-values of position dummies and tenure dummies only). We first note that auditors in small firms emphasize loyalty and collaboration with other directors significantly more than

Table 3.7 Estimation result (b): auditors included.

	Ability A	Ability B	Ability K	Ability C	Ability D	Ability H	Ability I	Ability J
TOP EXEC	−0.557	0.145	−0.278	−0.370	0.200	−0.252	−0.743[5]	0.839[5]
	[−1.497]	[0.388]	[−0.706]	[−0.966]	[0.560]	[−0.684]	[−1.996]	[2.233]
MANAGE	0.087	−0.075	−0.025	−0.115	0.447[10]	−0.490[5]	−0.659[5]	−0.020
	[0.346]	[−0.290]	[−0.094]	[−0.444]	[1.895]	[−1.994]	[−2.548]	[−0.082]
NOMANAGE	0.026	−0.157	−0.010	−0.077	−0.118	−0.439[10]	−0.820[1]	−0.158
	[0.111]	[−0.643]	[−0.039]	[−0.312]	[0.530]	[−1.880]	[−3.315]	[−0.681]
Small firm								
SHORT5	−0.012	0.493[10]	0.533[10]	−0.089	−0.147	−0.145	−0.106	−0.067
	[−0.045]	[1.680]	[1.801]	[0.307]	[−0.536]	[−0.515]	[−0.372]	[−0.243]
SHORT20	0.405[5]	0.432[5]	0.313	0.127	−0.365[10]	−0.187	0.004	0.140
	[2.032]	[2.132]	[1.510]	[0.622]	[−1.924]	[−0.973]	[0.020]	[0.710]
Pseudo-R^2	0.0510	0.0371	0.0338	0.0348	0.0280	0.0311	0.0418	0.0247
χ^2	65.94	43.15	37.85	40.24	43.33	45.03	50.79	31.17

TOP EXEC	-0.101	-0.116	0.021	0.579[5]	0.434[10]	0.353	-0.166	-0.100
	[-0.417]	[-0.463]	[0.087]	[2.336]	[1.885]	[1.511]	[-0.694]	[-0.416]
MANAGE	-0.161	-0.120	-0.195	0.267	0.084	-0.140	-0.165	-0.089
	[-0.927]	[-0.676]	[1.123]	[1.525]	[0.519]	[-0.842]	[-0.963]	[-0.519]
NOMANAGE	0.191	-0.163	0.170	0.309[10]	0.008	-0.198	-0.411[5]	-0.290[10]
	[1.128]	[-0.943]	[1.018]	[1.811]	[0.050]	[-1.226]	[-2.453]	[-1.735]
SHORT5	0.675[1]	0.643[1]	0.317	0.217	0.022	0.126	0.256	0.371
	[2.787]	[2.679]	[1.305]	[0.920]	[0.095]	[0.555]	[1.065]	[1.564]
SHORT20	0.264	-0.008	0.055	-0.237	-0.164	-0.000	-0.112	-0.159
	[1.552]	[-0.048]	[0.318]	[-1.349]	[-1.004]	[-0.003]	[0.665]	[-0.927]
Pseudo-R^2	0.0424	0.0262	0.0204	0.0210	0.0110	0.0378	0.0280	0.0297
χ^2	124.48	71.26	56.78	58.19	39.36	130.85	81.87	84.38

Large firm

Note: The figures in square parentheses are *t*-values.

Table 3.8 Estimation result(c): auditors included

	Goal K	Ability L	Goal E	Goal J	Ability M	Goal C
TOP EXEC	-0.110	0.032	0.185	-0.303	0.789[5]	0.560
	[-0.318]	[0.089]	[0.503]	[-0.834]	[2.042]	[1.487]
MANAGE	-0.303	-0.302	-0.399	-0.308	-0.215	0.188
	[-1.251]	[-1.231]	[-1.597]	[-1.228]	[-0.814]	[0.759]
NOMANAGE	-0.605[1]	-0.505[5]	-0.364	-0.567[5]	-0.388	-0.087
	[-2.614]	[-2.151]	[-1.525]	[-2.367]	[-1.534]	[-0.370]
SHORT5	0.322	0.103	0.414	0.046	-0.392	-0.601[5]
	[1.178]	[0.375]	[1.500]	[0.165]	[-1.327]	[-2.078]
SHORT20	0.066	-0.016	0.469[5]	0.128	0.134	-0.073
	[0.344]	[-0.081]	[2.331]	[0.643]	[0.639]	[-0.370]
Pseudo-R^2	0.0263	0.0229	0.0294	0.0252	0.0599	0.0175
χ^2	38.35	32.96	37.02	30.24	70.27	20.04

Small firm

TOP EXEC	0.145	-0.002	0.095	-0.200	-0.139	0.240
	[0.616]	[-0.007]	[0.415]	[-0.840]	[-0.544]	[0.986]
MANAGE	-0.136	-0.304[10]	-0.279[10]	-0.366[5]	-0.385[5]	-0.116
	[-0.805]	[-1.785]	[-1.647]	[-2.122]	[-2.127]	[-0.668]
NOMANAGE	-0.310[10]	-0.583[1]	-0.263	-0.476[1]	-0.433[5]	-0.258
	[-1.886]	[-3.511]	[-1.610]	[-2.824]	[-2.450]	[-1.517]
SHORT5	0.418[10]	0.611[1]	0.176	0.649[1]	0.015	0.143
	[1.771]	[2.650]	[0.765]	[2.688]	[0.060]	[0.613]
SHORT20	-0.143	0.264	0.012	-0.279	-0.079	-0.184
	[-0.838]	[1.603]	[0.074]	[-1.613]	[-0.436]	[-1.081]
Pseudo-R^2	0.0108	0.0203	0.0181	0.0258	0.0427	0.0203
χ^2	33.94	69.39	56.77	74.76	112.27	54.83

Large firm

Note: The figures in square parentheses are *t*-values.

73

other directors (abilities H and I). Second, for each variable in Table 3.8, there is no significant difference in large firms between auditors and top executives, and they both significantly emphasize each ability as well as goal J (and goal E although it is less significant) more than executive/managing directors and nontitled directors. In other words, auditors' opinions are close to top executives' in large firms. The only difference comes from value orientation (ability D and, in low degree of significance, ability H). However, we have already observed this in comparing top executives with other directors. The position dummies, in particular the top executive dummy, are also significant for the ability to produce new ideas in large firms (ability C): auditors in large firms are not expected to have creativity. The results are similar in small firms as well, except for the tendency that top executives emphasize personal relations more than auditors (abilities J and M), which feature was also observed previously in comparison with other directors. To summarize, we do not find evidence that supports auditor independence from other directors and the role of auditors as a monitoring and discipline device. The findings may actually imply the opposite conclusion: auditors may behave in accordance with other directors, in particular, with top executives in large firms.

3.4.3 Tenure Effects

There is a possibility that some of the directors with short tenure are those who are transferred from banks or group firms. We thus expect that these directors, along with directors who entered the company in mid-career, have different opinions about important abilities, qualifications and objectives of the director. The results reported in Table 3.8 are consistent, for the case of large firms, with the existence of directors transferred from banks and other financial institutions: in large firms, *SHORT5* is significant at the 1 per cent level for 'L. Credibility with shareholders and financial institutions' and goal J. As for small firms, the coefficients of the tenure dummies are positive for goal E, which observation may suggest that large shareholders provide directors. On the other hand, in small firms the coefficients are not significant for goal K. However, if we change the firm-size category, *SHORT5* is not significant in firms with 5,000 or more employees while it is significant with the t-value 2.034 in firms with less than 5,000 employees.[8] These results suggest that some directors are likely to be transferred from the core firm of the business group, an example of large shareholders.

As a second finding, we observe in Table 3.8 that directors with less than five years of tenure in small firms do not emphasize goal C and, with a low degree of significance, ability M. Seemingly this observation is consistent with the assertion that directors who are promoted from within make decisions from the standpoint of employees. However, we do not observe such a pattern in large firms. One interpretation is that directors may emphasize the interests of employees in large firms, independent of tenure, because large firms face social pressure to protect employment and there is an implicit rule that those who are not supported by subordinates cannot be promoted to directors.

Third, in Table 3.7, there is a tendency for directors with short tenure to emphasize knowledge and information-processing capabilities such as specialization (ability A), general knowledge (ability B) and ability to integrate diverse information (ability K). In small firms, this tendency is observed for directors with at least either less than five or less than twenty years' tenure. In large firms, directors with less than five years' tenure emphasize professional as well as general knowledge, while those with less than twenty years' tenure tend to favour specialist over generalist, although the significance level is low.

3.4.4   Effects of Reasons

We briefly mention the effects of other control variables. First, directors who think that 'I performed brilliantly in my field of specialization' is a reason for appointment, emphasize 'depth of professional knowledge'. Similarly, those who believe that 'experiencing a wide range of tasks' is a reason, think 'general knowledge' and 'ability to integrate diverse information' are important. Those who choose 'I worked hard without making serious mistakes' as a reason do not emphasize 'willingness to take a risk'. Almost all the abilities and qualifications are emphasized by those in large firms who believe they were on a fast track at the time when they were employed. For directors who think they won support from subordinates, 'popularity and credibility with subordinates' is an important qualification.

An economic interpretation of these observations is that promotion to director has a signalling effect: promotion of an employee with distinct characteristics to director transmits to others in the firm the information concerning what abilities and qualifications are important for directors. This signalling effect occurs intentionally or unintentionally. Promoting a particular employee may transmit a signal that was not intended by management.

One assumption behind this signalling story is that the abilities, qualifications and objectives emphasized by the firm are private information of management and are not precisely known to the employees. Another possible interpretation of the observations given above starts with the alternative assumption that they are well known to the employees, and what we have found are the outcome of the selection process: those who fit the firm's needs most were selected as directors. We shall study these alternative interpretations in future research.

Second, the success-orientated directors who 'worked hard so as to keep up with others in the same cohort in terms of promotion' emphasize 'raise the company's stock price' and 'increase budgets and personnel of the managing unit' significantly more. One possible interpretation of this observation is that these goals are relatively easily observed and hence those who desired success allocated their effort to the pursuit of these objectives. Furthermore in large firms, the success orientation is significant in 'Increase the number of managerial positions' and 'Improve the company's status in its business field' which observation may suggest that success orientation should be a source of growth orientation. Finally, we want to mention that the success-orientated directors in large firms do not emphasize value/belief or equity/fairness but they do emphasize the ability to organize and lead, and loyalty.

3.5 SUMMARY

We summarize the results of our analysis as follows:

1. Top executives (chairmen and presidents) tend to put more emphasis on both investors (such as shareholders) and employees than other directors do.
2. Top executives and executive/managing directors take a company-wide viewpoint and emphasize the performance of the business group as a whole, while nontitled directors think of depth of professional knowledge in a specific field as an important ability and qualification and emphasize the improvement of the status of their managing units.
3. In large firms, top executives take value orientation (sound value and belief, loyalty) in their leadership, and executive/managing directors consider the interpersonal skills (cooperation with other directors, equity and fairness) as more important than nontitled directors do.
4. Auditors in large firms place a greater emphasis on both investors and employees than directors do (with the exception of top directors). In this sense, their opinions and those of top executives are similar.
5. Auditors in small firms place more importance on loyalty and cooperation than directors do, and hence we do not observe auditor independence from management.

6. Directors with short tenure look upon knowledge and information-processing capacities as important abilities and qualifications.
7. In large firms, directors with short tenure emphasize credibility with stockholders and banks and raising the stock prices. This observation suggests that some directors should be transferred from financial institutions such as banks.
8. In small firms, directors with short tenure put more emphasis on the stock prices and the performance of the business group, which result suggests that some directors should be sent from the core firm in the business group.

In this chapter, we have focused on the effects of the directors' position and tenure, which have been ignored in the existing research on corporate governance of the Japanese firm. While the analysis based on opinion surveys such as ours is restrictive in various respects, there is little research that concentrates on the micro structure of top management. Our main assertion is that we should pay much more attention to the inside of the black box of top management which has mostly been analysed as a single entity. We hope that this chapter is a good starting-point for future research along the same lines.

NOTES

1. See, for example, the chapters by Itami (Chapter 7) and Komiya (Chapter 10) in Itami et al. (1993).
2. See Xu (1996), Kaplan (1994) and Kaplan and Minton (1994).
3. The distribution of firm size (in terms of the number of employees) is as follows: less than 300 (5.24 per cent), 300–499 (6.55 per cent), 500–999 (17.94 per cent), 1,000–4,999 (47.67 per cent), 5,000–9,999 (12.32 per cent), 10,000 or more (10.28 per cent).
4. One way to distinguish between those who started their career with the current employer (*haenuki*) and those who changed their jobs is to refer to the graduation year. Twenty-nine executives did not provide this data, and 34 graduated after they were employed with their current firm. Excluding these 63 from the data set, we find that the percentage of the executives who started their career with the current employer just after graduation is 48.22 per cent (284 persons) of the executives in small firms and 68.94 per cent (972 persons) of those in large firms. For presidents, however, the percentage is 20.83 per cent for small firms and 36.36 per cent for large firms.
5. In Table 3.1, there is no significant difference in the average tenure of the president between small firms and large firms. However, the president of the firm with 5,000 or more employees (although there are only three such firms) has an average tenure of 38.67 years, considerably larger than the average tenure of the president at the firm with less than 5,000 employees (21.98 years).
6. Using the same method as in note 4, we find that 67.03 per cent (61 persons) of auditors in small firms, and 40.36 per cent (67 persons) in large firms joined the current firm in mid-career.
7. A similar argument that the Japanese firm emphasizes value commitment is also found in Kagono et al. (1985), who made a comparison with a US firm.
8. *SHORT5* is also significant in firms with less than 500 employees.

REFERENCES

Aoki, Masahiko (1984), *The Co-operative Game Theory of the Firm*, Oxford: Oxford University Press.

Itami, Hiroyuki, Tadao Kagono and Motoshige Itoh (eds) (1993), *The Japanese Enterprise System. Vol.1. What Is The Firm?*, Tokyo: Yuhikaku (in Japanese).

Kagono, Tadao, Ikujiro Nonaka, Kiyonori Sakakibara and Akihiro Okumura (1985), *Strategic vs. Evolutionary Management: A U.S.–Japan Comparison of Strategy and Organization*, Amsterdam: North-Holland.

Kaplan, Steven N. (1994), 'Top Executive Rewards and Firm Performance: A Comparison of Japan and the U.S.', *Journal of Political Economy*, **102**, 510–46.

Kaplan, Steven N. and Bernadette A. Minton (1994), 'Appointments of Outsiders to Japanese Boards: Determinants and Implications for Managers', *Journal of Financial Economics*, **36**, 225–58.

Miyazaki, Hajime (1993), 'Employeeism, Corporate Governance, and the J-Firm', *Journal of Comparative Economics*, **17**, 443–69.

Xu, Peng (1996), 'Executive Salaries as Tournament Prizes, and Executive Bonuses as Managerial Incentives in Japan', mimeo, Forthcoming in *Journal of the Japanese and International Economies*.

4. Path to becoming a manager: promotion, advancement and incentives for office workers

Yoshinobu Kobayashi

4.1 INTRODUCTION

'Companies with strong managers are strong companies', is considered common knowledge. This is because managers are the leaders. President, chief executive, managing executive and director can do nothing without the work of the people on the frontlines. Thus, vitalization of managers as well as the allocation and education of personnel are critical points in any business.

The first target of employees in the struggle to climb the corporate ladder is to become a manager. Company employees have all kinds of targets in their lives: some may just want to become a manager; others will want to climb from senior manager to director, and even to the chair of the president. However, whether it is their first target or last, most employees would certainly like to become a manager, which also gives them an annual income of 10 million yen. Sooner or later, obtaining the title of 'manager' means that the desire for status has been satisfied, and at least one target in one's business life has been achieved.

This chapter focuses on the manager, looking at the intentions of both the employee and the employer. First we shall define the 'profile of a manager', and then discuss the making of a manager from the employer's point of view, while exploring how to become a manager via the internal corporate ladder. In this chapter, statistics were used only for under- and postgraduates, so that conditions for promotion are comparable.

4.2 PROFILE OF A MANAGER

Japan has 2 million managers. The Japanese Ministry of Labour reported in its 'Wage Packet Structure Basic Statistic Survey' that in 1992 there were

922,140 managers. This statistic is based on companies with 100 or more employees, where a manager is responsible for two or more subsections with ten employees or more. So, the above 2 million includes status-only managers without subordinates.

A typical manager is 45.6 years old, has 21.3 years of service, with an annual income of 8.5 million yen. This much we can see in the wage census.

Here, we shall examine in greater depth the profile of managers. Among the 262 managers sampled in this study, there were only five women, so Table 4.1 is based solely on men. The management positions will also be divided into those 'with subordinates' and those 'without subordinates'. Although the average age and average years of service do not differ much from those in the wage census, annual incomes were relatively high – 9 million yen, and nearly 10 million for those with subordinates, because the target population was managers of large enterprises. Most managers also took pride in their long service for the same company, and their undergraduate background. The existence of postgraduate science specialist managers (background statistics on men) may account for the existence of more university graduate managers without subordinates. This study reveals that most male employees (undergraduates) rise to the post of manager in their early forties. In the automotive company A, 88 per cent of those in their early forties are managers, 66 per cent in electronics company B, 80 per cent in chemical company C, 83 per cent in electric power company D, and 82 per cent (18 per cent of whom are senior managers) in department store E. The early forties is the age for rising to the post of manager. The 'Questionnaire on Japanese Managers' (Diamond) based on the study conducted by the Japanese Manager Study Group of managers in companies listed on the first section of the Tokyo Stock Exchange also shows that the average age of managers is 41.5.

Table 4.1 Profile of managers

	Manager (with subordinates)	Manager (without subordinates)
Sample	199	58
Age	44.6	43.6
Years of service	22.1	20.5
University graduates (%)	66.8	81.1
Loyalty (%)	95.5	89.7
Annual income (in 10,000 yen)	976	923

It might even be said that any university graduate can become a manager as soon as they reach their forties. Then, there would be another critical question: when does promotion occur? The study extracted from the sample university graduates who became managers, and reevaluated the group. The same was also done for submanagers as it is generally understood that the earlier one is appointed as a submanager, the earlier one rises to become a manager. Table 4.2 shows that employees become submanagers as early as 25, and up to 40. The model group was aged 31 to 33, which is generally considered the time for promotion. The first step to the post of manager is to become a submanager in one's early thirties. The age for promotion to manager is dispersed between early thirties and late forties, but the model group is concentrated between ages 37 and 38.

This study shows that it is the norm in most companies to be promoted to submanager in one's early thirties, and to manager in the late thirties. The early and late timing seems to be a difference in corporate culture. The coefficient of variation indicates this difference, with details of promotion by age given in Table 4.3. This table shows the age when submanagers and managers were promoted to their current position. The squared age is the age when most employees of the same age group are promoted, which is equivalent to the model value in the previous table. This table shows that most people are promoted to manager roughly 6 years after most people are promoted to submanager. In other words, a standard period for holding the submanager position can be considered roughly 6 years.

Table 4.2 Age when promoted to submanager and manager

		Automotive company A	Electronics company B	Chemical company C	Department store E
Sub-manager	Earliest	28	32	25	28
	Latest	38	40	36	45
	Mode	33	33	32	31
	Average	33.2	34.5	31.8	32.0
	Coefficient of variation	0.072	0.045	0.071	0.091
Manager	Earliest	35	35	30	31
	Latest	45	46	50	42
	Mode	38	38	38	37
	Average	38.4	39.6	37.2	37.2
	Coefficient of variation	0.048	0.061	0.098	0.056

Table 4.3 Promotion to submanager and manager, by age

Age	Automotive company A		Electronics company B		Chemical company C		Department store E	
	Sub-manager	Manager	Sub-manager	Manager	Sub-manager	Manager	Sub-manager	Manager
25					1			
26								
27					1			
28	1				1		1	
29	2				5	2	4	
30	4				6	2	12	
31	6				27	7	11	1
32	6		2		38	3	3	
33	8		10		21	2	2	
34	2		6		6	2	1	2
35	5	1	7	1		11	3	1
36	2	9	1		1	11		5
37	1	11		3		16	1	6
38	2	14		7		17		5
39		2		3		13		1
40		5	1	1		2		
41		1		2		1		
42		1		1		2		1
43				1		1		
44								
45		1						
46				1				
47								
48						1		
49						1		
50						1		
Total	39	45	27	20	110	95	39	22

What bears watching is the overlapping of the age of promotion to submanager and manager. For example, in automotive company A, the 35–36-year-old group still has some late-promoted submanagers at the same time as they have some early promoted managers. Such a trend is shared among the companies. This trend is especially prominent in chemical company C. Here, the age 31–33 submanager promotion group already has several people promoted to manager, implying a trend in early selection to promotion.

The background of the largely different process for promotion to manager at each company can be attributed to the different function qualification systems and their adaptation, especially the difference in application of duty positions, as described below.

4.3 FUNCTION QUALIFICATION SYSTEMS AND THEIR ADAPTATION

A qualification creates the order of the employees in the company. The ranking, based on the employee's capability to execute his functions is the function qualification system. This system was first introduced to Japan in the 1970s, and has rapidly become popular in the 1980s. It is now at the core of personnel administration.

4.3.1 Function Qualification System of Various Corporations

The five companies studied here are all large enterprises, and have strict function qualification systems. Generally, as the function qualification system gets established, the function qualifications become weighted more than the positions of manager, chief and so on. Therefore, the function qualification system of the enterprises must be thoroughly considered, for an understanding of the path to becoming a manager.

Figure 4.1 shows the function qualification systems of the corporations. Some corporations divide their lower qualifications (below manager class) into office workers and technical workers. This chart shows only the qualifications for office workers and technical workers, to avoid complications. The small figure at the left of the qualification name is the age for reaching the qualification (the average, earliest age, model is given here, according to the company). The charts show a rough correspondence of qualifications and positions. The bars at the middle of the qualification names show where screening is done for further promotion. The following describes the details of the systems.

Automotive company A
A has nine ranks from *syoki* to *sanji*, but qualifications override the positions. The managers are not called by their position titles, but by their qualification. As this would not be accepted outside the company, the corresponding positions (section head, manager and so on) are printed on the name cards for external use. University graduates start being pro-

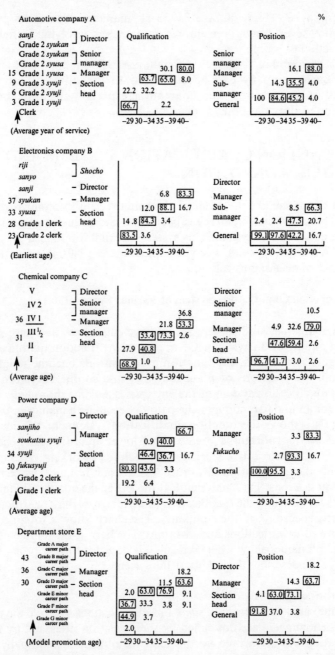

Note: The vertical total is basically 100 per cent, but may not always add up to 100 per cent due to rounding off.

Figure 4.1 Structure of qualification, position, by age

moted some time after they reach *syuji*. Screening is done at the stage of grade 1 *syusa*, which is roughly about 15 years after joining the company.

Electronics company B

The function qualification in B has seven ranks from grade 2 clerk to *riji*. The system is divided into the basic functions of clerk to *syusa*, and the specialist functions of *syukan* and above. The qualification for basic functions is reevaluated according to the length of service, training, interview and success of service; this is referred to as 'promotion'. When advancing to *syukan*, which corresponds to the manager class, the employee has to undergo 'screening' examinations – essay questions, quality evaluations and oral examinations. Then, *sanji* and above will be 'recognized' by management, and this is referred to as 'upgrading'. The function groups are divided into two, with the *syukan* as the dividing line; generally promotion procedures are applied until the *syukan* class, when screening starts.

Chemical company C

In C, the technical and office groups are categorized as grade I, and the specialist groups as II and above. An examination is given for promotion from grade I to II. Screening is done for promotion from grade III to the manager class, grade VI1. However, grade III became somewhat crowded, and was divided into two: grades III1 and III2. The upgrading from grade III1 to III2 was accelerated.

Electric power company D

D had the smallest university graduate population of the five target companies. Ranking starts to become apparent from the time of promotion from grade 2 clerk to *fukusyuji* (at about 30), and screening is conducted at the time of promotion from *fukusyuji* to *syuji*, which is about the mid-30s age group.

Department store E

At E, grades G to E constitute the minor career path, while grades above D constitute the major career path. Examinations are given for promotion from grade E minor career path to grade D major career path. The difference in age here is only some 3 years. The real screening comes at grade C (manager class) where the screening is based on a practical business assessment, resulting in up to a 10-year age difference.

4.3.2 Qualification Management and Positions

Here we shall see how the function and qualification system works to manage qualifications, as well as study the correspondence between qualification management and positions. Figure 4.1 shows the rate of qualifications and positions (vertically 100 per cent).

In automotive company A, the function qualification in the late twenties to early thirties age groups is *syuji* class, 20 per cent of which were promoted to grade 2 *syuji* in their twenties, and 67 per cent of which remain at grade 1 *syuji*. The difference becomes apparent in the early thirties group when 30 per cent are grade 2 *syuji* and 66 per cent are grade 3 *syuji*. In their late thirties, 30 per cent become grade 1 *syusa* (manager class), and 66 per cent are grade 3 *syuji* (section head class). The positions are largely rank and file for those in their early thirties, which diverges into manager, section head and rank-and-file class in their late thirties. When employees reach their forties, 80 to 90 per cent become grade 1 *syusa* – manager – making a neat match. In company A, the position does not catch up with the promotion by qualification in the thirties age group, but this can be considered the result of the internal banning of these positions.

Likewise, the rate of promotion starts becoming unequal at an early stage in chemical company C and department store E. Chemical company C starts seeing differences in promotion from as early as the twenties age group, and by the early thirties, half will be promoted to grade III and half will stay at grade II. In their late thirties, 70 per cent will be promoted to grade III (section head class), whereas 20 per cent will reach grade IV (manager class). The forties age group can also be divided into the grade IV1 and the grade IV2 groups. The shift of position is largely the same. Screening in company C at an early stage is also based on such promotion management.

Department store E also manages personnel by differentiating the qualifications and positions at an early stage. In other words, the qualifications start to differ from the twenties age group, with the early thirties group diverging into major career path grade D to section head and minor career path grade E.

On the other hand, the electronics and electric power companies do not differentiate as much among their employees. Electronics company B manages qualifications very neatly by age; those in their twenties are more or less grade 2 *syoki* (84 per cent), early thirties are grade 1 *syoki* (84 per cent), late thirties are *syusa*, and forties are *syukan*. With regard to positions, employees are mostly rank and file until the age of 35, and start having different rates of acceleration up the ladder from their late thirties, where, in their early forties their positions will vary from rank and file to manager. The company does not differentiate their people much by qualification, only making some later differentiation by position.

Electric power company D starts separating employees into *syuji* and *fukusyuji* in their early thirties, some will be promoted to *soukatsu syuji* in their late thirties, while others will remain *syuji*. However, the positions are strictly according to seniority: rank and file until the early thirties, *fukucho* in the early thirties, and manager in the forties. As company D is a public works corporation, employment conditions are more or less similar to civil servants, where management is based largely on seniority and supplemented by the qualification system.

As discussed above, the same function and qualification system combined with the position system can vary largely, even among only five corporations. Differences in history and culture, conventions of personnel management, and composition of the employees may explain the reason. Generally speaking, electronics company B and electric power company D are more or less balanced by age. Automotive company A, chemical company C and department store E start differentiating their employees from an earlier stage.

4.4 EMPLOYEES' IMPRESSIONS ABOUT PROMOTION

When we examine the path to becoming a manager, we must also study the question of how to become a manager from the employee's point of view, rather than only how to create a manager from the management side.

In this perspective, the subjects were asked questions about the possibility of promotion, the ranking of those starting in the same year, and if they could tell who would be promoted, as shown in Table 4.4.

First we shall look at the possibility of promotion – 'where will you end up in this company?'. The table shows that the undergraduate or postgraduate target group mostly expect to end up somewhere in the director class, or in the manager class. Delving deeper into the details, chemical company C and department store E have a large group, about 50 per cent, expecting to end up in the director class, indicating high expectations for promotion compared to the other three companies. On the other hand, automotive company A and electronics company B have some 40 per cent largely expecting to end up in the manager class. Electric power company D is somewhere in the middle, where expectations are divided among manager, senior manager and director.

Such differences may reflect the differences in the composition of the employees and personnel management, but differences in the sample in this study can also be a factor. In chemical company C, the questionnaire was distributed at their headquarters. Department store E has

Table 4.4 Promotion Factors

(1) Possibility of promotion

	Automotive company A	Electronics company B	Chemical company C	Electric power company D	Department store E
Managing director and up	3.3	5.4	8.2	0.6	10.6
Director class	23.5	23.9	47.3	23.7	56.1
Senior manager class	20.7	14.4	16.0	33.9	6.5
Manager class	44.1	42.3	19.7	29.4	20.3
Section head class	5.2	11.3	3.4	5.6	2.4
na	3.3	2.7	5.4	6.8	4.1
Total	100.0	100.0	100.0	100.0	100.0

(2) Manager orientated or specialist orientated

	Automotive company A	Electronics company B	Chemical company C	Electric power company D	Department store E
Manager orientated	53.5	31.1	39.8	45.8	43.1
Specialist orientated	16.9	42.8	31.3	26.0	31.7
Either	27.2	23.4	27.9	27.7	20.3
na	2.3	2.7	1.0	0.6	4.9

(3) Major in university

	Automotive company A	Electronics company B	Chemical company C	Electric power company D	Department store E
Law, economy	57.7	35.1	73.5	41.2	78.1
Technology, science	35.7	58.2	15.7	53.6	1.6

(4) Ranking of those starting in the same year is different

Age	1	2	3	4	5
24 and under	⎱ 11.1	9.1	⎱ 3.2	9.3	⎱ 7.8
25 to 29		5.9		27.3	
30 to 34	45.9	5.7	22.1	50.0	67.7
35 to 39	85.7	46.3	78.8	77.1	83.3
40 to 44	⎱ 89.6	86.3	86.7	⎱ 90.3	⎱ 88.0
45 and over		95.2	91.5		

(5) Can you tell who will be promoted to managing positions?

Age	1	2	3	4	5
24 and under	⎱ 44.4	54.5	⎱ 42.0	55.9	⎱ 39.9
25 to 29		42.1		65.7	
30 to 34	63.3	54.5	54.8	73.0	71.0
35 to 39	65.3	67.5	76.9	74.3	69.4
40 to 44	⎱ 66.7	70.6	78.4	⎱ 82.3	⎱ 74.0
45 and over		90.4	69.5		

(6) Why?

	1	2	3	4	5
According to the posts held	35.7	23.5	44.7	47.5	**40.3**
Superior results	**47.6**	**54.8**	**45.8**	21.2	44.4
Top in promotion race	**53.6**	20.0	30.0	13.6	4.7
Academic background	12.5	20.9	26.3	**64.8**	8.3
Training skills	34.5	**56.5**	28.4	30.5	44.4

(7) Do you think being a graduate of a leading university helps?

	1	2	3	4	5
	31.0	44.6	54.1	68.9	29.9

more female employees, and although there may be a difference of up to 10 years in the speed of promotion, they are likely to end up somewhere in the director class. The target of study of the two companies where people expect only to reach the manager class was the headquarters and sales department for automotive company A, and the headquarters and plant for electronics company B. Electronics company B has the highest rate of university graduates, with nearly 60 per cent of its employees being engineers: this may have some effect on the way they see their future there. Electric power company D has a low ratio of university graduates, and these graduates tend to take what is called the 'special fast track' to promotion. The reason why they still have different views about the future may lie in the fact that the management conducts de facto screening of university graduates at a comparatively early age. This matter will be discussed later.

In all of the companies surveyed, most university graduates expect to be promoted at least to the manager class, although some may go higher (to a director class). So, if most university graduates can be promoted to managerial positions, the problem then is how fast, and when?

Now let us examine when those who entered the company in the same year start noticing differences in their promotions. Table 4.4 (4) shows the rate of those who think that 'the ranking of those starting in the same year is already different'. This rate starts rising from the early thirties. The rise is especially apparent in department store E and automotive company A. Some 80 per cent of employees in these two companies, plus chemical company C, feel that they can see differences in their late thirties. However, only 50 per cent of those in electronics company B and electric power company D think so at this age level; this figure reaches 80 per cent only for those in their forties.

The speed of promotion can thus be divided into two groups: the fast groups of department store E, chemical company C and automotive company A, and the later groups of electronics company B and electric power company D. This largely coincides with the classification described in the function qualification system. The difference in personnel management is thus reflected in the eyes of individuals.

Generally speaking, the difference in ranking becomes apparent in the late thirties and early forties age groups, even though there may be some other differences. Such differences are mostly differences of the function qualification or position. When asked who would be most likely to climb up the corporate ladder, or who would go straight along the so-called 'élite course (fast track)', the trend seems apparent from a comparatively early stage. The result of this study also shows that 40 per cent of those in their twenties say that they can make a very good or vague guess about who will be promoted to a higher position, as can some 60 per cent in their early thirties and 70 per cent in their late thirties.

Then, how do they know? 'Superior results' is the most common answer, followed by 'top in the promotion race', 'training skills' and 'posts held'. However, electric power company D is a total exception. Here, 'academic background' ranks highest. In company D, 'academic background' (which in this company means which university a person graduated from, because the employees here are all university graduates) is a deciding factor which tells where each employee will end up (manager, director, and so on). They even know their final destination. This explains the reason why a surprising 70 per cent answered that 'being a graduate of a leading university helps' in company D.

4.5   PATH TO BECOMING A MANAGER

The important thing when climbing the path to become a manager is to be a part of the group of employees who joined the company in the same year, who are also promoted – and if possible, make a further step up from that group at as early a stage as possible. Never be late. So what do we do?

Here, we shall divide the 'manager age' group into three: early promotion group, late promotion group and not promoted group. We shall then reexamine these groups regarding work attitude, frame of mind and lifestyle, to see if these have any influence on their promotion (Table 4.5).

The results showed first, that the early promotion group make contributions to the company which are beyond expectations, have project proposals and suggestions adopted, and can make their own decisions. Second, they are determined to seek management posts, and have a clear ambition to climb up the corporate ladder, as shown by their future expectation to work as a line supervisor. Third, most do not take all of their paid holidays, and are negative about or simply disregard the need to have other things to do besides work.

Thus, this study shows that a typical manager is the 'workaholic' type. When considering the age of the current managers (in their forties), this may well be the only way to climb up the corporate ladder, and the quickest way to do so.

However, the above are only superficial reasons, given by those who succeeded. The watchword '343' whispered among employees reveals the true underlying reasons. The conditions for success are said to be 30 per cent luck, 40 per cent backup by a superior, and 30 per cent effort. Others insist on 70 per cent backup by a superior and the remaining 30 per cent of their own effort. In either case, backup by superiors speaks more than the employee's own capability and effort.

Table 4.5　Types of promotion for each group

	(A) Early promotion group	(B) Late promotion group	(C) Not promoted group
Work attitude			
Contributed to company beyond duty Chemical company C	33.9	12.8	16.7
Works just as or no more than expected Department store E	6.7	42.9	60.0
Paid holidays are not fully taken Electronics company B	100.0	66.7	76.9
Work progress			
Can make his or her own decisions Electronics company B	60.0	40.0	33.3
Project proposals and suggestions are adopted Automotive company A	63.6	33.5	38.5
Future expectation			
To work as a line supervisor Chemical company C	48.2	35.9	16.7
Department store E	66.7	28.6	0.0
Hobbies/interests			
Has other things to do besides work Electronics company B	9.1	22.2	53.8

Notes
Group (A) consists of those who reached a manager position by the median age of promotion.
Group (B) consists of those who failed to reach a manager position by the median age of promotion.
Group (C) consists of those who still remain in a submanager position at the end of their promotable age.

Table 4.6 Decisive factors for promotion to manager

	Automotive company A	Electronics company B	Chemical company C	Department store E	Total
Decisive factors for promotion					
Result of assessment	93.5	88.9	85.0	84.6	88.0
Age, seniority	58.9	64.3	66.4	66.7	64.4
Recommendation of superior	62.8	62.3	48.1	58.4	56.6
Achievement in examination	15.6	18.2	20.6	28.5	19.3
Academic background	16.9	17.8	28.6	13.8	20.8
Personality	45.5	40.4	31.6	28.5	37.0
na	1.7	2.4	5.0	4.1	3.3
Do you think being a graduate of a leading university helps?					
Early promotion group	37.1	36.4	37.5	13.1	35.0
Late promotion group	20.0	44.4	51.3	14.1	41.5
Not promoted group	26.7	46.2	50.3	20.0	36.8

93

The crucial factors for promotion to manager given in this study are 'result of assessment', 'age, years of service', and 'backup by a superior'. These are the three main factors. 'Assessment' and 'backup by a superior' become the two main factors for promotion beyond the post of manager. Although the most important factor for promotion is ' result of assessment' for all the surveyed companies, 'backup by a superior' ranks second or third in importance. Therefore, the superficial factor for promotion is always 'result of assessment', while the underlying factor seems to be 'backup by a superior'.

Academic background was generally not taken seriously in response to the question, 'do you think being a graduate of a leading university helps?'. The early promotion group especially showed negative responses of between 60 and 80 per cent. This implies that they were promoted not because of their academic background but because of their merit. However, three out of four companies affirm that academic background is a factor among the late promotion group and even more among the not yet promoted group; they do in fact think that it helps to be a graduate of a leading university.

Thus the above shows that to be promoted to manager at an early stage requires a person with determination to achieve, with both superior planning and execution skills, and who does not take many holidays. Besides being a workaholic, if this person also has the backup of his or her superior, and a good academic background, that will be an advantage when a promotion is being considered.

4.6 JAPANESE MANAGERS IN THE 21st CENTURY

American business economist Peter Drucker foresees that 'the Japanese hierarchical management organization system centring on the manager will soon become a constraint on effective management, and is doomed to extinction within some 15 years' (Drucker, 1993). Is it really true that managers will become extinct? The recent downsizing trend in organizations and revolution in information technology may be compelling proof of this possibility. The role of the Japanese manager who has supported corporate growth on the frontlines is gradually changing.

Actually, there are too many managers in Japan. Employees in managing positions of large businesses used to have an average of four subordinates; now it has decreased to 1.6. The major reason is the increased number of managers. The RIALS study, 'The Trials and Tribulations of Middle Management', also shows that the number of subordinates of a manager is between 1 and 4 or 5 and 9, even for line managers (the median is 7.1), and 3.9 for staff managers.

In addition, the traditional seniority approach is being reconsidered, forcing a change in the personnel management of promotion to manager. For example, Nissan Motors recently proclaimed a ban on the seniority system. In the traditional seniority management system, the bosses were asked to recommend a certain number of candidates for promotion from those who joined the company within a certain range of years, or certain percentages were allocated respectively to the primary screening, secondary screening and seniority levels. From now on, the years of service will not be taken into account. Honda has introduced a term system for the posts: 12 years for directors and 9 years for managers. Most noticeable in this new system is that age 45 was stated as the limit for promotion to manager. At Honda, a grade 4 exists under the manager class *syusa*, and the shortest time from grade 4 to *syusa* is 8 years. So it is understood that you must be at least grade 4 at age 37 to be promoted to *syusa* at age 45. In other words, 37 is the critical age for being promoted to manager in this new system.

The spring of 1994 saw a TV commercial showing a late-promoted new manager being tossed in the air by his seniors as well as his colleagues. This new manager looked about 50, and apparently had seen the promotion of his colleagues and juniors, but continued to do his very best in his work. They were saying, 'Oh you didn't even show your hangover' or, 'Congratulations, it's been a long wait'. But this will never happen under Honda's new system.

The fact that screening for promotion has become tough is confirmed not only by the short-range factor of restructuring under the prolonged recession, but also by the structural factor of white-collar university graduates; everyone is now a university graduate, and so many university graduates are being employed. This trend started in about 1970, when the baby boomers began to graduate. This triggered the employment of a large number of university graduates. Then, when the baby boomers reached the age of promotion to manager, the population of the manager class grew too large, creating what American Michael Hammer, known for his reengineering theory, referred to as the 'death zone' (Hammer,1993). One result of more and more people graduating from university has been the dilution of the quality of university graduates. These factors have driven management to make changes in personnel management. Even this study shows that electronics company B with the highest number of university graduates also has a greater number, compared to the other four companies, of those who have still not reached the position of manager (about 40 per cent). In the past, employees could be promoted to manager if they were university graduates; this is no longer the case.

With such trends, employees' ambitions can no longer be focused on becoming a manager. A recent trend shows that there are more employees studying at evening classes in vocational schools to gain relevant qualifications. In this era of transition in the corporate personnel management system, they find the need to learn special techniques in case they have to cope with restructuring. There is also a trend for employees to keep a psychological distance from the company. There is even a trend for mobilization of personnel.

The 'path to becoming president' is a success story only for a few select people. The 'path to becoming a manager' is a race that everyone participates in. Japanese corporate employees sweat blood in this regular race, because they expect, at the very least, that the management will promote them to manager. The 'path to becoming a manager' was the greatest incentive system for corporate employees. Now, however, the era in which everyone works hard to become a manager may have come to an end.

REFERENCES

Drucker, P.F, (1993), Comment in 'Japanese Manager', *Nikkei Sinbun* (newspaper), 28 November.

Hammer, M. and J. Champy (1993), *Reengineering the Corporation*, New York: Linda Michaels Literacy Agency.

5. Effort incentives: evidence from Japanese data*

Hideshi Itoh and Hiroshi Teruyama

5.1 INTRODUCTION

Many attempts have been made to explain practical pay and promotion systems in a firm as a consequence of rational behaviour of both the employer and the employee. Recently, incentive theory has played a key role in this literature. The main objective of incentive approaches is to explain how pay and promotion systems are organized in order to provide workers with incentives for greater effort.[1] Despite many theoretical contributions, there have so far been few empirical studies to examine the relevance of basic presumptions shared by many incentive models. One of the reasons is that most of the economic variables required for such empirical studies (for example, individual workers' effort levels and productivity) are, in general, difficult to measure quantitatively. In addition, even if there are appropriate proxy variables for those, they are usually unavailable to researchers because the data are closely related to the firm's personnel policy with factors such as salaries and performance ratings.

This chapter aims to investigate empirically whether the basic assumptions behind the incentive models are relevant in practice or not. The central assumptions are that a worker feels utility from earnings and disutility from effort and that a firm can make its workers put forth great effort by appropriately structuring its pay and promotion schemes as incentive devices. For this purpose we shall analyse how workers' effort levels are affected by their recognition of the firms' pay and promotion systems by using the data obtained from a questionnaire. The questionnaire forms

* The authors thank seminar participants at Hitotsubashi University, Osaka University and the University of Tokyo for helpful comments. Part of this research was done while Teruyama was visiting at the Department of Economics at Boston University.

This chapter is a translation of our previous paper in Japanese, which is Chapter 6 of *Shoshin no Keizaigaku* (*Economics of Promotion*) (ed. by T. Tachibanaki) published by Toyo Keizai in 1995, along with the following revision. A full description of a model in Section 5.2 and the comparisons of the distribution of questionnaire answers among companies in Section 5.3 have been added, and several explanatory variables in estimation equations in Section 5.4 have been altered.

were distributed to white-collar workers of five large Japanese companies: an automotive company, an electronics company, a chemical company, an electric power company and a department store (hereafter Companies A, B, C, D and E, respectively). Each is a representative company in the industry it belongs to in Japan. The questionnaire asked various questions about the respondents' work attitudes, and recognition and views about personnel policies in their firm, including self-evaluations of their effort levels and recognition of determinants of wages and promotion.

Since these answers are based on individual respondents' judgements, the data contain noises arising from differences in the respondents' subjective criteria. Although such a problem should be dealt with carefully, the data have a distinct desirable characteristic for our purpose. That is, in order to analyse the relation between effort levels and incentives, necessary information is how individual workers *subjectively* perceive the incentive devices. This is because personnel management schemes are not usually offered to the employees in unambiguous forms of contracts, and thus the recognition of the schemes may diverge among the employees.

The organization of this chapter is as follows. Section 5.2 will describe our hypotheses. Section 5.3 will explain how proxy variables are constructed by using the answers to the questionnaire in order to inspect the hypotheses, and compare the intra-firm distribution of the answers among the five companies. Estimation results of the ordered probit analysis will be presented in Section 5.4. Section 5.5 will conclude this chapter.

Table 5.1 Hypotheses

Hypothesis

(i)   The effort level increases with the size of short-term wage differentials on the basis of performance.

(ii) The effort level increases with the importance of performance as a determinant of short-term wages.

(iii) The effort level increases with the 'responsiveness' to wage differentials on the basis of performance.

(iv) The effort level increases with the importance of performance as a determinant of promotion probabilities.

(v)   The effort level increases with the expected hierarchical rank up to which the worker can be promoted.

(vi) The effort level increases with the size of long-term wage differentials due to differences in the hierarchical ranks on the basis of performance.

5.2   EFFORT LEVELS AND PAY AND PROMOTION SYSTEMS: HYPOTHESES

A firm is thought to provide effort incentives for its employees by compensating for their disutility of effort. From this viewpoint, the incentive models attempt to explore the economic rationales of observed personnel schemes in practice. The standard incentive models regard salaries as the compensation and explain that a firm provides its employees with effort incentives through the systems of wages, promotion and evaluations of workers' performance.

This section describes hypotheses about the determination of workers' effort levels responding to the incentive factors. These hypotheses should be accepted if the incentive view is realistic. Our six hypotheses to be examined are summarized in Table 5.1. Although they appeal intuitively, we will present a typical incentive model and explain each hypothesis along with the model in order to illustrate how they are logically derived from assumptions.

5.2.1   Short-term Incentives

We shall begin by considering short-term incentives with a single-period model. Let w be a worker's (real) wage level, and e be his or her effort level. The worker selects e. The higher value of e indicates the higher effort level. For simplicity, suppose that the worker's performance level takes only two values: either high or low. The (observed) performance level depends on the effort level and other uncertain factors (luck and/or measurement errors). We measure, for simplicity, e as the probability of achieving the high performance level. Therefore e is a continuous variable in [0,1]. The worker's (pecuniary) disutility of effort is $c(e)$, which is an increasing function of e. Let us assume $c(e) = e^2/(2R)$, where R is a positive constant.

A firm cannot observe its workers' effort levels directly. However it can observe the workers' performance levels (outputs) and thus can relate pay to performance. The wage level under the high performance level is w_H and under the low performance level is w_L. The worker is assumed to be risk neutral.[2] Then the worker's expected profit (expected utility) is $ew_H + (1-e)w_L - c(e)$. If an interior solution is assumed, the first-order condition of determining the effort level is $(w_H - w_L) - c'(e) = (w_H - w_L) - e/R = 0$ or:[3]

$$e = R(w_H - w_L). \tag{5.1}$$

The first-order condition (5.1) reveals the following. First, the condition, $w_H > w_L$, must be satisfied for $e > 0$. Second, e increases with the wage differential, $(w_H - w_L)$. This means that the effort level grows with the marginal revenue earned by an additional unit of effort. The condition (5.1) induces Hypothesis (i). The short-term wage differentials referred to in Hypothesis (i) are those made by 'bonuses' or 'regular raises' according to merit assessment and not by promotion (that is, the wage differentials which are not fixed in the long run).

In reality, especially for white-collar workers, it seems to be hard to obtain an exact and objective measure of individual performance level. Therefore, wages and performance cannot be accurately linked (that is, there exist noises in the evaluated performance, such as a supervisor's subjective judgement). Hypothesis (ii) is a restatement of Hypothesis (i) in this respect.

The first-order condition (5.1) also shows that the selected effort level rises with R. Differentiating equation (5.1) clarifies the meaning of R. That is, $\partial e / \partial(w_H - w_L) = R$, and this indicates that R is the 'responsiveness' of the worker's effort level to the incentive (the wage differential). In the above analysis, the pay scheme of the firm is given. However, the result with respect to R will not be altered when we consider endogenous determination of the firm's pay scheme. Suppose that, for some exogenous reason, a guarantee of minimum income (utility), $\underline{w}$, to each worker is imposed on the firm, independent of the worker's performance level.[4] Then under a given level of effort, e, the condition, $w_L - c(e) = \underline{w}$ or:

$$w_L = \underline{w} + \frac{e^2}{2R} \tag{5.2}$$

must be satisfied. From equations (5.1) and (5.2), the firm's expected profit is expressed by:

$$ex_H + (1 - e) x_L - ew_H - (1 - e) w_L = [ex_H + (1 - e) x_L] - \left(\underline{w} + \frac{3e^2}{2R}\right), \tag{5.3}$$

where x_H or x_L is the firm's profit when the worker's performance level is high or low, respectively. The second term in the right-hand side of equation (5.3) indicates that the firm must increase the average wage level if it wants to enlarge the wage differential, $(w_H - w_L)$, so as to raise the effort level. The first-order condition to the optimal effort level which maximizes the firm's expected profit is $(x_H - x_L) - 3e/R = 0$ (the interior solution is assumed). Thus the optimal effort level rises with R in the case of the endogenously determined firm's pay scheme. The above argument is summarized as Hypothesis (iii).

5.2.2   Long-term Incentives

However, the short-term pay-for-performance scheme is not always desirable for both the employer and the employee. It is likely that under the scheme a firm should incur many types of costs besides the cost assumed in the last subsection (that is, the cost of increasing the average wage level). Such costs may include, for example, the costs of monitoring or undesirable allocation of workers' effort to easily measured activities.[5] For a worker, the short-term performance evaluations may also be undesirable, if various noises are likely to preclude the fair evaluations in the short run (unless the risk is compensated enough).

If relating pay with performance in the short run is more costly than in the long run, a firm will adopt a system which differentiates long-term wages by using promotion based on the accumulated information on performance evaluations. In reality, Tachibanaki (1987, 1988) showed that the most influential factor for determining intra-firm wage differentials is the difference in hierarchical ranks, which means the long-term differentials in wages. (Throughout this chapter, the term '(hierarchical) rank' is used to refer to a hierarchical job position, such as section head, department head and so on.[6]) Thus we shall next consider the long-term incentives induced by wage differentials due to promotion by extending the model into a multi-period setting.[7]

Workers compete for moving up to higher ranks. The competition consists of R stages. Stage r ($r = 1, ..., R$) corresponds to each hierarchical rank in the firm. The worker's effort level at rank r is e_r. Let w_r be the (short-term) wage level at rank r, and P_r be the probability of promoting to the next higher rank $r + 1$. P_r is assumed to be an increasing and concave function of the effort level at rank r, e_r. The effort level, e_r, is unobservable for the firm in general, but both w_r and P_r can be tied to some verifiable performance measures (like the short-term incentive model above). Since performance measures vary with the effort level, w_r and P_r are functions of e_r. The lifetime utility of the worker at rank r is represented by v_r and thus:

$$v_r = \max_{e_r} \{ w_r(e_r) + P_r(e_r)v_{r+1} + [1 - P_r(e_r)] L_r - c_r(e_r) \}, \qquad (5.4)$$

where L_r is the present value of the lifetime utility (long-term wages) of a worker who loses the promotion competition at rank r and $c_r(e_r)$ is disutility of effort at rank r.[8] (We can adopt the same functional form $c_r(e_r) = e_r^2/(2R_r)$ as in Subsection 5.2.1.) Then the first-order condition to the effort level is:

$$w'_r(e_r) + P'_r(e_r)(v_{r+1} - L_r) = c'_r(e_r). \tag{5.5}$$

This equation means, under the standard assumptions, that the effort level, e_r, increases with w'_r, P'_r and $(v_{r+1} - L_r)$ and decreases with c'_r. The term w'_r can be measured by the short-term wage differentials on the basis of performance (as in Subsection 5.2.1). Let us represent the promotion probability in a more general form by $P_r(e_r; \theta)$. Here $\theta = (\theta_1, ..., \theta_K)$ indicates a vector of factors (uncontrollable by the worker) which may affect the promotion probability (for example, merit assessment factors). Factor θ_k is positive when it affects the promotion probability, and zero when it has no effect on the probability. If the marginal promotion probability with respect to e_r, $P'_r = \partial P_r / \partial e_r$, is larger with $\theta_k = 0$ than with $\theta_k > 0$, referring to factor θ_k upon promotion decisions becomes a negative effort incentive of the worker. That is because positive θ_k reduces the degree of dependence of the promotion probability on the effort level. Such factors may be the worker's academic background, length of service (tenure) and so on. For example some firms may differentiate promotion routes depending on workers' academic backgrounds for some reason, which is not necessarily irrational. However, workers' effort levels will be lower as the firm attaches more weight to such uncontrollable factors at the time of promotion decisions.

Many variables appearing in the first-order condition (5.5) may depend on the worker's length of service (hereafter tenure length), t. For example L_r can be a decreasing function of t under a given rank r, because the remainder period to the mandatory retirement is short for a worker with long duration of service. On the other hand we can think of the marginal probability, P'_r, as an increasing function of t (or c'_r as a decreasing function of t), because there are possibilities that human capital is accumulated with tenure length and that accumulated information about a worker's abilities enables the firm to assign a more suitable job to the worker.[9]

To look closer at the effect of $(v_{r+1} - L_r)$, following Rosen (1992), let us define $\mu_r = (\partial \ln P_r / \partial e_r)/(\partial \ln (c_r - w_r)/\partial e_r)$. Here we assume $(c_r - w_r) > 0$. Then the first-order condition (5.5) is expressed by $c_r - w_r = P_r \mu_r (v_{r+1} - L_r)$. Substituting this into equation (5.4) and rearranging give $v_r = \beta_r v_{r+1} + (1 - \beta_r)L_r$, where $\beta_r = P_r(1 - \mu_r)$, and $\beta_r \in (0,1)$ is assumed. For a worker expecting to be promoted up to rank R, $v_R = L_R$. Thus:

$$v_r = \prod_{s=r}^{R-1} \beta_s(L_R - L_{R-1}) + \prod_{s=r}^{R-2} \beta_s(L_{R-1} - L_{R-2}) + \ldots + \beta_r(L_{r+1} - L_r) + L_r.$$

Assume that $L_{r+1} > L_r$ for any r. This assumption means that the present value of the lifetime utility is larger when a worker will be promoted to the higher rank. We can prove $v_r > L_r$ for any $r(< R)$ by the mathematical induction as follows. By the assumption $L_R > L_{R-1}$, we obtain $v_{R-1} = \beta_{R-1}L_R + (1 - \beta_R)L_{R-1} > L_{R-1}$. Next suppose $v_{r+1} > L_{r+1}$, then, $v_r = \beta_r v_{r+1} + (1 - \beta_r)L_r > \beta_r L_{r+1} + (1 - \beta_r)L_r > L_r$.

Similarly $v_{r+1} > v_r$ can be proved. These results imply $v_{r+1} - L_r > 0$. If $R' > R$, then $v_{r+1} - L_r$ is larger for the worker with R' than the worker with R. Hence the higher is a worker's expected attainable rank, the higher is his or her current effort level. Hypothesis (v) states this property.

Furthermore the term, $L_{r+1} - L_r$, can be interpreted as the long-term wage differential between rank r and $r + 1$. If the differential expands, $v_{r+1} - L_r$ will also increase. (Note that this statement and equation (5.5) means that Hypothesis (iii) is also true with respect to the long-term wage differentials.) Consequently the effort level rises. This induces Hypothesis (vi), which is the long-term counterpart of Hypothesis (i).

5.3 ESTIMATION PROCEDURE WITH THE QUESTIONNAIRES AND THE DISTRIBUTION OF THE ANSWERS

This section explains the procedure to test the hypotheses in Table 5.1 by using the questionnaire data. As a preliminary investigation, this section also compares the distribution of the answers, which will be used in the statistical analysis, across the companies. The inter-firm comparisons will reveal that workers' effort levels and their recognition of personnel systems have quite different features among the companies. Furthermore the simple comparisons will give us the overall impressions that there may be relations between effort levels and pay and promotion systems as expected by the hypotheses.

One of our purposes is to examine the relationship between the effort levels and the wage differentials. The wage differentials theoretically mean the size of wage fluctuations responding to the effort levels (or performance) of an individual worker. Therefore when the wage differentials are empirically replaced by the cross-sectional dispersion of earnings, comparison should be among those who actually compete with each other, that is, employees whose relative positions in hierarchy can change upon the result of promotion competition. When tenure length of workers is not so long, the competitors in this sense are workers who have the same academic background and joined the company in the same year. [10] The questionnaire asks about the wage differentials across the respondent's colleagues with the same tenure length and academic background. Answers to this question can be used. However, when the promotion competition stage progresses with tenure length, it is not appropriate for such workers to be regarded as competitors. Therefore we restrict our attention to the workers who think that the promotion differences among such colleagues can be reversed. The following set of two questions is used to distinguish a worker competing with such colleagues. The first question asks:

- 'Are there promotion differences between you and your colleagues who have the same academic background and joined the company in the same year with you?'

The respondent selects an answer from the choice:

- '(1) There is no promotion difference. (2) There are promotion differences. (3) None has been promoted yet.'[11]

The respondent who selects answer (1) or (3) is categorized into the 'no promotion difference group'.

The second question asks the respondent who chooses (2) about the difficulty of catch-up:

- 'Among your colleagues with the same tenure length and academic background (including yourself), can the persons behind in promotion catch up with those in the fastest group?'

The respondent selects the closest recognition of the situation from four alternatives:

- '(1) Can catch up with no effort. (2) Can catch up easily with some effort. (3) May catch up with much effort. (4) Cannot catch up at all.'

The years of tenure of the respondents in each answer category are widely diverse. Some workers who have spent only a few years in the current firm feel that the promotion competition has already come to an end. Some workers who have been working for more than twenty years in the firm believe that the promotion differences change easily. It is ambiguous for the workers when the selection process is completed. A firm seems to give a little information on its selection policy to its employees. However, there is a common tendency that the proportion of workers thinking that catch-up is difficult (that is, selecting (3) or (4)), increases with their tenure length.[12] The respondent choosing answer (1) or (2) is classified into the 'promotion difference group'. Both 'promotion difference group' and 'no promotion difference group' can be interpreted as the promotion competitors with their colleagues with the same tenure length and academic background. For the respondent choosing answer (3) or (4), such colleagues are not competitors and thus these respondents are excluded from our samples. Table 5.2 summarizes the information of the demographic characteristics of the samples used in the following analysis.[13]

Table 5.2 Characteristics of the samples

	Company A: automotive company	Company B: electronics company	Company C: chemical company	Company D: electric power company	Company E: department store
Number of respondents	118	238	180	315	117
Number of females	3	18	4	25	21
Number of university graduates*	107	206	174	189	97
Average tenure (years)	12.0	8.2	10.1	10.9	10.3
Standard deviation of tenure	4.2	5.9	5.5	6.9	6.8
Distribution of tenure length (%)					
$1 < $ tenure < 10	38.1	72.3	52.8	60.3	59.8
$11 \leq$ tenure ≤ 15	50.0	16.0	32.8	19.4	20.5
$16 \leq$ tenure ≤ 20	5.1	7.6	8.3	10.2	7.7
$21 \leq$ tenure	6.8	4.2	6.1	10.2	12.0
Distribution of ranks (%)					
Ordinary worker	71.2	84.9	45.0	87.0	59.8
Section head	19.5	11.8	35.0	9.5	26.5
Department head	9.3	3.4	17.8	3.5	12.0
Deputy director	0.0	0.0	1.7	0.0	0.7
Director	0.0	0.0	0.0	0.0	0.7

Note: *Including the respondent who finished graduate school.

5.3.1   Index of Effort Level

The effort level, e, is the variable to be explained in our analysis, but it is not directly observable. Therefore the answer to the following question, which is a respondent's self-evaluation of the effort level, is used. The question and the alternatives are:

- 'Which of the following most closely describes the way you work?'

- '(1) Contribute considerably more than the assigned level of job. (2) Contribute somewhat more than the assigned level of job. (3) Do just the assigned level of job. (4) Need somewhat more effort to complete the assigned level of job. (5) Need much more effort to complete the assigned level of job.'

Since the question sets a judgement standard of the effort level at the 'assigned level of job', the individual self-evaluations can be regarded as normalized and comparable with each other. Figure 5.1 shows the distribution of the answers in each company. It should be noted that the

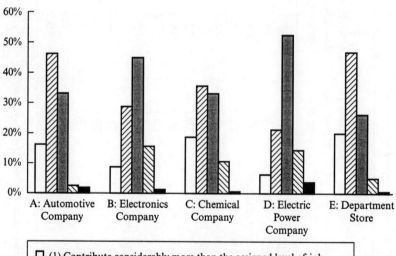

Figure 5.1 Effort level

distribution is quite dissimilar across the companies. The proportion of workers attaining the effort level over their assigned level is clearly higher in Companies A and E and lower in Companies B and D. That in Company C is at the intermediate rate between them. In particular the proportion is the lowest in Company D.

Achieving the assigned level of job may be a result due to not only effort but also the degree of matching between the job and the worker's abilities and qualifications. If the degree of mismatch is large, the worker may contribute less than a worker at a suitable job even with the same effort level. To avoid this bias, the respondents with an effort level less than or equal to the assigned level (that is, the respondents who selected an answer from (3) to (5)) are gathered. This is because if a worker provides an effort level over the assigned level regardless of the degree of matching, such a worker is thought to be responding to some effort incentives. Accordingly, our index of the effort level consists of three ranks: (1) Contribute much more than, (2) Contribute somewhat more than and (3)' Contribute less than or equal to, the assigned level of job.[14]

5.3.2 Estimation Procedure

The index of effort level used as a dependent variable is discrete and ordered. The ordered probit method is thus employed. Let e_j be an underlying effort level of the jth worker. The effort level, e_j, is unobserved. What is observed is a category, $I_j = i$ ($i = 1$, 2 or 3), where i corresponds to the three-ranked answer to the above question of the jth worker based on e_j. If the respondent's answer belongs to category (3)', (2) or (1), I_j is coded as 1, 2 or 3, respectively. The relations between the effort levels and their determinants described in Section 5.2 are linearly approximated. That is, the latent regression is $e_j = \beta X_j + \varepsilon_j$ where β is a vector of parameters, X_j is a vector of factors affecting the effort level, which will be explained below, and the disturbance term ε_j is assumed to normally distribute with mean 0 and variance 1. Suppose that there are threshold values, $\kappa_0, ..., \kappa_3$ ($\kappa_{i-1} < \kappa_i$), such that if $\kappa_{i-1} < e_j \le \kappa_i$ then $I_j = i$. The parameters, βs and κs, are simultaneously estimated by the maximum likelihood method based on the relation: $\Pr\{I_j = i\} = \Pr\{\kappa_{i-1} < e_j \le \kappa_i\}$, where $\Pr(.)$ means probability, and $\kappa_0 = -\infty$ and $\kappa_3 = \infty$. Here the larger is the value of the estimated coefficient of each dummy variable, the higher is the expected effort level of a worker with the attribute corresponding to the dummy variable.[15]

Our purpose is to investigate how different pay and promotion systems affect workers' effort incentives. Therefore if a firm applies a single pay and promotion system to all the workers, comparison of the effort levels should be carried out across companies which have different systems. As we shall see below, however, workers in the same firm do not always answer similarly. The fact suggests that even in the same firm, individuals recognize its personnel management system differently. The differences may arise simply because of different workers' subjective recognition of the same system. Or if the degrees of difficulty of the performance evaluations differ depending on, for example, departments, regional offices and workers' length of tenure in the same firm, the different degrees may induce different features in the acting incentive systems for the employees with various attributes. Since workers' effort is affected by their *subjectively recognized* pay and promotion systems, if these systems matter, the different recognition should be dealt with as different systems irrespective of the actual states. Accordingly, the intra-firm differences in both the recognition and the effort levels should be examined as well as the inter-firm differences. For this reason the samples in each company are pooled together and the ordered probit estimation is applied to the pooled samples. Among these factors, however, the inter-firm differences in the incentive schemes are thought to be most consequential. Therefore, as a preliminary investigation, we shall compare the intra-firm answer distribution across the five companies along with the following description of the explanatory variables.

5.3.3   Wage Differentials: Hypotheses (i) and (vi)

The explanatory variables, X_j, are constructed from the answers to the questionnaire with respect to each hypothesis. Hypotheses (i) and (vi) say that the effort level is high when the short- and/or the long-term wage differentials (on the basis of performance) are large. The question about the wage differentials is:

- 'How wide is the range of annual salaries among your colleagues with the same tenure length and academic background?'

The respondent chooses the answer closest to his or her recognition of the range from the alternatives:

- '(1) Almost no difference. (2) About 10 per cent. (3) About 20 per cent. (4) About 30 per cent. (5) More than or equal to 40 per cent.'

The distribution of the answers is compared across the companies in Figure 5.2. In Companies B, C and D, more than 60 per cent of workers feel that there are few wage disparities among their colleagues. Company

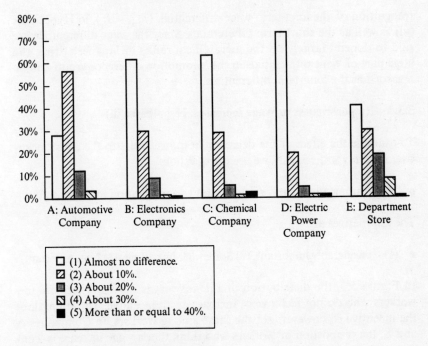

Figure 5.2 Range of annual salaries

D has the highest proportion. On the other hand, about 15 per cent of workers in Company A and about 30 per cent in Company E think that there are wage differentials more than or equal to 20 per cent. As shown in Figure 5.1, the proportion of workers contributing over their assigned levels is higher in both Company A and Company E, and it is the lowest in Company D. This seems consistent with Hypotheses (i) or (vi).

Since the number of workers who selected answer (5) is very small (about 1 per cent of the whole sample), they are classified together with the respondents selecting (4) into one category: '(4)' More than or equal to 30 per cent.' This aggregation is done in order to avoid the situation that the peculiarity of a few workers may strongly influence the result. Variable WD takes 0, 1, 2 or 3, corresponding to the respondent's answer (1), (2), (3) or (4)', respectively. The square of WD (WD^2) is also included to consider the possibility that the assumption of linear dependence between the recognition of wage differentials and the effort level may be too restrictive.

For the 'no promotion difference group', WD can be interpreted to represent the recognition of the short-term wage differential, $(w_H - w_L)$, in Hypothesis (i).[16] For the 'promotion difference group', WD reflects the recognition of the long-term wage differential, $(L_{r+1} - L_r)$, in Hypothesis (vi) as well as the short-term differentials. Since the wage differentials are said to depend largely on the hierarchical ranks in Japanese firms, the large part of wage differentials in the 'promotion difference group' can be regarded as the long-term differentials.[17]

5.3.4 Responsiveness to Wage Increases: Hypothesis (iii)

To examine the effect of the degree of responsiveness to the effort incentive, R, in Hypothesis (iii), we use the question:

- 'How important is a pay raise for you as a motivation for working?'

The alternatives are:

- '(1) Considerably important. (2) Somewhat important. (3) Not important.'

In Figure 5.3, the distribution of the answers is shown. There are few workers who do not feel a wage increase as an incentive. The strength of the incentive is, however, not the same among workers. In Companies A and E, the proportion of workers who think that a wage increase is 'con-

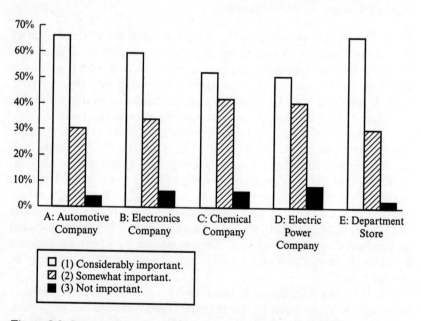

Figure 5.3 Importance of a pay rise as a motivation for working

siderably important' is nearly 70 per cent and higher than in other companies. In Company D, the proportion is the lowest. By comparing Figure 5.3 with Figure 5.1, we can find that these features are consistent with Hypothesis (iii). A dummy variable indicating the strong responsiveness to the incentive is *RESPONS* which takes the value 1 for the respondent who selects answer (1) and takes the value 0 otherwise. (Similarly all the explanatory dummy variables constructed below take 1 when the respondent belongs to the category and otherwise 0.)

5.3.5 Performance Evaluations and Short-term Wage Differentials: Hypothesis (ii)

The respondent is asked about the importance of his or her performance as a determinant of wage differentials:

- 'How important is achieving excellent performance for wage differentials among workers doing the same job?'

The respondent selects the closest answer from:

- '(1) Considerably important. (2) Somewhat important. (3) Not so important. (4) Not important at all.'

Since the question asks about the wage differentials among workers 'doing the same job', such wage differentials can be interpreted as the short-term differentials. The proportion of workers who feel that their performance is considerably important for wage determination is high in all the firms, as shown in Figure 5.4. Among them, the proportion is the lowest in Company D whose workers' average effort level is also the lowest. However, it is the highest and more than 80 per cent in Company C, while its workers do not provide high effort levels on average. This may be because the resulting wage differentials are not so large in the company as in Company A or E. *PERFORM* is a dummy for the respondent who selected answer (1). This dummy is included to test Hypothesis (ii).

5.3.6 Performance Evaluations and Promotion Differences: Hypothesis (iv)

To test Hypothesis (iv), the following question is used:

- 'Which of the following factors do you think are important for promotion decisions in your company? Select the top three factors in order of importance for promotions both up to and beyond department head.'

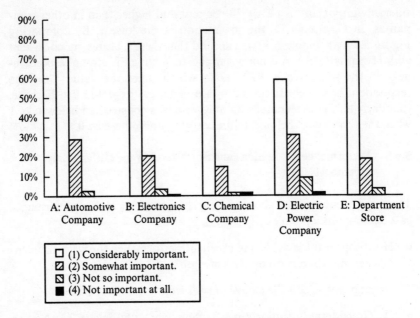

(1) Considerably important.
(2) Somewhat important.
(3) Not so important.
(4) Not important at all.

Figure 5.4 Importance of performance for short-term wage differentials

Among factors in the alternatives, 'result of merit assessment' can be interpreted as the importance of a worker's performance to his or her promotion probability (in so far as merit assessment is done accurately enough). The alternatives also include 'tenure length and age' and 'academic background'.[18] These factors are not controllable by a worker and thus are expected to have negative effects on the effort level, as the effects of θs on e_r through P'_r in Hypothesis (iv). The proportion of workers feeling these factors to be important is shown in Figures 5.5 and 5.6. A noticeable feature is the low evaluation of the role of merit assessment in Company D for promotion both 'up to' and 'beyond department head'. In the company, seniority and an academic background are the most effective factors with regard to promotion up to department head. This suggests the relationship between the company's workers' average low effort level and its personnel policy, as expected by Hypothesis (iv).

As for seniority, it is not a distinct feature of Company D that this factor is recognized as an important factor by many workers. In each company, many workers recognize that the tenure length is an important determinant especially for promotion 'up to department head'. This seems compatible with the traditional explanation that the seniority system and the late selection policy are distinct characteristics of Japanese firms. However, it should be noted that all the companies except D are thought

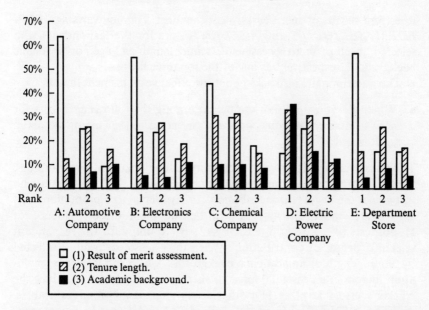

Figure 5.5 Important factors for promotion decisions: up to department head

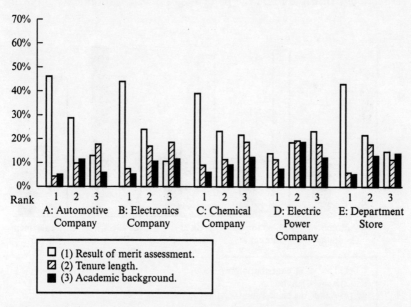

Figure 5.6 Important factors for promotion decisions: beyond department head

to esteem results of merit assessment the most. Dummy variables, *PER-FORM*, *SENIORITY* and *ACADEMIC*, are for the respondents who selected 'result of merit assessment', 'tenure length and age', or 'academic background', respectively, as one of the top three factors.[19]

The questionnaire also asks about the effective assessment factors:

- 'Which do you think are important among the following factors for merit assessment in your company? Select up to four major factors in random order.'

The questionnaire lists twelve factors including 'degree of contribution', 'tenure length and age', and 'academic background'.[20] If the worker who recognizes the degree of contribution closely related to a promotion decision exerts more effort, this will be the most direct evidence of Hypothesis (iv). *ASSESS_PERFORM* is a dummy for the respondent selecting 'degree of contribution'. When the assessment result is affected by tenure length or an academic background, which should not be evaluation factors in an essential sense of merit assessment, it may reduce the worker's effort level as Hypothesis (iv) suggests. Dummy variables, *ASSESS_SENIORITY* and *ASSESS_ACADEMIC*, are for the respondent selecting 'tenure length and age' and 'academic background', respectively. In Figure 5.7, the percentages of the respondents choosing

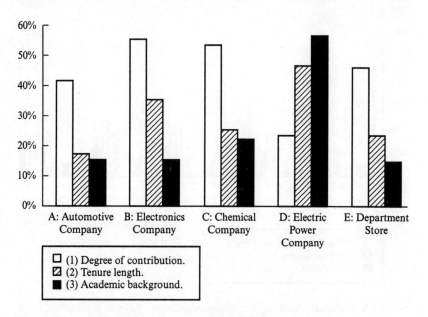

Figure 5.7 Important factors for merit assessment

these three factors are shown. In respect of the assessment contents, Company D is the exceptional here again. The recognition of the lower weight on contribution and the recognition of the higher weight on both tenure length and academic background are shared by many workers in the firm, which seems consistent with Hypothesis (iv). However, not so many employees in Companies A and E feel that their degree of contribution is an important factor in their companies' assessment policies, in spite of their average high effort levels.

The evaluations of the individual's performance may not always be accurate and unambiguous. They may suffer from the difficulty of exact measurement of performance, or subjective opinions and arbitrariness of the evaluators. If a worker feels his or her performance is not correctly evaluated in the pay and promotion decisions, his or her effort incentives will decline. The questionnaire also asks whether the respondent is satisfied with appraisals of his or her results by his or her superiors and colleagues. In order to examine this effect, a dummy *EVALUAT*, for the respondent who chooses the answer 'considerably satisfied' to the question is introduced.

5.3.7 Career Concerns: Hypothesis (v)

Hypothesis (v) says that a worker's expected future career can have an incentive effect on his or her current level of effort (the career concern effect). This is because the higher is the expected attainable rank, the longer is the promotion competition duration, and thus it induces the worker to put forth greater effort. The following question asks about which rank the respondent expects to be promoted up to:

- 'Which rank do you expect you will attain?'

The respondent selects from:

- '(1) Section head. (2) Department head. (3) Deputy director. (4) Director. (5) Higher rank than director.'

A dummy variable, *CAREERCON*, is for the respondent who expects that he or she can be director or a higher rank, that is, who selects (4) or (5). (If the respondent is director now, the dummy is for the person expecting to move up to a higher rank than the director.)

A variable, *TENURE*, represents the years of tenure length and is included in the explanatory variables in order to consider the following two effects. First long tenure length means the remaining period of competition is short and it weakens the career concerns (with all other things being equal) and lowers the effort incentives.[21] Second, as we have already mentioned in Subsection 5.3.1, it may be easier for a worker with long tenure to provide greater effort than the assigned level.[22] One reason is that the human capital accumulates along with tenure length. Another reason is that the improved learning about a worker's abilities and qualifications with tenure length enables the firm to assign the worker a more suitable job. Since these two effects act in opposite directions, the effort level may depend on tenure length in a nonlinear way. To capture this, the square of tenure length ($TENURE^2$) is also included.

5.4   EMPIRICAL RESULTS

In addition to the variables explained in the last section, the following dummy variables are involved. *FEMALE* is a dummy for a female and *EDUCATION* is one for a worker who is a college graduate or who finished graduate school. A mismatch between a worker's aptitude and his or her current job may cause a downward bias in the effort level index. Thus *MISMATCH*, which is a dummy for the respondent who is dissatisfied with the suitability of job to aptitude, is added.[23] These dummies are included to consider the possibility that workers' abilities and qualifications influence the distances between their actual and assigned effort levels. In addition, company dummies are also included to capture other factors inducing the inter-firm differences in the effort levels (for example, the differences in incentive systems which are not reflected by the other explanatory variables).

The estimation result is shown in column (a) in Table 5.3. The coefficients of *FEMALE*, *EDUCATION* and *MISMATCH* are not statistically significant and this suggests that sex, educational level and the mismatch do not affect the effort level index when other factors are controlled. To examine Hypotheses (i), (iii) and (vi), we first included *WD*, WD^2 and *RESPONS* separately in the estimation equation. The result was that only the coefficient of *RESPONS* was significant.[24] However, since the effect of responsiveness to wage increases and that of the recognition of wage differentials may be strongly interdependent, their effects should be considered simultaneously. Thus, instead of these dummies, dummy variables, *RESPONS*WD* and *RESPONS*WD^2*, were included next. Here '*'means the multiplication of two dummies. With respect to these dummies, a worker who thinks 'a pay raise is not considerably important' is taken as a reference case.[25]

The result is that the coefficient of *RESPONS*WD* has a positive and that of *RESPONS*WD^2* has a negative sign and both are significant, as shown in column (a) in Table 5.3. Judging from these estimated parameter

Table 5.3 Ordered probit estimation results

	(a) Whole sample case	(b) No promotion difference group	(c) Promotion difference group
FEMALE	–0.0843	–0.0836	–0.463
	[0.64]	[0.68]	[0.26]
EDUCATION	0.0418	–0.0783	0.432
	[0.76]	[0.61]	[0.13]
TENURE	0.118	0.134	0.0526
	[0.00]	[0.00]	[0.00]
TENURE^2	–0.00232	–0.00265	–
	[0.00]	[0.00]	
MISMATCH	–0.0351	0.0320	–0.328
	[0.73]	[0.78]	[0.17]
*RESPONS*WD*	0.436	0.490	0.396
	[0.00]	[0.00]	[0.05]
*RESPONS*WD^2*	–0.0940	–0.122	–0.0510
	[0.01]	[0.00]	[0.44]
EVALUAT	0.426	0.468	0.356
	[0.00]	[0.00]	[0.11]
PERFORM	0.587	0.0785	0.475
	[0.17]	[0.47]	[0.02]
ASSESSMENT	0.147	–0.0884	0.0717
	[0.33]	[0.96]	[0.04]
SENIORITY	0.199	0.316	–0.106
	[0.03]	[0.01]	[0.53]
ACADEMIC	–0.318	–0.373	–0.183
	[0.00]	[0.00]	[0.40]
ASSESS_PERFORM	–0.0762	–0.0353	–0.127
	[0.40]	[0.74]	[0.46]
ASSESS_SENIORITY	–0.270	–0.242	–0.399
	[0.01]	[0.02]	[0.05]
ASSESS_ACADEMIC	0.208	0.238	0.197
	[0.08]	[0.08]	[0.46]
CAREERCON	0.587	0.516	0.824
	[0.00]	[0.00]	[0.00]
FIRM_A	0.246	0.409	–0.506
	[0.08]	[0.02]	[0.09]
FIRM_C	0.192	0.335	–0.596
	[0.13]	[0.02]	[0.06]

Table 5.3 (continued)

	(a) Whole sample case	(b) No promotion difference group	(c) Promotion difference group
FIRM_D	−0.155	−0.102	−0.772
	[0.22]	[0.49]	[0.01]
FIRM_E	0.458	0.810	−0.604
	[0.00]	[0.00]	[0.05]
Pseudo-R^2	0.397	0.331	0.427
No. of observations	968	733	235
Average tenure of samples (years)	10.2	8.57	15.1
Average value of effort level index I_j	1.57	1.51	1.76

Notes: The number in square brackets indicates the p-value of the t-test. A Pseudo-R^2 used here is the Aldrich–Nelson's measure normalized by Veall and Zimmermann (1992). This measure can be interpreted as an analogue to the OLS-R^2.
The explanatory variables are:

FEMALE = dummy for a female
EDUCATION = dummy for the respondent whose educational level is a college education or higher
TENURE = length of service
MISMATCH = dummy for the respondent who is dissatisfied with the suitability of the current job in relation to aptitude
RESPONS = dummy for the respondent who thinks that a pay raise is considerably important
WD = recognition of the degree of wage differentials (1 for almost no difference, 2 for about 10 per cent, 3 for about 20 per cent or 4 for more than or equal to 30 per cent)
EVALUAT = dummy for the respondent who is considerably satisfied with appraisals of results by superiors and colleagues
PERFORM = dummy for the respondent who thinks that excellent performance is considerably important as a determinant of short-term wage differentials
ASSESSMENT = dummy for the respondent who thinks that merit assessment is included in the top three important determinants of promotion decisions
SENIORITY = dummy for the respondent who thinks that length of service is included in the top three important determinants of promotion decisions
ACADEMIC = dummy for the respondent who thinks that an academic background is included in the top three important determinants of promotion decisions
ASSESS_PERFORM = dummy for the respondent who thinks that contribution is important for merit assessment
ASSESS_SENIORITY = dummy for the respondent who thinks that length of service is important for merit assessment
ASSESS_ACADEMIC = dummy for the respondent who thinks an academic background is important for merit assessment
CAREERCON = dummy for the respondent who expects to be promoted to director or highter
FIRM_i = dummy for the respondent belonging to Company i (i = A, C, D or E).

values, we can say the following. First the effort levels of workers with strong responsiveness to wage increases (that is, *RESPONS* = 1) rise with the wage differentials when the range of wage differentials is less than 20 per cent. Second their effort levels differ little between the 10 per cent and the 20 per cent range of wage differentials, while they decrease when the range is more than 20 per cent. Third, their effort levels do not decline below the level of workers with weak responsiveness to wage increases (that is, *RESPONS* = 0). We can thus conclude that the effort levels are higher for workers with strong responsiveness to wage increases. Moreover, the effort levels do not exhibit a monotonous increasing pattern for such workers. In consequence, Hypothesis (iii) is supported but neither Hypothesis (i) nor (vi) are literally consistent with the result. We shall return to this point later.

The coefficient of *PERFORM* is positive but its significance level is not so high. Thus the differences in recognition of the degree of short-term dependence between performance and wages are not so influential for the effort level. Neither coefficients of *ASSESSMENT* and *ASSESS_PERFORM* are significant. This means that the tighter relation of the evaluations of performance (or abilities) with promotion decisions (that is, the long-term wage differentials) does not affect the effort level. We can find no clear evidence to support Hypotheses (ii) and (iv) with respect to *PERFORM*, *ASSESSMENT* and *ASSESS_PERFORM*. The coefficient of *EVALUAT* is positively significant, and thus the recognition of accurate performance appraisal induces the worker to provide more effort. The results of these parameters mean that the effort-level elasticity to the recognition of the intensity of relationship between the performance evaluations and the wage and promotion determination is partly supported but the evidence is weak.

The coefficient of *SENIORITY* has a significant positive sign and this seems to contradict Hypothesis (iv). The positive effect, however, can be explained from another viewpoint of the incentive theory. Lazear (1979), for example, argues that the seniority-based wage system in which a firm pays workers less than their marginal product when they are young and greater than their marginal product when they are old can prevent shirking, because the cost of dismissal is high when shirking is disclosed. Therefore the seniority-based promotion system may provide an effort incentive. On the contrary, the coefficient of *ASSESS_SENIORITY* is significantly negative as expected by Hypothesis (iv). These results suggest that the seniority provision generally increases the effort levels, while it reduces the effort levels if it is recognized to appear in merit assessment. *ACADEMIC* has a significantly negative effect. If a worker feels his or her academic background affects promotion probability, then effort level decreases. However, the coefficient *ASSESS_ACADEMIC* has the

opposite sign, although the significance level is not so high. It seems difficult to explain the latter fact directly by the incentive hypothesis.

Both coefficients of *TENURE* and *TENURE*^{2} are significant: *TENURE*
has a positive sign and that of *TENURE*^{2} has a negative sign. The effort level
increases with tenure length at early stages in one's career and then decreases.
The effects of human capital accumulation and learning are thought to dom-
inate for a short-tenure worker. When the mandatory retirement age draws
near, the career concern effect dominates and reduces the effort level. These
parameter values indicate that the effort level peaks at about twenty-five
years of service. In addition, *CAREERCON* shows a significantly positive
effect. This also supports the career concern Hypothesis (v).

Next we conduct the ordered probit analysis of the 'no promotion difference group' and the 'promotion difference group' separately. These
separate estimations are made to consider the possibility that the elasticity of effort to the incentive factors may differ between the two groups.
The estimation results are shown in columns (b) and (c) in Table 5.3. In
the 'no promotion difference group' (b), the result is not so very different
from the whole sample case (a). The statistical significance level of each
coefficient is not so much altered, and the estimated values are close as
far as the significant coefficients are concerned. It can be said that the
character of this group dominates the result in the whole sample case.

As for 'promotion difference group' (c), the result is quite dissimilar to
that of the whole sample case. The major difference points are, as a whole,
favourable for our hypotheses and summarized as follows. First the coefficient of *RESPONS*WD* is significant and positive, whereas that of
*RESPONS*WD*^{2} is insignificant. Therefore the fact that the effort level
increases with the wage differentials, is observed. As argued earlier, most of
the wage differentials in this group can be regarded as long-term differentials. Thus it can be said that the fact is consistent with Hypotheses (iii) and
(vi). Second, both coefficients of *PERFORM* and *ASSESSMENT* exhibit
the significantly positive sign, as expected by Hypotheses (ii) and (iv). While
the recognition of the importance of merit assessment improves the workers'
effort, *ASSESS_PERFORM* does not show a significant effect. The reason
might be that merit assessment is thought to evaluate workers' acquired
abilities (expected future contributions) more than their current realized
performance. If this means that the noises (such as unlucky results) appearing in the realized performance levels are taken carefully into consideration
in the assessment, such property of assessment may be desirable in order for
workers to exert a lot of effort. Third, the coefficient of neither *ACADEMIC*
nor *ASSESS_ACADEMIC* is significantly different from zero. The
academic background consciousness in promotion decisions does not show a
negative incentive effect. Fourth, the coefficient of *SENIORITY* is insignifi-

cant, whereas that of *ASSESS_SENIORITY* is negatively significant. The seniority system does not directly affect the effort level. However, the recognition that the seniority rule emerges through merit assessment reduces the effort level, as predicted by Hypothesis (iv). In addition to these results, both *EVALUAT* and *CAREERCON* display positive effects, although the significance level of the coefficient of *EVALUAT* is not as high.[26]

In summary, the estimation regarding the 'promotion difference group' shows consistent results for all the hypotheses in Table 5.1. As for the 'no promotion difference group', on the other hand, although the estimation indicates some favourable results for Hypotheses (iii) and (v), we cannot find the conclusive evidence for Hypotheses (i), (ii) and (iv). In particular, large wage differentials over the 20 per cent range decrease the effort levels in this group. Furthermore, workers also raise their effort levels under the seniority-based promotion system. A large number of workers in the 'no promotion difference group' had relatively short tenure. Therefore we can say that workers have a tendency to prefer a system in which earnings and promotion are not so much differentiated according to performance in the early stages in the promotion competition.

The questionnaire also asks the respondent's opinion about wage and promotion systems. To the question, 64 per cent of workers answer that they agree with the view: 'large differentiation of wages and promotion is not desirable in the early stages of one's career, and it should start at a higher rank'. In fact our results with regard to short-tenure workers indicate that if a worker happens to recognize the great extent of differentiation in the short run for some reason, such recognition will show a perverse incentive effect. This can be said to coincide with the common view that the slow speed of promotion and egalitarian treatment for employees early in their careers are prevalent among Japanese firms.

5.5 CONCLUSION

This chapter analysed whether the basic assumptions which many incentive models share are appropriate in practice. To this end we tested the hypotheses derived from a typical incentive model, by using the data of a questionnaire sent to white-collar workers in five large Japanese companies.

The results as a whole supported the hypotheses at least for the workers differentiated with respect to hierarchical ranks among their colleagues with the same tenure length and academic background. If the workers feel that a pay raise is an important effort incentive and if they believe that pay and promotion differences are contingent on their firm's performance evaluations and the evaluations are fair, they are motivated enough to put forth high levels of effort. The recognition of both larger wage differentials and a higher attainable hierarchical rank encourages the workers to work harder. We therefore reasonably conclude that the assumptions in many incentive models have realistic foundation for these long-tenure workers.

On the other hand, for short-tenure workers who have not yet confronted the realized promotion differentiation, some estimation results were not in favour of our hypotheses. That is, large wage differentials do not always stimulate the effort level. The degree of the linkage between performance evaluations and wages or promotions does not exhibit a significant incentive effect. Workers seem to prefer egalitarian treatment early in their careers. However, it should be noted that these facts can also be explained from the viewpoint of the incentive theory. Itoh (1994) summarizes the several reasons why the immediate pay-for-performance schemes have perverse incentive effects. Further research is necessary to reveal what reasons are empirically important.

In addition, by comparing the distribution of the answers to the questionnaire across the companies, it was shown that the wage and promotion systems (recognized by workers) have quite different features. The differences are probably responsible for the different average attained levels of workers' effort, as predicted by the incentive theory (see also Chapter 6 by Mitani). It may be another interesting point to investigate why some firms accept particular systems (such as the education-conscious promotion system[27]) which reduce employees' effort and what environment induces firms to adopt different systems for personnel management.

NOTES

1. For surveys, see Baker, Jensen and Murphy (1988) and Itoh (1994). Itoh (1994) examines characteristics of Japanese firms' pay and promotion systems from the viewpoint of the incentive theory.
2. In the case of a risk-averse worker, we can also induce the same hypotheses mentioned below.
3. We assume R is sufficiently small so as to satisfy $e \in [0, 1]$ at the optimum.
4. Because of the minimum income condition, the firm must increase the average wage level in order to raise the effort levels of its workers. Hence there is a tradeoff between the incentive and the cost, and thus the incentive problem arises. In the case of a risk-averse worker, without the minimum income condition, the firm confronts the incentive problem, because it must compensate its workers for the risk premium of fluctuating wages due to uncertain factors in order to raise their effort levels.
5. Itoh (1994) discusses the possible reasons why the immediate reward structure is not desirable, particularly in Japanese firms.
6. Usually there is another kind of hierarchical rank ('grade') in Japanese firms. Since the questionnaire does not contain questions related to promotion with respect to grades, we shall analyse incentive effects of promotion only in terms of moving up to higher job positions. Generally grades and positions are closely related.

7. Throughout this chapter we restrict our attention to the effort incentives in terms of pecuniary rewards. From this standpoint only an aspect of promotion as a device for long-term pay increases is concerned. This is because the standard economic models assume that only pecuniary rewards (earnings) are sources of utility. Thus our testing hypotheses are also based on this assumption so as to examine the appropriateness of the economic approach. However, we do not intend to deny the possibility that non-pecuniary factors can operate as effort incentives. Motivations for working may not be derived solely from earnings. From the broader point of view, Ishikawa (1994) discusses 'job worth' and 'job satisfaction' with respect to both pecuniary and non-pecuniary factors and investigates how workers' attributes affect their job satisfaction in Japanese firms.

8. We assume, for simplicity, L_r is exogenously given. It is possible to extend the model so that we can allow for the dependence of L_r on the future effort of the worker.

9. In the above model we assume the promotion competition as a tournament among the workers who joined the firm at the same year. That is, only the winners in the competition at rank r can go to the next at rank $r + 1$ and all the competitors have the same tenure length. This assumption simplifies the analysis, but effects of different tenure length on the effort decision (within the same rank) are ignored. It is possible to extend the model to allow for the promotion competition among workers with a different tenure length. However, the analysis will be more complicated.

10. The model in Subsection 5.2.2 assumes that the selection from rank r to rank $r + 1$ is carried out once and for all. Therefore the model does not consider the possibility of 'revival'. In the empirical part of this chapter the range of long-term wage levels for an individual worker is represented by the wage differentials among workers with the same tenure length and different ranks. This treatment is appropriate if the (lifetime) earnings corresponding to a particular rank do not vary so much according to the workers' tenure length when they are promoted to that rank.

11. The questions and answers we refer to are translated from their originals in Japanese.

12. For detailed descriptions of different characteristics of the worker selection processes across the five companies, see Chapter 4 by Kobayashi.

13. The respondents who did not answer all the questions used in the analysis are dropped from the samples. Although the respondents having pre-company experiences of working are included in the samples, the number is very small (the fraction is less than 4 per cent), as is the usual case in large Japanese firms. Thus we shall not distinguish between respondents' length of tenure at the current firm and length of experience of working.

14. For the same purpose, tenure length and dummies about educational level, sex and the degree of the mismatch will be included so as to adjust the biases arising from the possibility that a worker whose abilities are more suitable for the job, or whose potential abilities are higher, can contribute more by less effort. These variables will be explained later.

15. The estimated value of coefficient of a continuous variable (*WD* or *TENURE*, which is explained below) means the marginal effect of increase in the variable.

16. Since the regular raises and bonuses are in part based on the current basic salaries, the wage differentials even in this group are not purely transient. However it is natural to think that pay differences within the same rank can be reversed more easily than those across different ranks.

17. Strictly speaking, the wage differentials are not those in lifetime earnings, $(L_{r+1} - L_r)$, in the model in Subsection 5.2.2, but those in annual earnings in a certain year. However, the wage differentials associated with the hierarchical rank differences influence future earnings. In this sense the wage differentials in 'promotion difference group' can be said to reflect the long-term wage differentials.

18. Other factors in the alternatives are 'pull of superiors', 'result of examination' and 'personality'.

19. If the respondent is now department head or at a higher rank, only the answer corresponding to 'beyond department head' is considered. If he or she is below department head, each dummy is constructed as 1 for the respondent choosing the respective factors about either 'up to' or 'beyond department head'. This is because even the worker below department head may think that information of the previous and current assessment is accumulated and will be referred to in decisions of future promotions. In fact, to a question about the important

factors of merit assessment (mentioned just below), the proportion of the respondents who think that the 'previous results of assessment' are important for the current assessment is about 40 per cent in each company.

Regarding promotion to higher ranks beyond department head, the fraction of workers feeling the 'pull of superiors' to be important becomes much higher. This feature is observed commonly across the firms. However, since it is unclear how the pull of superiors relates to workers' performance and effort we do not examine the effects of this factor.

20. Others are factors related to one's abilities such as 'know-how and skills', 'ability to make proper judgement', 'ability to make effective plans' and so on. These can be regarded as evaluations of the potential probabilities of high contributions. The exception is 'previous results of assessment'.
21. Gibbons and Murphy (1992) explain that the career concern effect will arise if workers are concerned about the effects of their current performance on their future careers, because the current performance is used to update the firm's belief about the workers' abilities.
22. In the context of the model in Section 5.2, $c_r{}'$ (P'_r) may decrease (increase) with tenure length.
23. *MISMATCH* is a dummy for the respondent who chooses 'dissatisfied' as the answer to a question that 'the suitable job is assigned'.
24. If our effort-level index mainly reflects the differences in workers' abilities to attain the assigned levels of job, *RESPONS* cannot be expected to show the statistically significant positive effect, because there is no reason for the linkage between the workers' abilities and their responsiveness to effort incentives. Hence the result of *RESPONS* also means that our explanatory variable represents the worker's effort level appropriately.
25. That is, for a set of the dummies, *RESPONS*WD* and *RESPONS*WD^2*, *WD* is 1 (not 0) if the wage differential recognition is 'almost no difference' and rises to 4 if it is 'more than or equal to 30 per cent'.
26. The coefficients of *TENURE* and *TENURE^2* are insignificant if both are included, while *TENURE* shows a significant positive effect if *TENURE^2* is dropped. This is probably because both variables are closely correlated in this group since the range of *TENURE* in the samples is narrow.
27. Chapter 8 by Ohashi argues why the graduates from prestigious universities are so evaluated in promotion in Japanese firms.

REFERENCES

Baker, G.P., M.C. Jensen and K.J. Murphy (1988), 'Compensation and Incentives: Practice vs. Theory', *Journal of Finance*, **63**, 593–616.

Gibbons, R. and K.J. Murphy (1992), 'Optimal Incentive Contracts in the Presence of Career Concerns: Theory and Evidence', *Journal of Political Economy*, **100**, 468–505.

Ishikawa, T. (1994), 'Interindustry and Firm Size Differences in Job Satisfaction among Japanese Workers', in T. Tachibanaki (ed.), *Labour Market and Economic Performance – Europe, Japan and the USA*, London: Macmillan, pp. 183–215.

Itoh, H. (1994), 'Japanese Human Resource Management from the Viewpoint of Incentive Theory', in M. Aoki and R. Dore (eds), *The Japanese Firm; Sources of Competitive Strength*, Oxford: Oxford University Press, pp. 233–64.

Lazear E.P. (1979), 'Why Is There Mandatory Retirement?', *Journal of Political Economy*, **87**, 1261–84.

Rosen, S. (1992), 'Contracts and Market for Executives', in L. Werin and H.

Wijkander (eds), *Contract Economics*, Oxford: Basil Blackwell, pp. 181–217.

Tachibanaki, T. (1987), 'The Determination of the Promotion Process in Organizations and of Earnings Differentials', *Journal of Economic Behavior and Organization*, **8**, 603–16.

Tachibanaki, T. (1988). 'Education, Occupation, Hierarchy and Earnings', *Economics of Education Review*, **7**, 221–9.

Veall, M.R. and K.F. Zimmermann (1992), 'Pseudo-R^2's in the Ordinal Probit Model', *Journal of Mathematical Sociology*, **16**, 333–42.

6. Work incentives for white-collar workers: wages and promotion

Naoki Mitani

6.1 INTRODUCTION

During the recent recession, there have been many arguments insisting that we should change wage/promotion systems for white-collar workers into more performance-related ones. Moreover, some companies have already changed their wage systems, for example, with the introduction of annual salary systems. It is questionable whether these changes have resulted in an improvement in the workers' morale and the firms' profits.[1]

Labour-incentive mechanisms are already incorporated into the wage/promotion system, since wage increases and promotion are linked to the performance of the worker. But the problem is to what extent should they be linked to performance and how should the performance of the worker be measured? If wages or promotion are strongly linked to the ability and the performance of the worker, then there will be more risk that they may be affected by factors beyond the worker's control, because the worker's performance tends to be influenced by uncontrollable factors such as the general economic situation or changeable weather. Therefore, it is not necessarily efficient to determine wages and promotion only by the ability or the performance of the individual worker. None the less, if we neglect totally ability and performance and determine wages or promotion automatically according to age or length of service, then there will be no incentive for workers to work hard. Thus the wage/promotion system is considered to be optimum when it reflects to some extent the performance/ability of the worker. First of all, we shall investigate which factors determine the optimum linkage between performance and wages/promotion.

Second, we shall discuss the problem of the evaluation of performance, that is, how evaluation elements affect workers' efforts. In addition, we shall investigate the influence of satisfaction about wages and/or promotion. It will be considered whether evaluation elements affect a worker's incentive to work, and consequently his or her work effort. We can suppose that effort will be greater when the evaluation involves performance and/or ability than when it involves age and/or enterprise tenure. Further, the objectivity or accuracy of the evaluation may greatly influence the workers' efforts. In fact, in the case of white-collar workers, it is often difficult to evaluate objectively their performance or ability. Although there is an objective index of the performance for sales staff, such as the amount of goods sold, there are few objective quantitative measures of performance for many other occupations such as planning, accountancy, personnel, advertising, research and development. In most cases, the performance is measured by the subjective merit rating of the supervisor. The less objective the evaluation is, the less enthusiastically the worker works under a wage system which links wages to the results of the evaluation. Thus, we shall investigate the relation between evaluation elements and work effort, by examining how the latter is affected by the former. Moreover, it is of great concern to the workers how fairly they are treated in the wage and promotion systems. How do they consider the merit ratings? This is also an important issue in considering the future system of wages and promotion for white-collar workers. In addition, it is also a very important point to verify whether the incentive mechanism for skill formation is incorporated into the wage and promotion system for white-collar workers. We wonder if it is possible to verify this point through the analysis of the relationship between evaluation elements, work effort and satisfaction.

Third, what is the relation between unpaid overtime and work effort? It is a great problem for workers' welfare that there is persistent unpaid overtime, as well as long working hours and a low rate of take-up of paid annual leave – only about 50 per cent. It is possible to explain the practice of unpaid overtime as an economically rational behaviour which will be recompensed by future promotion. Thus it may be possible to regard such behaviour as the results of increased effort, when evaluation elements are related to performance. On the other hand, such behaviour may be the consequence of the lack of objective evaluation elements for wage increase and promotion, except for hours worked. In the latter case, unpaid overtime may be performed reluctantly with little effort. Thus we should like to investigate the relationship between unpaid overtime, unused annual paid leave, work effort and evaluation elements.

All the data which we use in this chapter is from the 'Survey of white-collar employees', conducted by RIALS in July 1993. This survey was conducted for the sampled employees in one company for each of the following five industries: automotive, electronics, chemical, electric power and commerce (referred to throughout this book as automotive company A, electronics company B, chemical company C, electric power company D, and department store E). We use the data for the employees whose job ranks are up to section head, because the behaviour of the employees whose ranks are equal to or above department head may be somewhat different.

The structure of the chapter is as follows: first of all, we shall analyse the wage/promotion system and the work incentive. Then, in Section 6.3 we shall investigate the relation between evaluation elements, work effort and workers' satisfaction. We shall analyse the significance of unpaid overtime, and unused annual paid leave in Section 6.4. Finally, we shall summarize the results and infer some policy implications. A definition of variables can be found in the appendix.

6.2   WAGE/PROMOTION SYSTEM AND WORK INCENTIVE

6.2.1 Theory

The problem of a wage/promotion system, that is, how to determine wage increases or promotion, is closely related to the problem of how to motivate workers to work hard. In the wage/promotion system of modern enterprises, an incentive mechanism for work effort is incorporated by linking pay to the performance or the ability of the worker. If the wages of workers with low ability and who make little effort were the same as those of the workers with high ability and who make strenuous efforts, there would be no incentive to work hard. By contrast, if the work efforts are appropriately evaluated and the wages and/or promotion are determined on that basis, the workers' morale will increase, they will work hard and the profits of the company will increase.

However, if wages and/or promotion is linked to performance and ability, there would be greater risk: wages and/or promotion would be affected by uncertainties which the worker cannot control. The first reason is that it is difficult to measure correctly the performance of the worker. Of course, we can use some test to obtain an objective measure, but it is only a partial measure to show the ability and/or the performance of the formal, repetitive and general operations which can easily be measured by such a test. Business abilities can be measured only by the performance on the job, and this may be even more applicable in the case of managerial staff. Moreover, it is difficult to measure objectively the performance of individual workers, when they work in a team. Even if it is possible to measure the performance of a particular worker, the subjective judgement of the supervisor may enter into the assessment.[2] Further, various external factors may affect the indices which are used for measuring the performance of the workers. For instance, in the case of car sales, the number of cars sold is affected by the consumption behaviour of the clients as well as by the macroeconomic situation and the weather.

Thus, the performance-related pay or promotion system may promote the work efforts of the workers, resulting in the efficiency of the production activity on the one hand, but on the other hand, it may introduce uncertainties in the determination of pay or promotion. If wages and promotion are determined solely on performance, then the income or the social status of the workers becomes unstable. This may be undesirable for workers, who want to have a secure livelihood avoiding any uncertainty. Nevertheless, it may lower the morale of the workers if the same wage were paid to all the workers regardless of their performance and in consequence result in lower profits for the firm, ultimately having adverse effects on the income and employment of the workers. In effect, the extreme egalitarianism in Eastern European countries under the ex-communist regimes is considered as one of the causes which has made the economies of these countries stagnate.

Therefore, it is necessary to strike a balance in the wage system between work incentives which promote morale and the workers' risk-averse attitudes, in order to increase the efficiency of the companies' activities and to ensure stability for the workers. For this purpose, it is necessary to find an appropriate index to measure the performance of the workers and find the optimal linkage between the wages and the index of the performance.

We shall look further into the issue by taking the case of wages. Now, we assume that the wage w is determined by the following formula:

$$w = \alpha + \beta \ (z + \gamma y)$$

where α, β and γ are constants, z is an index showing the effort of the worker (for example, the amount of sales), and y is an index of the factors which affect z but have nothing to do with the effort of the workers, such as the weather or the macroeconomic situation. Both z and y are assumed to be observable. z and y contain a part which the worker cannot control, and can be considered to be stochastic variables. z can be represented as $z = e + x$, with e and x, being the effort and the error terms, respectively. In this wage system, α is the part of the fixed wage which is paid regardless of the performance of the worker. $\beta \ (z + \gamma y)$ is the part which is linked to the performance, in other words, a performance-based payment. γy is the term which adjusts z so that external effects are excluded. β is a coefficient which determines the extent to which the wage reflects the performance. If β is zero, the same wage is paid to all workers regardless of their performance, and there will be no incentive for workers to work hard. On the other hand, if β is large, the performance-related part of the wage is large and the incentive to work hard will be greater, while the uncertainties will increase with the greater part of wages being dependent on uncontrollable factors. According to the economic theory of incentives, the optimal β is determined by the following four factors:[3]

1. the degree of risk-averse behaviour shown by the worker,
2. the importance of the performance of the worker to the profits of the firm,
3. the objectivity of the evaluation, and
4. the sensitivity of the worker to the wage incentive (the extent to which the worker increases his or her effort in response to the amount of β).

The degree of risk-averse behaviour is the index which shows the extent to which the worker tends to avoid the risks of the uncertainties in wage determination due to uncontrollable factors. The degree of risk-averse behaviour depends on attributes of the worker, such as age and sex. For example, heads of household with the responsibilities for their family may be considered to be more risk-averse than a single worker because they prefer a stable income. Other factors are the firm and the occupation. Workers who are more risk-averse tend to search for a job in a firm which has a less performance-related wage system. The more risk-averse the worker is, the less β sought by the worker, and the more stable the income.

The importance of the worker's effort to the profits of the firm shows the extent to which the effort of the worker increases the profits of the firm. It is measured by the increments in the profits caused by a unit of increase in effort. The greater this value is, the greater the profit of the firm is when the same amount of effort is increased. As a result, it will contribute to the total pie to make β larger so as to induce higher effort.

The objectivity of the evaluation indicates the correctness of the measurement of the effort of the worker. If the effort is measured correctly, there will be less uncertainty due to uncontrollable factors, even when β is large. Rather, it would be better to have a larger β so that effort is reflected in wages to a greater extent. For instance, if it were possible to measure the performance of the worker objectively and correctly by some test, the worker would be better off with a larger β.

The sensitivity of the worker to the wage incentive shows the extent to which wages and/or promotion are related to the evaluation element. In other words, it indicates the extent to which the value of β induces the work effort. The larger this value is, the larger is the extent to which the incentive of β induces the worker to make an effort. Thus it would be better to make β greater.

What we should like to verify is how different are the values of β across different firms, and whether they are related to the above factors as shown by the theory. That is, do the firms in which the workers are less risk-averse, the importance of work effort is higher, the measurement of the effort is more correct, or the sensitivity of the worker to the incentive is higher, tend to have greater β, that is, a higher proportion of performance-related pay?

6.2.2 Empirical analysis

Here, we estimate the value of β and the values of the factors which affect β for five different companies, and we shall verify the hypothesis by comparing these values across five companies. The survey does not give the values of the theoretical variables. Therefore, we consider the proxies as follows.

1. *Value of β* We recognize the variances of wages or promotion. We assume that the larger the variance, the larger the β. In the survey, we ask about the differentials in wages (the variance of wages) as well as about the differentials in promotion (the variance of promotion).
2. *Risk-aversion of workers* Although there is no appropriate variable in the survey, we use as a proxy the worker's attitude towards wage/promotion differentials. In the survey, the subjects were asked to choose one of the following answers concerning the existence of wage/promotion differentials among those who had joined the enterprise at the same time: 'it is better to make early wage/promotion differentials among those who have entered the firm at the same time', 'it is better to make little differentiation up to certain levels, and to make differentials thereafter', 'it is unavoidable to make differentials in promotion, but making large ones in wages should be avoided' and 'making any differentials in wages or promotion should be avoided'.
3. *Importance of the worker's effort to the profits of the firm* There is no appropriate variable. Thus, we use as a proxy what is most appreciated as an evaluation element. We can consider that the most appreciated element must be that of effort. When performance or skill is appreciated, the importance of effort to the profits can be considered to be greater than either age or tenure.
4. *Objectivity or accuracy of the evaluation* We cannot use an appropriate direct variable. Therefore, as above, we use the workers' own assess-

Table 6.1 Ordered probit analysis of the variances in wages/promotion, recognition of factors, job satisfaction and degree of intolerance for wage/promotion differentials

	Important factors determining wage differentials				Important factors determining promotion		
	Wage differentials	Promotion differentials	Worked earnestly	Worked harder and achieved more	Improvement in skills and knowledge	Age/tenure	Contribution to the firm
Female dummy	0.37 **	0.24 *	0.13	-0.12	0.31 **	-0.22 *	-0.30 **
Age	0.10 **	0.13 **	0.00	0.00	-0.01	-0.01	0.00
University graduate dummy	-0.27 **	-0.17 *	-0.34 **	0.29 **	-0.31 **	0.40 **	0.18
Section head dummy	0.19 *	0.23 **	0.09	0.09	-0.02	-0.11	0.10
Salesperson dummy	0.03	0.03	-0.02	-0.03	0.02	-0.33 **	0.13
Technician dummy	0.19 *	0.07	-0.10	-0.15	0.00	-0.23 **	0.05
Automotive dummy (company A)	0.73 **	0.82 **	0.01	-0.30 **	-0.10	-0.26 **	-0.45 **
Chemical dummy (company C)	-0.16	0.44 **	-0.23 *	-0.17	0.10	0.04	-0.28 **
Electrical power dummy (company D)	-0.45 **	0.16	0.37 **	-0.53 **	0.07	0.31 **	-1.03 **
Commerce dummy (company E)	0.51 **	0.56 **	0.28 *	-0.28 **	0.38 **	-0.15	-0.31 **
Constant	-3.22 **	—	-0.44	0.85 **	-0.20	0.63 **	-0.24
Number of samples	1,277	1,436	1,436	1,436	1,436	1,436	1,436
Pseudo R^2	0.2138	0.1964	0.0413	0.038	0.0295	0.0437	0.08

Important factors determining promotion (cont.)

	Ability and examination results	Supervisor's favouritism	Educational attainment	Character	Consider that a wage increase is important for job satisfaction	Consider that promotion is important for job satisfaction	Intolerance of wage/promotion differentials
Female dummy	-0.31 **	-0.01	0.30 **	-0.21 *	-0.22 *	-0.31 **	0.12
Age	-0.01	0.02 **	0.01	0.00	0.01	0.01	0.01
University graduate dummy	-0.19 *	0.10	-0.81 **	0.35 **	-0.33 **	-0.03	-0.22 **
Section head dummy	0.16	-0.05	0.03	0.06	-0.01	0.09	-0.12
Salesperson dummy	-0.04	0.31 **	0.05	0.02	0.17 *	-0.04	0.10
Technician dummy	-0.02	-0.03	0.18 *	0.04	0.13	-0.17 *	0.19 **
Automotive dummy (company A)	0.56 **	0.02	-0.13	0.10	0.09	0.45 **	0.13
Chemical dummy (company C)	0.05	-0.47 **	0.25 **	-0.26 **	-0.05	0.14	0.23 **
Electric power dummy (company D)	-0.79 **	-0.06	0.79 **	0.02	-0.29 **	0.18 *	0.34 **
Commerce dummy (company E)	0.05	-0.02	-0.22	-0.22	0.07	0.31 *	-0.03
Constant	1.53 **	-0.47	-0.27	-0.63 *	0.17	-0.96 **	—
Number of samples	1,436	1,436	1,436	1,436	1,436	1,436	1,409
Pseudo R^2	0.097	0.0241	0.14	0.0195	0.023	0.023	0.0184

Notes

* Significant at the 10 per cent level.
** Significant at the 5 per cent level.

ment about what is the most important element which makes a differential in wages or promotion, because the elements considered as important must be objective and accurate. If evaluation elements such as age or tenure are regarded as important, then other elements monitoring effort can be considered relatively less objective and accurate.
5. *Sensitivity to the incentive* We use as a proxy the importance of wage increase or promotion in the satisfaction of the work.

Table 6.1 shows the results of the ordered probit analysis using the above variables. The dependent variables are those variables mentioned above and the explanatory variables are the attributes of the workers, occupations and the firms. The occupation dummy and the firm dummy are normalized to zero for department store E and electronics company B, respectively. From this table, we can infer the following.

1. *Wage differentials (the value of β)* The probability that the wage differentials are large is higher when the worker is female, older, a high-school graduate, and a section head or technician. By firm, compared with electronics company B, the wage differentials are greater for automotive company A, department store E, and roughly the same for chemical company C. In contrast, the wage differentials are fairly small for electric power company D, compared with electronics company B.
2. *Promotion differentials (the value of β)* Females, older workers and section heads are more likely to recognize that promotion differentials are large. By firm, promotion differentials are larger for companies A, E and C; compared with electronics company B.
3. *Wage differential factors (evaluation element)* Females tend to consider that an improvement in skills and knowledge is a factor in wage differentials and high-school graduates also feel that working earnestly and an improvement in skills and knowledge are relevant factors, whereas university graduates tend to consider that performance is the important factor in wage differentials. By firm, companies B and C regard performance as an important factor for wage differentials, but in company C, working earnestly is not considered as important a factor for wage differentials, compared with company B. On the other hand, in company D, working earnestly is regarded as an important factor, while performance is not considered to be so important. In company E, working earnestly is considered as a somewhat important factor.
4. *Determinant factors of promotion (evaluation element)* Compared with males, females tend to give greater importance to educational attainment, but less importance to the contribution to firm's profits, ability and examination results, age/tenure, and character as determinant fac-

tors of promotion. The older the worker is, the more importance she gives to supervisor's favouritism. High-school graduates regard educational attainment and ability and examination results as important determinant factors of promotion, whereas university graduates give greater importance to age/tenure and character. By occupation, compared with clerical workers, sales workers and technical workers tend to consider that age and tenure have little to do with promotion, whereas sales workers and technical workers tend to give greater importance to supervisor's favouritism and educational attainment, respectively. By firm, in company A, the workers tend to give less importance to age and tenure but greater importance to ability and examination results as determinant factors of promotion, compared with the workers in company B, who give significant importance to contribution to the firm. In company C, they tend to give less importance to contribution to the firm, supervisor's favouritism and character, but give greater importance to educational attainment, in comparison with those in company B.[4] In company D, the workers tend to consider that age and tenure are important but contribution to the firm, ability and examination results are less important determinants of promotion.

5. *Work satisfaction and wage increase (sensitivity)* Males, high-school graduates, and sales workers consider that wage increase is important for work satisfaction. By firm, the number of workers in company D who agree with this is relatively small, compared with those in the other companies surveyed.

6. *Work satisfaction and promotion (sensitivity)* Males, sales workers and clerical workers consider that promotion is fairly important for work satisfaction. By firm, the workers in companies A and D are more likely to agree with this, compared with those in company B. To a lesser extent the workers in company D are also more likely to agree.

7. *Non-acceptance of differentials in wage increase or in promotion (risk-aversion)* University graduates tend to consider that there may be differentials among those who entered the company in the same year. In contrast, workers in technical occupations, (companies C and D), consider that less differential is better.

As seen above, the variances in wage and promotion are affected by factors such as sex, age, education, occupation and status, and the type of firm. We can summarize the differences across five companies as shown in Table 6.2. This table shows that in firms such as companies A and E, where variances in wages and promotion, namely the incentive β, are large, the evaluation elements tend to be performance related and sensi-

Table 6.2 Variances in wages/promotion, sensitivity to evaluation elements and degree of intolerance to the differentials

	Wage variances	Promotion variances	Evaluation element for wage	Evaluation element for promotion	Sensitivity to wage increase	Sensitivity to promotion	Degree of intolerance to wage/promotion differentials
Automotive company A	Large	Large		Appreciating skills		Large	
Chemical company C	Somewhat small	Somewhat small	Not appreciating age or tenure	Appreciating educational attainment and non-personal elements	Small		Somewhat large
Electric power company D	Small	Small	Appreciating age and tenure	Appreciating age, tenure and educational attainment	Small		Large
Department store E	Large	Large	Appreciating skills and knowledge			Large	
Electronics company B	Medium	Small	Appreciating performance	Contribution to the firm		Small	

tivity to promotion tends to be high. On the other hand, in firms such as company D, where the wage or promotion variances, or the incentive β, are small, the evaluation elements tend to be age related, the sensitivity is small, and the workers tend to be more risk-averse. This table shows that the empirical results are roughly consistent with the theoretical hypothesis mentioned earlier.

6.3   EVALUATION SYSTEM AND WORK INCENTIVE

6.3.1   Theoretical Hypothesis

In this section, we investigate the relationship between the evaluation system and work effort.[5] The degree of risk-averse behaviour and the sensitivity to incentives are different across workers. From the theory that has given the optimal incentive β, we can derive the hypothesis regarding the determinants of work effort as follows:[6]

1. risk-aversion: higher risk-aversion leads to less work effort;
2. importance of the workers' performance to the profits of the firm: greater importance leads to greater work effort;
3. objectivity of the evaluation: greater objectivity leads to greater work effort;
4. sensitivity of the worker to the incentive β: greater sensitivity leads to greater work effort.

Given the data limitations, we shall verify empirically only how objectivity and sensitivity affect the effort of the worker. Especially, it is important to know how the effort of the worker is affected by evaluation elements, in order to investigate the mechanism of the work incentive of the wage and promotion system in the firm. If age and tenure are important determinant factors of wage increase and promotion, then the incentive to work hard can be considered small. When performance and ability are important determinants, then the incentive to work hard is large.

The important thing is whether the incentive to accumulate skills is incorporated into the wage and promotion system. Namely, skill formation is achieved through education and through training in the company – on-the-job training (OJT) is particularly important. Such OJT is conducted most efficiently through experiencing different but closely related jobs, because such an experience tends to widen and deepen a particular skill. It is indispensable for such a training system to work efficiently that the incentive to encourage workers to enhance their skills in this way is built into the wage and promotion system. That is, the change in job must not result in a wage cut, even if productivity decreases during training. In addition, promotion and an increase in wages should keep up with improvements in skill level. Thus it is important to see whether the wage and promotion system incorporate the incentive system for the human capital accumulation of the worker.

Further, it is necessary to take into consideration objectivity or fairness, when we consider evaluation elements. Workers are very concerned about whether they are treated fairly in the wage and/or promotion system. Especially, excessive differentials in wages or promotion may not be compatible with the worker's own estimation of the fairness of the system.[7]

6.3.2 Empirical Analysis

As mentioned above, it can be considered that work effort is affected by evaluation elements which determine wages and promotion. In addition, the worker's behaviour may be influenced by educational attainment. Therefore, we tried probit analysis of educational attainment, with work effort as the dependent variable and the worker's attributes and evaluation elements as explanatory variables. The results are shown in Table 6.3. This table shows, in the case of high-school graduates, that work effort is high when the employee is older, the factors for wage differentials are to have accomplished lots of work or to have achieved good results, and when the factors for promotion determination are 'supervisor's favouritism' or 'wage increase is important for job satisfaction' or the promotion probability is high. In the case of university graduates, work effort is high when they are older, or section head, or when the promotion determinant factors are ability and examination results, or when the wage increase is important for job satisfaction or when the promotion probability is high. In any case, the coefficients are not statistically significant when the factor for wage differentials is to have worked hard, or when the determinant factor of promotion is age or tenure. Thus, these results are also roughly consistent with the theoretical hypothesis.

On the other hand, given the positive relation between incentive and effort, it is assumed that work effort increases under the wage/promotion system, where the incentive is large with a strong linkage between wage/promotion and performance. In order to verify this, we estimated the model with the firm dummies as independent variables. According to the results, in firms such as companies A and E, where the wage/promotion system is performance related, work effort tends to be high *ceteris paribus*. On the contrary, in firms such as company D, where

Table 6.3 Results of the estimation of effort functions by educational attainment (a) (Dependent variable = effort dummy)

Explanatory variables	High-school graduates	University graduates
	Estimated coefficients	Estimated coefficients
Female dummy	0.35	0.18
Age	0.05 **	0.05 **
Section head dummy	–0.06	0.28 **
Factor for wage differential = hard work	–0.09	0.14
Factor for wage differential = lots of work/good performance	0.39 **	–0.03
Factor for wage differential = improvements in skills or knowledge	–0.25	0.04
Determinant factor for promotion = age/tenure	0.01	0.07
Determinant factor for promotion = contribution to the firm	–0.27	–0.06
Determinant factor for promotion = ability/examination	0.37	0.27 **
Determinant factor for promotion = supervisor's favouritism	0.50 **	0.02
Determinant factor for promotion = educational attainment	0.28	–0.05
Determinant factor for promotion = character	0.18	0.17
Wage increase is important for job satisfaction	0.70 **	0.32 **
Promotion is fairly important for job satisfaction	–0.05	0.07
Probability of promotion	0.28 **	0.34 **
Satisfaction about the freedom of the job	0.07	0.20
Constant	–3.53 **	–3.25 **
Number of samples	248	889
Pseudo R^2	0.1559	0.1296

Notes
* Significant at the 10 per cent level.
** Significant at the 5 per cent level.

139

the incentive β is small, the work effort is low (Table 6.4). In consequence, we have obtained a result which is roughly consistent with the theoretical hypothesis.

In order to see whether the worker regards the evaluation element as fair or not, we tried a probit analysis with satisfaction for the wage increase and satisfaction for promotion as dependent variables. The result shows that satisfaction is high when the evaluation element is the improvement in skills and knowledge and it is low when the promotion is made because of the supervisor's favouritism or there is a promotion gap which cannot be caught up. By firm, company D, where the promotion is by seniority, satisfaction is high for wage increase as well as for promotion. In company C, dissatisfaction about promotion is high (see Tables 6.5 and 6.6).

It can be said that the fact that work effort is high when the skill accumulation is the evaluation element, and satisfaction is high when it is the improvement in skills and knowledge that is important, indicates that the incentive mechanism for skill formation is built into the wage/promotion system for white-collar workers.

6.4   UNPAID OVERTIME AND WORK EFFORT

6.4.1   Theoretical Considerations

The low rate of taken to given paid annual leave and unpaid overtime means working without compensation. There may be various reasons for this. One, based on economics, is that unpaid overtime may increase the probability of promotion associated with higher wages and therefore compensation is received later. In other words, unpaid overtime or unused paid annual leave constitutes rational behaviour, if the recompense in the future through the increased probability of being promoted with higher wages is sufficiently large, although there is no present compensation. In this case, it can be assumed that work effort is high and evaluation elements are performance related. None the less, the problem is that number of hours worked tends to be used as a measure of performance, when there is no objective and accurate evaluation element. In this case, since the important thing is to stay in the workplace, the worker endeavours to increase the number of hours by putting in long hours of unnecessary overtime (or by working inefficiently during office hours but working hard after five o'clock), or by taking less paid annual leave, even if it is possible to take more. This includes the case in which workers do unpaid overtime simply to maintain good relationships with colleagues during

Table 6.4 Results of the estimation of effort functions by educational attainment (b) (department variable = effort dummy)

Explanatory variables	High-school graduates Estimated coefficients	University graduates Estimated coefficients
Female dummy	−0.23	0.13
Age	0.05 **	0.05 **
Section head dummy	−0.16	0.22 *
Salesperson dummy	−0.70 **	0.03
Technician dummy	0.02	0.10
Automotive dummy (company A)	−0.30	0.31 **
Chemical dummy (company C)	−0.34	0.15
Electrical power dummy (company D)	−0.56 **	−0.30 **
Commerce dummy (company E)	0.86 *	0.38 **
Wage increase is important for job satisfaction	0.86 **	0.28 **
Promotion is fairly important for job satisfaction	0.01	0.05
Probability of promotion	0.23 *	0.34 **
Satisfaction about the freedom of the job	−0.03	0.23 *
Constant	−2.18**	−2.92 **
Number of samples	248	889
Pseudo R^2	0.1593	0.1409

Notes
* Significant at the 10 per cent level.
** Significant at the 5 per cent level.

Table 6.5 Probit analysis of satisfaction of wage increase (dependent variable = satisfaction for wage increase dummy)

Explanatory variables	Estimated coefficients
Female dummy	0.27 **
Age	0.00
University graduate dummy	0.00
Section head dummy	0.26 **
Salesperson dummy	–0.17 *
Technician dummy	–0.15 *
Automotive dummy (company A)	0.09
Chemical dummy (company C)	–0.03
Electric power dummy (company D)	0.65 **
Commerce dummy (company E)	0.41 **
Factor for wage differential = hard work	0.08
Factor for wage differential = lots of work/good performance	–0.10
Factor for wage differential = improvements in skills or knowledge	0.14 *
Factor for wage differential = education of subordinates	0.08
Wage differential	–0.04
Number of samples	1,268
Pseudo R^2	0.0522

Notes
* Significant at the 10 per cent level.
** Significant at the 5 per cent level.

the hours when supervisors or colleagues are at the workplace. This type of the non-take-up of paid annual leave or unpaid overtime takes place when work effort is not high, and when evaluation elements are not performance related.

6.4.2 Empirical Analysis

Here we classify the unused paid annual leave and unpaid overtime according to the reason, in order to estimate the changes in the probability due to the differences in the evaluation elements and the worker's effort, and verify the theoretical hypothesis mentioned above. Essentially, reasons for type 1 unused paid leave are: 'Because I would like to work more than the average', 'Because I cannot finish the work during the

Table 6.6 *Probit analysis of satisfaction for promotion (dependent variables = satisfaction for promotion dummy)*

Explanatory variables	Estimated coefficients
Female dummy	0.24 **
Age	−0.01 *
University graduate dummy	0.10
Section head dummy	0.45 **
Salesperson dummy	−0.14
Technician dummy	−0.05
Automotive dummy (company A)	−0.09
Chemical dummy (company C)	−0.32 **
Electric power dummy (company D)	0.29 **
Commerce dummy (company E)	−0.04
Determinant factor for promotion = age/tenure	−0.02
Determinant factor for promotion = contribution to the firm	0.02
Determinant factor for promotion = ability/examination results	0.07
Determinant factor for promotion = supervisor's favouritism	−0.19 **
Determinant factor for promotion = educational attainment	−0.09
Determinant factor for promotion = character	0.11
Existence of overtakable promotion differential	−0.01
Existence of nonovertakable promotion differential	−0.23 **
Number of samples	1,413
Pseudo R^2	0.0379

Notes
* Significant at the 10 per cent level.
** Significant at the 5 per cent level.

scheduled working hours', 'Because I would be an inconvenience to my colleagues and supervisor'. This type of behaviour is exhibited when a worker wants to demonstrate good performance in the anticipation of recompense through future promotion. Reasons for type 2 unused paid leave are: 'Because it is more pleasant to stay at the workplace', 'Because it is too expensive to take holidays', 'Because I save up paid leave so as to be ready for eventualities such as illness'. This type of behaviour is exhibited when a worker considers that the number of hours worked is of prime importance in the merit rating. Similarly, reasons for type 1 unpaid overtime are: 'Because it will be compensated for in the future by promotion', or 'Because the supervisor would look displeased if I required compensation'. This type can be considered as overtime which will be paid for by future promotion. Reasons for type 2 unpaid overtime are: 'Because the procedures are troublesome', 'Because I may be shunned, if I require recompense', or 'Because what I do is not worth claiming for'. This type of unpaid overtime occurs when the worker is not working hard to achieve a good performance but simply because he or she believes that staying at the workplace is appreciated by the supervisor. We estimated the probit model in which we took these indices as dependent variables, with the worker's attributes, evaluation elements, and work effort as explanatory variables.

Tables 6.7 and 6.8 show the results. In the case of unused paid annual leave, the probability of the incidence of type 1 is high for those workers who consider that the amount of work and good performance are important factors for wage differentials or that the favouritism of the supervisor and the character of the worker are fairly important for the promotion. It is lower for those workers who consider that skills and knowledge are important for wage differentials. On the other hand, the probability of the occurrence of type 2 unused paid annual leave is higher for the worker who considers that promotion is determined by age or tenure or whose work effort is low.

In the case of unpaid overtime, the probability of type 1 is high for those workers who consider that much work accomplished or good performance are important factors for wage differentials and it is low for those who consider that age or tenure are important factors for promotion. It is high when effort is high. The probability of type 2 is high for those who consider that the supervisor's favouritism or ability and examination results are important factors for promotion. However, work effort is not statistically significant, so it is not related to unpaid overtime of type 2.

In sum, the probability of unused paid annual leave of type 1 or unpaid overtime of type 1 is high when the evaluation factor is performance and it is low when the evaluation factor is age or tenure. It tends to be high for those who work hard. On the other hand, the probability of type 2 unused paid annual leave or type 2 unpaid overtime is high when the evaluation factor is age, tenure or the supervisor's favouritism and it is irrelevant with work effort. In other words, the hypothesis mentioned above is basically supported.

These facts imply that unnecessary unpaid overtime and intensive effort exist when the evaluation element is based on the number of hours worked with no objective evaluation of ability and performance, while there are other cases where unpaid overtime is undertaken and big efforts are made in the belief that they will be recompensed by future promotion.[8]

Table 6.7 *Probit analysis of unused paid annual leave (dependent variable = annual leave of type 1, unused annual leaves of type 2)*

Explanatory variables	Unused annual leave (type 1) (Because I would like to work more than the average, because I cannot finish the work during the scheduled working hours, because I would inconvenience my colleagues and supervisor)	Unused annual leave (type 2) (Because it is more pleasant to stay at the workplace, because it is too expensive to take holidays, because I save up paid leave so as to be ready for eventualities such as illnesses)
Female dummy	−0.65 **	−0.06
Age	0.02 **	0.00
University graduate dummy	0.63 **	0.06
Section head dummy	0.12	−0.06
Factor for wage differential = hard work	−0.01	0.00
Factor for wage differential = lots of work/good performance	0.21 **	−0.06
Factor for wage differential = improvements in skills or knowledge	−0.24 **	0.07
Determinant factor for promotion = age/tenure	0.06	0.28 **
Determinant factor for promotion = contribution to the firm	−0.03	−0.01
Determinant factor for promotion = ability/examination results	0.11	−0.09
Determinant factor for promotion = supervisor's favouritism	0.20 **	−0.03
Determinant factor for promotion = educational attainment	0.13	0.24 **
Determinant factor for promotion = character	0.15 *	0.09
Effort dummy	−0.01	−0.17 *
Constant	−1.47 **	−1.35 **
Number of samples	1,238	1,238
Pseudo R^2	0.0775	0.0223

Notes
* Significant at the 10 per cent level.
** Significant at the 5 per cent level.

Table 6.8 Probit analysis of unpaid overtime (dependent variable = unpaid overtime of type 1, unpaid overtime of type 2)

Explanatory variables	Unpaid overtime (type 1) (Because it will be compensated for in the future by promotion, or because the supervisor would look displeased if I required compensation)	Unpaid overtime (type 2) (Because the procedures are troublesome, because I may be shunned if I require recompense or because what I do is not worth claiming for)
Female dummy	−0.47 *	−0.14
Age	0.01	0.02 **
University graduate dummy	0.29	0.25 **
Section head dummy	−0.03	0.08
Factor for wage differential = hard work	0.06	−0.07
Factor for wage differential = lots of work/good performance	0.29 *	0.03
Factor for wage differential = improvements in skills or knowledge	−0.02	0.03
Determinant factor for promotion = age/tenure	−0.23 *	0.03
Determinant factor for promotion = contribution to the firm	−0.08	0.13
Determinant factor for promotion = ability/examination results	−0.01	0.18 *
Determinant factor for promotion = supervisor's favouritism	−0.05	0.19 **
Determinant factor for promotion = educational attainment	−0.19	0.10
Determinant factor for promotion = character	−0.19	0.01
Effort dummy	0.42 **	0.07
Constant	−2.05 **	−0.80 **
Number of samples	1,238	1,238
Pseudo R^2	0.0548	0.0226

Notes
* Significant at the 10 per cent level.
** Significant at the 5 per cent level.

6.5 CONCLUSION

In this chapter, we investigated the issues of the wage/promotion system of white-collar workers.

First, we analysed the determinant factors of the optimal work incentive in the wage/promotion system. Linkage of wages and promotion to ability and performance increase the morale of the worker and promote performance on the one hand, but on the other hand it may increase the uncertainty of the income because of the difficulty in measuring ability or performance, and other factors which the worker cannot control. According to economic theory, the appropriate incentive is determined by the risk-aversion of the worker, the profitability of the incremental effort and the responsiveness of effort to incentives. We obtained evidence which basically supports the hypothesis, by comparing the variances of wages and promotion, attitudes to the promotion differential, evaluation elements and the importance of the wage increase or the promotion for job satisfaction as proxies of the explanatory variables.

Second, we investigated the influence of the difference in the evaluation elements on work effort and satisfaction. The work incentive and work effort are considered to be higher when the evaluation element is ability or performance rather than when it is age or tenure. Empirical analysis shows the results, which are roughly consistent with the theoretical hypothesis. In addition, satisfaction is higher when the evaluation element is ability enhancement, and it is lower when the evaluation element is supervisor's favouritism. Moreover, it is shown that the incentive to the investment in human capital is inherent in the wage/promotion system for white-collar workers.

Third, we analysed the relationship between unused paid annual leave, unpaid overtime and work effort. In consequence, the probability of not taking paid annual leave and doing unpaid overtime to achieve a good performance is high when the evaluation element is performance or when effort is high. On the other hand, the probability of not taking paid annual leave and doing unpaid overtime not to achieve a good performance but simply to stay longer at the workplace is high when the evaluation element is age or tenure, but it is irrelevant to work effort. These facts imply that unnecessary unpaid overtime and intensive effort exist when evaluation is based on the number of hours worked with no objective evaluation of ability and performance, while there are other cases where unpaid overtime is undertaken and big efforts are made in the belief that they will be recompensed by future promotion.

From the above findings, we can deduce the following implications. First, the appropriate incentive to induce the worker to work hard in the linkage between wage/promotion and ability/performance is dependent on various factors such as the worker's risk-aversion, the reliability of measurement of performance and the sensitivity of the worker to the work incentive. In consequence, the simple modification towards the merit system may not necessarily result in a higher effort being made by the worker and the improvement of the profits of the company. If you want to increase the work incentive, then these factors must be changed. In particular, reform may be insufficient unless it is accompanied by reform of the evaluation system with an improvement in the reliability of the evaluation, and what to evaluate.

Second, it is shown that skill improvement is assessed and the incentive to skill accumulation is built in to the wage/promotion system for white-collar workers. When we consider the wage/promotion system in the future, it is necessary to retain such a skill accumulation system in order to promote the skill accumulation of white-collar workers.

Finally, the results of the analysis imply that the reasons for unused paid annual leave and unpaid overtime are that there is no objective evaluation element for ability and performance, and the duration of hours worked is used as the proxy. It is necessary to formulate a system which enables us to evaluate the ability/performance not by the number of hours worked but by the content and the quality of the work, although it is an important issue to promote the full take-up of paid annual leave and the abolition of unpaid overtime.

NOTES

1. Sasajima (1994) discusses recent trends and issues mainly from the institutional point of view. Ito (1992) and Milgrom and Roberts (1992) review the recent studies on the wage/promotion system in the field of the economics of firm.
2. Subjective evaluation by supervisors tends to be lenient, ambiguous and inaccurate. In the United States, a study has shown that in a firm with a rating system of four ranks, 94.5 per cent of the workers are rated as 'Good' or 'Outstanding' , the best two ranks. In another firm with six ranks, 98.8 per cent of the workers are related in the best three ranks (Abraham and Medoff, 1980).
3. The appropriate β is given by the following formula (Migrom and Roberts, 1992):

$$\beta = \frac{P'(e)}{[1 + rVC''(e)]}$$

where $P'(e)$ = the incremental profits created by additional effort, V = Var $(x + \gamma y)$ = the precision with which the desired activities are assessed, r = the worker's coefficient of absolute risk aversion, and $C''(e) = d\beta/de$ = the inverse of the worker's responsiveness to incentives.
4. One of the reasons, why educational attainment is considered as an important element of promotion, may be that chemical company C, which we surveyed, is a research and development branch with many graduate engineers (the proportion of graduates to all workers is 11 per cent).

5. Itoh and Teruyama (1998) analysed the elements of the work incentive from a different point of view.
6. We postulate that the cost of the effort is given by the following equation of the effort *e* (where *a*, *b* and *c* are constants):

$$C(e) = \frac{1}{2}ae^2 + be + c.$$

Then, C"(e) = the inverse of the worker's sensitivity to the incentive = *a*. Further we postulate that $P'(e)$ = the incremental profits created by additional effort is given by a constant *m*. Then, the effort function can be calculated as follows:

$$e = \frac{m}{a(1 + rVa)} - \frac{b}{a}.$$

7. Ishida (1990) says that the equity behind the Japanese 'pay for skills' system is the basis for the ideology which approves of wage differentials depending on skill differentials.
8. According to the survey, the proportion of workers who did not take all type 2 paid annual leave and those who did take type 2 overtime was 14.6 per cent and 64.7 per cent, respectively.

REFERENCES

Abraham, K.G. and J.L. Medoff (1980), 'Experience, Performance and Earnings', *Quarterly Journal of Economics*, **95**, December, 703–36.

Ishida, M. (1990), *Chingin No Syakaikagaku: Nihon To Igirisu* (The Social Science of Wages; Japan and the United Kingdom), Tokyo: Chuo-Keizaisya, (in Japanese).

Itoh, H. (1992), 'Satei Syousin Chingintaikei No Keizairiron – Joho To Incentive No Kenchi Kara' (Economic Theories on Merit Rating, Promotion and Wage Systems: From the Point of View of Information and Incentive) in T. Tachibanaki (ed.), *Satei, Syosin, Chingin Kettei* (Merit Rating, Promotion and Wage Determination), Tokyo: YuhiKaku, pp. 207–29.

Itoh, H. and H. Teruyama (1998), 'Effort Incentives: Evidence from Japanese Data', Chapter 5 in this book.

Milgrom, P. and J. Roberts (1992), *Economics, Organization and Management*, Englewood Cliffs, NJ: Prentice-Hall.

Sasajima, Y. (1994), *White Collar No Ikinokori Sakusen – Jiritsugata Jinzai O Mezase* (A Strategy of Survival for White-Collar Workers: Towards Independent Human Resources), Tokyo: Seisansei Press.

APPENDIX 6A DEFINITION OF VARIABLES

Wage differentials
0	Little differential.
0.1	About 10%.
0.2	About 20 per cent.
0.3	About 30 per cent.
0.4	About 40 per cent.

Worked earnestly
1	It is an important factor for wage differential to have worked earnestly.
0	Others.

Worked harder and achieved more
1	It is an important factor for wage differential to have done more work than others or to have achieved good work.
0	Others.

Improvement in skills and knowledge
1	It is an important factor for wage differential to have improved skills or knowledge.
0	Other.

Age/tenure
1	One of the most important determinant factors of promotion up to department head is age or tenure, or it is the merit rating result for age/tenure.
0	Others.

Promotion differentials
0	'Is there any promotion differential among those who have entered the firm in the same year as you?': There is no differential; No one has been promoted.
1	There are differentials; We can catch up with them without particular effort.
2	There are differentials; We can catch up with them with some effort.
3	There are differentials; We may be able to catch up with them but it is fairly difficult."
4	There are differentials; We cannot catch them up.

Contribution to the firm
1	One of the most important determinant factors of promotion up to department head is the merit rating result for contribution to the firm.
0	Other.

Ability and examination results
1   One of the most important determinant factor of promotion up to department head is the merit rating results for ability/skill, judgement ability, planning ability, cooperation ability, negotiation ability, presentation ability, leadership, educational ability, or examination results.
0   Others.

Supervisor's favouritism
1   One of the most important determinant factors of promotion up to department head is supervisor's favouritism.
0   Others.

Educational attainment
1   One of the most important determinant factors of promotion up to department head is educational attainment.
0   Others.

Character
1   One of the most important determinant factors of promotion up to department head is character.
0   Others.

Intolerance of wage/promotion differentials
1   It is better to make early wage/promotion differentials among those who have entered the firm at the same time.
2   It is better to make little differentiation up to certain levels, and to make differentials thereafter.
3   It is unavoidable to make differentials in promotion but making large ones in wages should be avoided.
4   Making differentials in wages or promotion should be avoided.

Consider that a wage increase is important for job satisfaction
1   Wage increase is fairly important for job satisfaction.
0   Others.

Consider that promotion is important for job satisfaction
1   Promotion is fairly important for job satisfaction.
0   Others.

Satisfaction with wage increase dummy
1   I am fairly satisfied with wage increase.
0   Others.

Satisfaction with promotion dummy
1   I am fairly satisfied with promotion.
0   Others.

Effort dummy
1   I contribute to the firm more than expected for my job.
0   I work as much as expected for my job.

7. White-collar careers in a large electronics company

Hisakazu Matsushige

7.1 INTRODUCTION

In this study, we shall attempt to examine the promotion process and the role of job rotation in it, taking male university graduates in a Japanese electronics company as an example.

The efficiency of a company will be improved to a great extent when workers are correctly assigned to the jobs where they can best bring their competency into play. Selection of workers, job allocation and training mechanisms are, therefore, always a subject of discussion not only among academics but also within companies.

In the recent restructuring process in Japanese companies, these aspects of white-collar workers, in particular, have been central agenda in the field of labour economics and human resource management. The study by Koike (1991b), which can be cited as a seminal study on this topic, examines the career development of white-collar workers in Japan and presents many new findings obtained through interviews and analysis of documents carried out inside companies. Sano and Kawakita (1993), on the other hand, attempt broad surveys of the workers in large companies listed on the Japanese stock markets, deducing details of their working lives and examining those factors which are work incentives.

There have been, however, only a few studies which have collected statistical information on job rotation and promotion. The Japan Institute of Labour Research (1993) conducted two questionnaires, one on the management of companies belonging to the same group as that analysed by Sano and Kawakita, and the other on those companies' workers. Their study is the first to attempt to capture the details of workers' careers, statistically, on such a large scale. The project of Imada and Hirata (1995) is another example. They obtained a full set of employment files from one of the largest iron and steel companies in Japan, and analysed a complete panel data of a group of workers who were recruited in a certain year, with respect to their job experience and promotion. This is the most informative data set on company internal information about workers that is available for this sphere of labour economics in Japan.

However, since Imada and Hirata's study is confined to only one company, we need to extend our analysis to cover other cases in order to understand the mechanism of job rotation and promotion in Japanese companies as a whole. In this study, therefore, we shall attempt another career analysis, of the workers in one of the largest electronics companies in Japan.

Two aspects of promotion have to be considered. One is that promotion means selection; only a few out of many can be selected for higher positions. The other is that promoted workers need to be sufficiently skilled to pursue more responsible tasks.

Regarding the first aspect of promotion, the studies of Rosenbaum (1984) in the United States on one hand, and Hanada (1987) in Japan on the other, are frequently cited as representative. Describing the patterns of promotion in detail, they closely examine not only the question of at which stage of employment workers are most likely to be promoted, but also whether later opportunities can enable earlier losers in career competition to redeem themselves. However, the investigation of the factors which make the difference between winners and losers was not their main purpose.

Wakabayashi (1986) compensates for the shortcomings in these studies. He attempts to identify the abilities and characteristics of workers who are promising candidates for future promotion and examines the relationship between their scores in the aptitude test which they took soon after recruitment and the probability of promotion in the future. He argues that selection probably begins in the first few years.

Selection is also determined on the basis of assessment within the company. Medoff and Abraham (1980, 1981) examined the importance of assessment in determining who is promoted in the United States. Tomita (1992) attempted a similar study in Japan. In both studies, it is found that promotion is significantly affected by the results of assessment. The difference between these two studies is that whereas Tomita argues that tenure is one of the main factors affecting promotion in Japan, Medoff and Abraham do not give much endorsement for the tenure argument as regards the United States. Koike (1993) emphasizes that the difference between the two countries lies in the fact that Japanese companies do not apply fast-track promotion to their workers and promotion in Japan occurs at a much later stage of employment than it does in the United States. He indicates that Japanese workers devote themselves to longer-term competition than do US workers.

Many studies analyse job rotation within companies from the viewpoint of training. Through experiencing a number of jobs, workers can synthesize their knowledge about different tasks and learn the mechanism of production. Workers in higher positions have to examine the efficiency of production of their subordinates and observe their performance, and so for higher-ranking workers, experiencing different jobs is inevitable.

This idea was used by Koike and Inoki (1987) in an analysis of skill formation in South East Asian countries. Subsequently, Koike (1991a, 1991b) extended this study to the case of white-collar workers.

In the analysis of job rotation and skill formation, it is also important, as Inoue (1982) and Nakamura (1987) argue, to take into account the fact that transferring workers to new jobs which are completely unconnected to their previous ones may seriously impair their productive efficiency. Such workers have to spend considerable time mastering a new job. This has the result that the effort and time devoted to mastering their previous jobs is largely wasted, and in addition they have less time to reap the rewards of the effort invested in their new jobs. What makes things worse is that this kind of job rotation does not help workers' understanding of the overall process of production and the relationships between jobs in the company. Because of these considerable costs associated with the transfer of workers to new jobs, it can be safely said that promising workers show a pattern of job rotation different from others. This implies that at a given point we may be able to identify those who are more likely to be promoted in the future if we examine closely the jobs which they have been allocated so far.

It is often said that with respect to promotion, Japanese companies treat workers entering the company in the same year equally in the early stage of their careers and that they prevent information on promotion leaking out as a matter of tactics. But it might be that patterns of job rotation reflect a company's assessment of its younger employees.

This implies that we need to examine types of promotion as well as frequency of promotion in discussing the relationship between job rotation and promotion. It is, however, nearly impossible to obtain a relevant data set which can adequately explain the various careers of workers within a single company, and the relationships between their careers.

In this study, we are fortunately able to present such a data set for a company, and attempt statistical analysis of it. Furthermore we are able to investigate the pattern of job rotation and identify the period when competent workers are selected. In Section 7.2, we shall describe the company which is analysed in this study and discuss the characteristics of the data on its workers. An outline of the promotion process will also be presented. We shall then examine the question of whether workers are able to identify their more able colleagues before promotion, in Section 7.3. We shall also examine the relationship between job rotation and promotion in Section 7.4. Finally, we shall summarize our findings and draw conclusions regarding the Japanese promotion system.

7.2 PERIOD OF PROMOTION

The data used for the analysis in this study was collected through questionnaires conducted on white-collar workers in the company in question in 1993.

This company is one of the largest electronics companies in Japan and was established before the Second World War. It comprises more than ten branches, about 30 factories and several R&D centres, and employs more than 50,000 workers. Our survey was carried out on 2,000 workers in one of the company's plants.

The number of useful samples obtained was 406, consisting of 222 male university graduates, 75 male postgraduates and 25 female graduates. The female graduates were excluded from the consideration since their number was too small for application of statistical analysis.[1]

The male graduates consisted of 221 non-managerial personnel, 37 section heads, 20 middle managers without subordinates, nine middle managers with subordinates and eight workers with other positions, the remaining two being of unclear status. A drawback of our data was that it did not include workers promoted above the level of director.

We examined the humanities and social science graduates as a separate category from science and technology graduates, since we supposed that in an electronics company the promotion mechanisms differ considerably between these two groups. The postgraduates were also analysed as a separate category since they are more likely to be in R&D sections and less likely to be involved in managerial tasks.[2]

Among subjects who stated their educational qualifications, 184 were engineering graduates (of whom 70 were postgraduates), 18 were natural science graduates (of whom three were postgraduates), and five were graduates of other branches of science and technology. There were in addition 85 humanities and social science graduates, 54 in economics, management, or commerce, 24 in law or political science, five in literature, one in education and another in another humanities subject. There were no humanities and social science postgraduates.

Before beginning analysis of the questionnaires, it was necessary for us to grasp two special promotion policies of this company. First, promotion to middle manager with subordinates occurs at a certain fixed age, in the late thirties in almost all cases. As a result, there is very little variation in the age of promotion, and it is extremely difficult to be promoted once the fixed age is passed. Second, graduates are promoted at the same age as postgraduates, in theory at least.

We needed to confirm that these policies were carried out in practice. Accordingly we classified workers according to their positions and length of service, reasoning that the workers with the shortest length of service among those with the same position would probably represent the most successful cases, with the fastest promotion.

First, we looked at the science and technology graduates. Among the workers who had been working for the company since graduation, the youngest section head had 12 years of service, the youngest middle manager without subordinates had 19 years of service and the youngest middle manager with subordinates had 17 years of service. That is, promotion to section head would seem to require more than ten years, while that to middle manager does indeed start after 15 years of service or in the late thirties, as per the policy.

There was the possibility that some of the above workers had already spent some years in their positions since promotion, so we also needed to examine their past careers. It should be noted, however, that the workers' answers may not be reliable since they were recalling what happened a long time ago. In addition, since many of them did not answer certain questions, the number of samples was limited.

One worker answered that he was promoted to section head after nine years of service. Seven workers were promoted after ten years of service and three after 11 years. One said that he was promoted after 12 years of service. Another said that he was promoted after 16 years and another after 17 years.

As regards promotion to middle manager without subordinates, the fastest promotion occurred after ten years, two others occurred after 13 years and two more after 14 years.

Four workers stated when they were promoted to middle manager with subordinates. One was promoted after 14 years of service and the other three after 15 years.

As a result, it may be concluded that promotion to section head starts after approximately ten years of service, that to middle manager without subordinates after 13 years, and that to middle manager with subordinates after 14 years.

Next, we examined the science and technology postgraduates. The youngest postgraduate section head was in the tenth year of service, the youngest middle manager without subordinates in the 13th year, and the youngest middle manager with subordinates also in the 13th year.

The figures for their promotion to section head are presented in Table 7.1. Twenty-one of the postgraduate workers stated details of their career history which are relevant for the analysis. None of them had worked for other companies.

Table 7.1 Promotion of science and technology postgraduates to section head (number of employees)

Year of service	Age 23	24	25	26	27	29
4th			1			
5th						
6th				1	1	1
7th						
8th			4			
9th			6	1	1	
10th		1	1	1		
11th	1	1	1			

Age appears to be a significant factor in this case as well. Since the postgraduates' length of stay in graduate school varied, the ages at which they started to work for the company were not the same. Except for one worker who entered the company at the age of 25 and was promoted in the fourth year of service, workers who entered at a younger age were more likely to require a longer time to be promoted. It can also be pointed out that a worker who spent, say, two years in a postgraduate course usually requires eight or nine years for promotion. If we recall that a graduate has to wait 11 years or so for the same promotion, then the postgraduates need a shorter length of service for the promotion than graduates, by a few years. In the end, they are promoted at a similar age.

As regards promotion to middle manager, the youngest postgraduate middle manager without subordinates was in the 13th year of service, and the youngest middle manager with subordinates was also in the 13th year.

In the past career records of postgraduates, it is recorded that one of the two workers who entered the company at the age of 24 was promoted to middle manager without subordinates after 13 years of service and the other was promoted after 14 years. In addition, workers who were employed at the age of 25, 26 and 27 were promoted to the position after 13, 14 and 10 years of service, respectively. Three workers who were recruited at the age of 25 were promoted to middle managers with subordinates after 13 years of service and one who was recruited at the age of 27 was promoted to the position after ten years. These facts imply that the policy of adding the years spent in postgraduate education to the length of service in determining promotion was adhered to in this case as well.

Finally we trace the careers of humanities and social science graduates. All of them entered the company soon after graduation. The five youngest section heads were promoted to their current positions after 11 years of service. The worker with the shortest length of service among middle managers without subordinates was in the 14th year of service. There was only one middle manager who answered the questionnaire. He had been working for the company for 19 years.

Eight workers stated when they were promoted to section head. Two were promoted after nine years of service, three after ten years, and the others after 11, 17 and 18 years. Only one worker stated when he was promoted to middle manager without subordinates – after 22 years of service. None of these workers stated that he had been promoted to middle manager with subordinates. Accordingly, in the case of humanities and social science graduates, ten years or so are required for promotion to the position of section head. It may be noted that the findings in this section are mostly in accordance with those of other research in this sphere of study. They also suggest that Japanese companies do not apply unequal treatment to their workers in terms of promotion during the first ten years of employment.

We next extended our analysis to the workers' careers after ten years of service. We were especially interested in the question of whether workers who fail in competition for promotion at early stages can catch up with their competitors later. We examined the extent to which the company's policy concerning promotion to middle manager is followed. If it were followed without exception, the differences in promotion occurring before the late thirties would vanish and all workers would end up on the same level once again.

Table 7.2 presents the lengths of time which workers waited for promotion to section head as well as the lengths of time they waited for promotion to middle manager. Unfortunately, the number of samples of humanities and social science graduates was too small for statistical analysis.

There were only three science and technology graduates who stated when they were promoted to section head and to middle manager without subordinates.[3] The table clearly shows that the worker who was promoted to section head fastest was also fastest in promotion to middle manager without subordinates. Furthermore the differences in the length of time required for the promotion to section head were more or less repeated for the next promotion. That is, the order of promotion among workers does not change up to this level.

The pattern of promotion to middle manager with subordinates is somewhat unclear. Three other workers gave details of their career. The one who was promoted to section head fastest took longer to be promoted to middle manager with subordinates than the other two. However all three were promoted to middle manager with subordinates at the age of 37 or 38, as per the company's policy.

Table 7.2 Promotion to section head and to middle manager (number of employees)

Science and technology graduates

Promotion to section head	Promotion to middle manager without subordinates		
	16th year	17th year	19th year
11th year	1		
12th year		1	
13th year			1

Promotion to section head	Promotion to middle manager with subordinates	
	15th year	16th year
10th year		1
11th year	2	1

Science and technology postgraduates

Promotion to section head	Promotion to middle manager without subordinates		
	11th year	14th year	15th year
6th year	1		
10th year		2	
11th year			1

Promotion to section head	Promotion to middle manager with subordinates		
	11th year	14th year	15th year
4th year		1	
6th year	1		
8th year		1	
11th year			1

Next, we investigated the promotion of science and technology post-graduates. There were four cases of promotion to middle manager without subordinates. Three of these were promoted to section head in the 10th or 11th year of service and then promoted to middle manager without subordinates in the 14th or 15th year. The exception was one who was promoted to section head in the 6th year of service. He entered the company at the age of 27 after spending a few more years in postgraduate education than those who started to work straight after graduating from MA courses. It seems that these years of education were counted in determining his promotion. This means that all of these workers were promoted at a similar pace without age variation.

Four other workers gave their promotion history up to middle manager with subordinates. Although the time waited for the promotion to section head varied, three became middle manager with subordinates in the 14th or 15th year of service, the exception being one who became a section head in the 6th year. He was recruited when he was 29 years old. Again, if the time which he spent in the postgraduate course is taken into account, it becomes clear that he was promoted at almost the same age as the others.

In summary, the pace of promotion differs among workers up to the level of middle manager without subordinates, but all workers need to wait until their late thirties for promotion to middle manager with subordinates – exactly as per the company's promotion policy.[4]

7.3   WHEN IS SUPERIOR COMPETENCE REVEALED?

Once promotion is carried out, it is distinctly clear who excels. However, the competence of workers is presumably gauged by the company beforehand in order to determine the candidates for promotion. The question is whether the candidates are made clear to the workers or not, and if so, at what point.

In the questionnaire, we asked, 'Were you able to identify those of your colleagues who would be promoted to high managerial positions?'. There was a choice of three answers: 'Yes, definitely', 'Yes, to a certain extent' and 'No'. Examination of the answers to this question will clarify the period when workers become aware of the differences in their competence.

Table 7.3 sets forth the answers from workers with up to 10 years of service. It is meaningful to focus on this period since promotion to section head starts after 10 years or so of service (see above). It may also be useful to assess the argument that in Japanese companies there is no markedly unequal treatment of workers in the first 10 years of employment.

Table 7.3 *When workers realize who is promising**

Year of service	Science and technology graduates				Science and technology postgraduates				Humanities and social science graduates			
	Yes, definitely	Yes, to some extent	No	Total	Yes, definitely	Yes, to some extent	No	Total	Yes, definitely	Yes, to some extent	No	Total
1st	0 (0.0)	3 (42.9)	4 (57.1)	7 (100.0)	0 (0.0)	0 (0.0)	1 (100.0)	1 (100.0)	0 (0.0)	3 (60.0)	2 (40.0)	5 (100.0)
2nd	1 (6.7)	5 (33.3)	9 (60.0)	15	0 (0.0)	3 (60.0)	2 (40.0)	5 (100.0)	0 (0.0)	4 (40.0)	6 (60.0)	10 (100.0)
3rd	2 (8.7)	4 (17.4)	17 (73.9)	23 (100.0)	0 (0.0)	3 (60.0)	4 (40.0)	7 (100.0)	1 (7.1)	4 (28.6)	9 (64.3)	14 (100.0)
4th	2 (33.3)	2 (33.3)	2 (33.3)	6 (100.0)	0 (0.0)	3 (42.9)	4 (57.1)	7 (100.0)	1 (20.0)	1 (20.0)	3 (60.0)	5 (100.0)
5th	0 (0.0)	3 (60.0)	2 (40.0)	5 (100.0)	0 (0.0)	3 (60.0)	2 (40.0)	5 (100.0)	0 (0.0)	1 (25.0)	3 (75.0)	4 (100.0)
6th	0 (0.0)	3 (60.0)	4 (40.0)	7 (100.0)	1 (20.0)	2 (40.0)	2 (40.0)	5 (100.0)	0 (0.0)	4 (50.0)	4 (50.0)	8 (100.0)
7th	2 (22.2)	3 (33.3)	4 (57.1)	9 (100.0)	0 (0.0)	1 (50.0)	1 (50.0)	2 (100.0)	0 (0.0)	3 (60.0)	2 (40.0)	5 (100.0)
8th	0 (0.0)	4 (50.0)	4 (44.4)	8 (100.0)	1 (25.0)	3 (75.0)	0 (0.0)	4 (100.0)	0 (0.0)	0 (0.0)	3 (100.0)	3 (100.0)
9th	0 (0.0)	1 (50.0)	5 (50.0)	6 (100.0)	0 (0.0)	0 (0.0)	7 (100.0)	7 (100.0)	0 (0.0)	3 (60.0)	2 (40.0)	5 (100.0)
10th	0 (0.0)	4 (16.7)	1 (83.3)	5 (100.0)	0 (0.0)	4 (100.0)	0 (0.0)	4 (100.0)	0 (0.0)	1 (50.0)	1 (50.0)	2 (100.0)
Total	7 (7.7)	32 (80.0)	52 (20.0)	91 (100.0)	2 (4.3)	22 (46.8)	23 (48.9)	47 (100.0)	2 (3.3)	24 (39.3)	35 (57.4)	61 (100.0)

Note: *Number of employees; percentage in parentheses.

Table 7.4 How and when competent workers show their ability (number of employees)

Science and technology graduates

Year of service	Jobs and positions	Outstanding performance	Fast promotion	University and educational qualifications	Training courses	Others
1st	0	0	0	0	0	0
2nd	0	1	0	0	3	0
3rd	0	1	0	2	3	0
4th	1	0	1	0	3	0
5th	0	2	0	1	3	0
6th	1	1	0	2	2	0
7th	0	1	0	0	1	0
8th	2	3	0	1	1	1
9th	0	0	0	0	0	0
10th	1	2	0	0	3	1
Total	5	11	1	6	19	2

Science and technology postgraduates

Year of service	Jobs and positions	Outstanding performance	Fast promotion	University and educational qualifications	Training courses	Others
1st	0	1	0	2	2	0
2nd	0	2	1	1	5	2
3rd	0	4	0	2	5	0
4th	0	4	0	0	2	0

Year of Service	Jobs and positions	Outstanding performance	Fast promotion	University and educational qualifications	Training courses	Others
5th	0	3	0	2	1	0
6th	1	1	0	0	1	1
7th	0	4	0	3	3	0
8th	0	3	0	1	3	0
9th	1	1	0	0	1	0
10th	1	3	0	0	3	0
Total	3	26	1	11	26	3

Humanity and social science graduates

Year of Service	Jobs and positions	Outstanding performance	Fast promotion	University and educational qualifications	Training courses	Others
1st	0	2	1	0	2	0
2nd	1	2	0	5	3	0
3rd	2	2	0	2	3	0
4th	1	1	0	3	1	0
5th	2	0	0	0	1	1
6th	0	3	0	0	4	1
7th	1	2	0	0	3	0
8th	0	0	0	0	0	0
9th	2	1	0	0	2	0
10th	0	1	0	0	1	0
Total	9	14	1	10	20	2

Three out of seven science and technology graduates in the first year of employment answered 'Yes, to a certain extent'. Among those in the second year of service, the answer 'Yes, definitely' appears. Of all the workers with up to 10 years of service, more than 40 per cent were able to identify promising colleagues. The science and technology postgraduates showed the same pattern as the graduates apart from the fact that none with less than 6 years of service answered 'Yes, definitely'. More than half became aware of the differences in their competence within the first ten years of service. The humanities and social science graduates were not very different from others. On the whole, it can be concluded that workers know their future prospects from a relatively early stage of their employment.

Naturally, we next became curious as to how they come to possess these perspectives on the future. In the questionnaire, respondents who answered 'Yes, definitely' or 'Yes, to a certain extent' to the question above were further asked, 'How did you identify them?'. They could choose two out of six responses: 'from the jobs and positions which they had had', 'from their outstanding job performance', 'because they had always been promoted first', 'from their educational qualifications and the names of their universities', 'from their high competence shown at training courses and other opportunities' and 'for other reasons'.

Table 7.4 presents the answers from workers with up to 10 years of service. The response which science and technology graduates chose most was 'from their high competence shown at training courses and other opportunities'. The second most common response was 'from their outstanding job performance'. 'From their educational qualifications and the names of their universities' and 'from the jobs and positions which they had had' came next.

There are three major noteworthy findings. First, in the second year of service, workers have already started assessing their colleagues on the basis of their performance on the job and on training courses. Second, in the fourth year of employment, some of them start paying attention to the jobs and positions to which they are rotated. Finally, educational background is also used as a signal of competence for a certain length of time.

What distinguished the science and technology postgraduates from the rest was that 11 of them gave 'educational qualifications and the names of their universities' as the basis of assessing competence. We suppose that since most of these workers pursue their careers as professional researchers and engineers, the level of their competence is more directly linked to the universities from which they graduated than in the case of other workers.

The humanities and social science graduates were similar to the others in that they also stressed 'jobs and positions' in and 'outstanding job performance'. However, they differed in that none of them with more than five years of service responded with 'educational qualifications and the names of their universities'. Instead, 'the jobs and positions which they had had' and 'outstanding job performance' were more important for these respondents. In addition, more of them start according importance to the jobs and positions which they are assigned at an earlier stage than the science and technology postgraduates.

The findings in this section imply that workers may start assessing their colleagues many years ahead of the time of promotion. They also show that there are some differences in the way that groups with different educational qualifications make these assessments.

7.4   JOB ROTATION AND SELECTION

It is a natural conjecture that the company itself assesses its workers more precisely than they do themselves, since it has to select the workers who deserve expensive training through job rotation. The workers who are given the training are therefore more likely to be promoted. Since we had data on the workers' history, we were able to attempt a statistical test on this point.

In the questionnaire, job changes were categorized into four types: job change within the establishment, job change between establishments, job change with transfer to an affiliate and job change with transfer from an affiliate.

There were two shortcomings in the data, however. The sample set of the promotions to high managerial positions was not large enough and we were able to apply statistical analysis only to the promotion to section head. We therefore focused on job rotation before promotion to section head, that is, job rotation in the first 10 years of service. Unfortunately in this period no transfer of workers from an affiliate is recorded and this restricts our analysis to the three other types of job rotation.

We created a dependent variable by designating the workers who were section heads or higher as units, and the others as zero, and applied probit analysis to identify the factors which foster the promotion of workers. In order to make the number of job rotations exogenous, only workers with more than $n + 1$ years of service were used for analysis of the effects of job rotation in the first n years of employment. In addition, workers who were promoted without waiting n years were dropped from the samples to exclude job rotation after promotion.

Table 7.5 Job rotation and promotion of science and technology graduates

	Workers with more than 3 years of service	Workers with more than 5 years of service	Workers with more than 6 years of service
Number of samples	82	74	74
Pseudo R^2	0.45	0.46	0.46
Explanatory variables			
Length of service	0.5807 [3.869] {0.000}	0.6315 [3.907] {0.000}	0.6277 [3.895] {0.000}
(Length of service)^2	−0.0122 [−3.013] {0.003}	−0.013 [−3.048] {0.002}	−0.0131 [−3.039] {0.002}
Job rotation within establishment frequency in 4th year	0.0451 [0.071] {0.943}		

frequency in 6th year		0.2609 [0.335] {0.738}	
Job rotation between establishments frequency in 4th year	−1.3347 [−1.638] {0.101}		−0.6916 [−0.704] {0.482}
frequency in 6th year		−1.8386 [−2.455] {0.014}	−1.6312 [−2.003] {0.045}
Constant term	−5.6519 [−4.557] {0.000}	−6.1366 [−4.499] {0.000}	−6.0497 [−4.495] {0.000}

Notes
[ ] indicates *t*-value.
{ } indicates *p*-value.

Table 7.5 shows the case of science and technology graduates.[5] Several points should be noted. First, the coefficients of length of service are positive and statistically significant. This implies that the longer a worker works for the company, the more likely he is to be promoted, which concurs with the argument in Tomita (1992). However, the coefficients of length of service powered to two are negative and statistically significant. This means that the effect of length of service decreases the longer workers stay.[6]

Second, rotation within the establishment does not have an effect on promotion. This seems to contradict the opinion that workers are generally rotated to jobs similar to their previous ones so as to minimize the cost entailed by mastering new skills. We expected, therefore, that rotation within the establishment, which tends to include cases of skill enrichment, would have a more positive effect on promotion than the other three types of rotation. One reason for this contradiction, which an employee familiar with personnel matters in the company pointed out, is that the way the types of job rotation are defined does not properly apply to science and technology graduates, who are transferred to similar jobs within the same job section in almost all cases and gradually improve their skills there. Possibly they do not regard this kind of job change as job rotation and did not include it in the category of job rotation within the establishment.

Third, rotation between establishments in the fourth and sixth years has a negative effect on promotion. Science and technology graduates work as engineers and build up their speciality within their work section, as explained above. If moving to another establishment involves a major change in their duties and their new job is not relevant to their previously established speciality, their skill and career development will be hindered.

Finally, we may recall that Table 7.3 showed that workers start to identify those of their colleagues who are promising candidates for future promotion after a few years of service. It would not seem to be a matter of coincidence that job rotations in the same period were found to be significant for promotion prospects in our estimate as well.

Table 7.6 shows the relationship between job rotation and promotion in the case of science and technology postgraduates. This contrasts with that for graduates in the same subjects in several ways. First, age has the same effect on promotion as does length of service. This may be due to the company's policy that the extra years of education are added to the length of service in determining who is to be promoted, which has the result that promotion occurs at the same age in almost all cases.

Table 7.6 Job rotation and promotion of science and technology postgraduates

	Workers with more than 5 years of service	Workers with more than 6 years of service
Number of samples	52	47
Pseudo R^2	0.70	0.66
Explanatory variables		
Years in other companies	0.4461 [0.198] {0.843}	0.4126 [0.162] {0.871}
Age	0.3945 [1.377] {0.168}	0.3642 [1.245] {0.213}
Length of service	0.3344 [1.087] {0.277}	0.3855 [1.202] {0.229}
Job rotation within establishment		
total frequency up to 5th year	0.1732 [0.421] {0.674}	
total frequency up to 6th year		−0.0878 [−0.258] {0.797}
Job rotation between establishments total frequency up to 5th year	1.0964 [0.909] {0.364}	
total frequency up to 6th year		0.221 [0.244] {0.807}
Transfer to affiliates		
total frequency up to 5th year	2.9449 [2.139] {0.032}	
total frequency up to 6th year		2.8285 [2.033] {0.042}
Constant term	−18.667 [−2.263] {0.024}	−17.918 [−2.144] {0.032}

Notes
[ ] indicates *t*-value.
{ } indicates *p*-value.

Table 7.7 Job rotation and promotion of humanities and social science graduates

	Workers with more than 4 years of service	Workers with more than 5 years of service	Workers with more than 7 years of service
Number of samples	56	56	39
Pseudo R^2	0.5	0.48	0.37
Explanatory variables			
Length of service	1.022	1.12	1.1087
	[2.449]	[2.317]	[2.189]
	{0.014}	{0.021}	{0.029}
(Length of service)^2	−0.0276	−0.0294	−0.0294
	[−2.100]	[−1.991]	[−1.887]
	{0.036}	{0.047}	{0.059}
Job rotation within establishment frequency in 4th year	0.8446		
	[1.274]		
	{0.203}		

	(1)	(2)	(3)
total frequency up to 4th year		0.5529 [1.063] {0.288}	
frequency in 7th year			1.0859 [1.592] {0.111}
Job rotation between establishments frequency in 4th year	1.9091 [1.645] {0.100}		
total frequency up to 4th year		0.9517 [1.785] {0.074}	0.9245 [1.742] {0.082}
Constant term	-8.8532 [-2.811] {0.005}	-10.026 [-2.628] {0.009}	-9.8505 [-2.482] {0.013}

Notes
[ ] indicates *t*-value.
{ } indicates *p*-value.

Second, transfer to an affiliate during the first five years of employment has a positive effect on promotion. Since the majority of these workers are masters course graduates, such transfers occur when they are about 27 years old. This also was confirmed by the employee familiar with the company's personnel management, who added that they transferred young workers to affiliates in order to promote productive coordination between them. In the case of postgraduates, the young workers are assigned managerial posts in their new workplaces, as a by-product of which they receive training as managers through on-the-job experience. He also mentioned that in some cases young workers are deliberately sent to such posts to give them managerial training as well.

Table 7.7 summarizes the case of humanities and social science graduates. First, it proves that length of service has a positive relationship with promotion consistently in all estimates in the case of science and technology graduates. Second, job rotation within the establishment has a positive effect on promotion in contrast to other cases, although the coefficients are not significant. Finally, in sharp contrast to the science and technology graduates, job rotation between establishments is positive and significant. This implies that experiencing jobs in other establishments increases the skills and knowledge which humanities and social science graduates require. As a matter of fact, this type of job rotation happens quite frequently in this company. As Nakamura (1994) described in his study of other Japanese companies, the more able workers in the sales and marketing section are often deliberately sent to the production plants in order to promote their understanding of production processes and products.

The finding that the job rotation which affects the promotion of workers occurs in the fifth year of service recalls the result in Table 7.4. Some workers answered that they could identify colleagues who were promising candidates for promotion when they looked at the jobs they had had in the first few years.

In summary, the job rotation in the first five years or so is crucial for the future promotion of all groups, whatever their educational backgrounds. This reflects the fact that in this company, the workers' careers are reviewed in the fifth year of employment. It seems that the company closely examines its workers in this special year and puts them on different job rotation paths.

7.5 CONCLUDING SUMMARY

In this chapter, we have analysed the pattern of selection and promotion in a Japanese electronics company. First, we examined the worker promotion process and found that in this company age is one of the main parameters in determining promotion. Promotion to section head starts about the tenth year of service, that is, at about 33 years old and promotion to middle manager with subordinates occurs at about 37 or 38 years old regardless of workers' educational qualifications. The promotion scheme which this company applies is similar to those adopted by other Japanese companies.

We next examined the period of selection and found that, in a very early stage of employment, 30 to 40 per cent of workers could identify those of their colleagues who were promising candidates for promotion. This is not consistent with the argument that Japanese companies try to treat all workers equally at least in the first 10 years of employment and to prevent them noticing that some are viewed differently from others.

We extended the analysis to how the workers are able to notice the differences in their competence. We especially focused on the fact that some workers pointed to the jobs which workers have been assigned as an indicator of competence and we examined the relationship between job rotation and promotion. The analysis found that some types of job rotation at an early stage of employment have significant effects on workers' future promotion and that the effects differ among workers with different educational qualifications.

NOTES

1. There were two female managers. One had a BA in education and had worked for the company for 23 years and the other had a BA in science and had worked for the company for 21 years.
2. Imano (1986, 1991), Nihon-seisansei-honbu, Seisansei-jyokyu-gijyutsusha-mondai-kenkyukai (1990) and Muramatsu (1986) analysed the skill formation of engineers within companies.
3. There was a worker who was promoted to section head in the 18th year of service and promoted to middle manager without subordinates in the 25th year of service. However, calculations based on his length of service and age show that he entered the company at 19, which conflicts with his statement that he graduated from university. Although it is possible that he obtained a degree at night school or by correspondence, his case was omitted from the sample set since the possibility of a false answer could not be ruled out.
4. The position of middle manager with subordinates appears distinctly different from that of middle manager without subordinates. The latter would seem to be allocated to senior workers who cannot be promoted to responsible positions and may be nothing but a title without actual responsibility. Further investigation is necessary to confirm this.
5. In this estimation, the variable of experience in other companies is not included in the set of explanatory variables since the number of workers who have such experience is in most

cases too small to subject to statistical analysis, and even where it is not, the effect of this variable is not statistically significant. In addition, the variable of age is omitted from many estimates since length of service is more likely to be significant and to have a stronger effect on promotion in such cases in spite of the correlation between the two variables.

6. Although we applied statistical analysis to various sets of variables and to different groups of workers, only representative cases are selected and shown in Tables 7.5 to 7.7.

REFERENCES

Hanada, M. (1987), 'Jinji-seido ni okeru Kyoso-genri no Jittai – Shoshin, Shokaku no Shisutemu kara mita Nihonkigyo no Jinji-senryaku' (How does the principle of competition work in personnel systems? – Strategies of personnel management in Japanese companies from the viewpoint of promotion and upgrading systems), *Soshiki-kagaku*, **21** (2) , 44–53.

Imada, S. and S. Hirata (1995), *Howaito-kara no Shoshin-kozo* (Promotion structure for white-collar workers), Tokyo: Nihon-Rodo-Kenkyu-Kikou.

Imano, K. (1986), 'Gijitsusha no Jinzai-Keisei' (Human resource development of engineers), in Kazuo Koike (ed.), *Gendai no Jinzai-keisei* (Human resource formulation of today), Tokyo: Toyokeizaishinposha, pp. 49–70.

Imano, K. (1991), 'Gijitsusha no Kyaria' (Careers of Engineers), in Kazuo Koike (ed.), *Daisotsu-howaito-kara no Jinzai-kaihatsu* (Human resource development of graduate white-collar workers, Tokyo: Toyokeizaishinposha, pp. 29–62.

Inoue, S. (1982), 'Naibu-Rodo-Shijo no Keizai-teki-Sokumen – Howaito-kara no Jirei' (Economic aspects of internal labour markets – a case study of white-collar workers), *Nihon-rodo-kyokai-zasshi*, **282**, 2–13.

Koike, K. (1991a), *Shigoto no Keizai-gaku* (The economics of work in Japan), Tokyo: Toyokeizaishinposha.

Koike, K. (ed.) (1991b), *Daisotsu-howaito-kara no Jinzai-kaihatsu* (Human resource development of graduate white-collar workers), Tokyo: Toyokeizaishinposha.

Koike, K. (1993), *Amerika no Howaito-kara* (White-collar workers in the United States), Tokyo: Toyokeizaishinposha.

Koike, K. and T. Inoki (1987), *Jinzai-keisei no Kokusaihikaku* (International comparison of human resource formation), Tokyo: Toyokeizaishinposha.

Medoff, J.L. and K.G. Abraham (1980), 'Experience, performance, and earnings', *Quarterly Journal of Economics*, **95** (4), December, 703–36.

Medoff, J.L. and K.G. Abraham (1981), 'Are those paid more really more productive? The case of experience', *Journal of Human Resources*, **16** (2), 186–216.

Muramatsu, K. (1986), 'Ei, Bei no Gijitsusha-shijo ha Kyoso-teki ka' (Are the markets for engineers really competitive in the UK and US?), in Kazuo Koike (ed.), *Gendai no Jinzai-keisei* (Human resource formation of today), Tokyo: Toyokeizaishinposha, pp. 71–93.

Nakamura, M. (1987), 'Howaito-kara no Kigyonai-kyaria – Sono Rontenn to Bunseki-wakugumi' (Careers of white-collar workers within companies – arguments and analytical framework), *Kobegakuin-keizaigaku-ronshu*, **19** (1), 109–39.

Nakamura, M. (1994), 'Howaito-kara no Ido – Kigyobetsudeta kara' (Job rotation of white-collar workers – data analyses of individual companies), in *Koyo-sokushinjigyo-dan, Sutokku-choukei-ka no Koyo to Rodoryokuhaibun* (Employment and labour force allocation in stock adjustment process), Osaka: Kansai-keizai-kenkyu-senta, pp. 75–95.

Nihon-rodo-kenkyu-kiko (1993), 'Daisotsu Howaito-kara no Ido to Shoshin-Howaito-kara no Kigyo-nai-Haichi-Shoshin ni kansuru Jittai-Chosa-Kekka-Hokoku' (Job rotation and promotion of university graduates – research report of internal job rotation and promotion of white-collar workers), *Chosahokokusho,* No. 37, Tokyo: Nihon-rodo-kenkyu-kiko).

Nihon-seisansei-honbu, Seisansei-jyokyu-gijyutsushamondai-kenkyukai (1990), *Eikoku no Gijyutsusha Nihon no Gijyutsusha – Gijyutsusha no Kyaria to Noryoku-kaihatsu* (Engineers in the UK and Japan – career and ability development of engineers), Tokyo: Shakai-seisansei-honbu.

Rosenbaum, J.E. (1984), *Career Mobility in a Corporate Hierarchy*, Orland: Academic Press.

Sano, Y. and J. Kawakita (eds) (1993), *Howaito-kara no Kyaria-kanri* (Career management of white-collar workers), Tokyo: Chuokeizaisha.

Tomita, Y. (1992), 'Shoshin no Shikumi' (Mechanism of promotion), in Takatoshi Tachibanaki (ed.), *Satei, Shoshin, Chingin-kettei* (Assessment, promotion and wage determination), Tokyo: Yuhikaku, pp. 49–65.

Wakabayashi, M. (1986), 'Daisotsu-shinnyu-shain no Kyaria O Saguru' (Investigation of careers of new university graduates), *Gekkann Rikuruto*, February and March, pp. 14–19.

8. Does the name of the university matter?

Isao Ohashi

8.1 INTRODUCTION

Economics provides two explanations for the economic functions of education in a society. One is that education endows people with more knowledge and skills, augmenting their human productive capacity. From this perspective, human capital theory, which has been developed since the early 1960s, formalizes the cost–benefit relation of human investment in education. The main motivations of this theory are to show how labour quality can be improved in order to accomplish a high rate of economic growth, and to analyse how people's earnings are determined. The other explanation is provided by the signalling theory of education, which emphasizes that in the absence of good information on labour quality, educational attainment is used to sort and allocate workers to different kinds of jobs, signalling information about their inherent productivity to employers.

It is important to note here that these explanations are not contradictory, although they do emphasize different aspects of education. That is, both can apply at the same time. For example, Spence (1974) presented a signalling model to explore the conditions under which education can function to signal information on labour quality, assuming that education can also raise labour productivity. In turn, according to the job competition hypothesis proposed by Thurow (1975), workers compete for good jobs in which they can have access to favourable training opportunities, while employers attempt to hire more capable workers in order to minimize the cost of on-the-job training. In particular, employers choose and hire applicants from the most to the least capable in the labour queue according to education, race, age and so on. Thus both human capital theory and signalling theory can be combined in one model. Therefore, if there is any conflict between them, it is the problem of which theory is more effective in explaining reality.

From the sociological perspective, education has been interpreted as a motive element for forming cliques in an organization. According to Takeuchi (1988), the acquisition of an academic career is governed by meritocracy, that is, determined on the basis of what a person can do, but once it has been acquired, it becomes attributive, representing what that person is. This social standing hallmarked by academic careers motivates people to form rank groups such as academic cliques in a society. The rank group means a collection of people who share a common culture such as language, clothes, manners, topics of conversation, opinions, value systems, sports and arts. They have a sense of unity through feeling a common bond with the same rank group.

As discussed above, we now have three main explanations for the functions of education in a society. Since they are not contradictory, our attention is drawn to the problem of which explanation is the most realistic among them. This chapter will analyse how education and academic career are relevant to the process of university graduates being promoted to higher positions such as president and chief executive in companies, using the data obtained from a questionnaire sent to executives in the listed companies of the Tokyo Stock Market. This is called the 'Toyokeizai Top Executive Survey'.

8.2 PREPARATION FOR THE ANALYSIS

We here define academic career in terms of the type of university from which one graduated. This is because most of the executives in the listed companies received a bachelor's or higher degree. More specifically, in our data, university graduates (including the holders of a master's degree or a doctorate) compromise 89.7 per cent of 2,246 respondents, junior college graduates 2.8 per cent, high-school graduates 7.2 per cent and junior high-school graduates 0.2 per cent. Thus we shall focus on how differences in the type of university from which one graduated affect promotion to executive status, rather than how differences in educational level do.

Against our expectation there are only a few empirical studies analysing how academic career affects getting a job and the subsequent promotion in companies, although the harmful influence of attaching great importance to academic career is often stressed by many people. Among them, Koike and Watanabe (1979) showed that when the number of graduates of each university is controlled, those from élite universities such as Tokyo and Waseda do not necessarily have an advantage in getting jobs in the companies of the first rank while the graduates of non-élite universities such as Nanzan have a higher probability of being promoted to department head after entrance. On the other hand, Higuchi (1994) obtained the opposite results. That is, he first calculated the ratio of the number of the managers who were in positions higher than director in the listed companies and the government offices in 1985 to the total number of graduates who left their universities between 1965 and 1969, and regressed it on the deviation value of each university which shows the difficulty of the entrance examination. His conclusion is that the graduates of the universities whose entrance examinations are hard to pass are more likely to be promoted to director or a higher position. He also analysed the effect of academic career on promotion in the big companies with 5,000 employees and more and the government offices, and came to the conclusion that academic career has positive effects both on the entrance probability and on the promotion probability in the organizations, and that the former effect is larger than the latter, judging from the values of the coefficients and the adjusted R-square. The main purpose of this chapter is to explore why a 'good' academic career gives graduates an advantage in promotion, accepting Higuchi's conclusion that in practice it is a favourable factor.

As a first step we categorize academic career into three types, that is, graduation from an élite university, from a non-élite university and from other establishments such as a foreign university, a high school or a junior high school. Based on the difficulty of the entrance examination, reputation and tradition, the élite universities are defined specifically as the seven Old Empire Universities (Tokyo, Kyoto, Thoku, Kyushu, Hokaido, Osaka and Nagoya), plus Hitotubashi University, Kobe University, Tokyo Engineering University, Waseda University and Keio University. We may question whether some of the private universities such as Chuo University should be included among the élite universities on the basis of their reputation and the difficulty of the entrance examination, but we excluded them because the number of the executive respondents who graduated from them are less than half of those from the private and élite universities such as Keio and Waseda.[1] Furthermore, even if they are included, our conclusions do not change substantially.

Table 8.1 shows the number and the percentage of respondents according to academic career. The percentage of élite university graduates, that is, 47.0 per cent, is higher than that of non-élite university graduates, that is, 43.2 per cent, by 3.8 per cent, but we cannot say that the former have a greater chance of becoming executives because we do not know the total number of graduates in each university category.[2]

What we can do using our data is to take a look at how the percentages of executives classified by position such as president and chief executive, by company size and by annual salary, differ depending on their academic career. By these we can know if there are any differences among

Table 8.1 Composition of respondents

	Elite	Non-élite	Other
Number	1,056	970	220
Percentage	47.0	43.2	9.8

Note: In Tables 8.1–9 élite = graduates of élite universities; non-élite = graduates of non-élite universities; other = other graduates.

Table 8.2 Cross-table by academic career and position (percentages)

Position	Elite	Non-élite	Other
Chairman	1.7	0.3	0.9
Vice-chairman	0.7	0.1	0.0
President	3.4	1.7	1.8
Vice-president	5.8	2.0	2.3
Chief executive	12.5	7.8	9.6
Managing executive	24.2	20.5	25.5
Executive	36.7	55.6	38.7
Auditor	14.9	11.9	21.4
Other	0.3	0.2	0.0
Total	100.0	100.0	100.0

the companies where they are executives at present. Tables 8.2–4 show the percentages of executives with different academic careers by position, company size and salary, respectively.

From Table 8.2 we know that élite university graduates command higher positions (such as chairman, president and chief executive) than the non-élite university graduates. For example, in the former, 48.3 per cent are managing executives or higher while in the latter 32.4 per cent are. However, this tendency is not noticeable in the executives of the younger generation because only a small number of them could be promoted to higher positions.

Table 8.3, which shows the percentages of executives with different academic careers by company size, tells us that élite graduates have the highest probability of becoming executives of large companies. More specifically, 33.3 per cent of them are executives of companies with more than 5,000 employees, while only 14.9 per cent of non-élite graduates and 5.9 per cent of other school graduates are. We find this phenomenon across all age groups.

Table 8.3 Cross-table by academic career and firm size (percentages)

Firm size	Elite	Non-élite	Other
more than 10,000	15.9	6.2	2.3
5,000–9,999	17.4	8.7	3.6
1,000–4,999	43.4	50.5	50.9
500–999	14.3	20.6	22.3
300–499	4.3	8.3	12.3
less than 300	4.7	5.8	8.6
Total	100.0	100.0	100.0

Note: Firm size is measured by the number of employees.

Table 8.4 Cross-table by academic career and salary (percentages)

Annual salary (yen)	Elite	Non-élite	Other
more than 70 million	0.2	0.1	0.0
50–69 million	1.1	0.3	0.0
30–49 million	9.2	3.8	3.7
20–29 million	35.2	19.2	16.0
15–19 million	35.2	38.8	30.6
10–14 million	17.2	34.1	43.8
less than 10 million	2.0	3.6	5.9
Total	100.0	100.0	100.0

Note: Annual salary includes taxes.

According to Table 8.4, élite graduates tend to be paid more than non-élite graduates. For example, 45.7 per cent of élite graduates are paid more than 20 million yen while only 23.4 per cent of the non-élite are. The élite graduates are also paid more than executives who graduated from other schools with the exception of the younger generation. But in the case of the younger generation the sample size is not large enough to draw any conclusions.

In order to test statistically the advantage that élite graduates have over other graduates, we conducted an ordered probit analysis by regressing the dummy variable of the élite graduates on the orders of position, company size and salary, respectively, and obtained the result that the positive effect of the dummy variable is statistically significant at the 5 per cent level of confidence in all the estimations, judging from the value of χ^2 with one degree of freedom.

Based on the above discussion, we hereafter assume that élite graduates have an advantage over other graduates in getting favourable and
stable jobs and promotion to higher positions which are well paid.

8.3   EVALUATION OF ELITE UNIVERSITY
GRADUATES

Now our problem is to analyse why élite university graduates are more
likely to be promoted to executive, focusing on two aspects of the problem. One is to ask how ability and attributes of élite graduates vary from
non-élite ones, and the other is why élite graduates are more likely to be
promoted in their companies even in the case where their ability to do the
job is the same as the others.

First, using the results of our questionnaire survey, we analyse how
élite graduates are evaluated by executives on their abilities and characteristics such as technical knowledge and emotional strength. To each of
nine questions concerning abilities or characteristics of élite graduates,
the respondents revealed their opinions by answering one of five options:
'I definitely agree', 'If anything, I agree', 'I cannot give a definite answer',
'If anything, I disagree' and 'I definitely disagree'.

In order to see which abilities or characteristics are evaluated highly,
we gave a score to each answer and calculated the average in both cases.
That is, in case A the given scores are 2 for 'I definitely agree' 1 for 'If
anything, I agree', 0 for 'I cannot give a definite answer', –1 for 'If anything, I disagree', and –2 for ' I definitely disagree', and in case B the
given scores are 1.5, 1.5, 0, –1.5 and –1.5 for each answer, respectively.

The results are shown in Table 8.5, where the average scores for abilities and characteristics are ordered from top to bottom. First of all it
should be noted that the order is the same in both cases. According to
this table, the item 'élite graduates know a wide range of helpful people'
(networking in the table) achieves the highest average score (0.839),
implying that most respondents are in agreement, and the item which
scored second highest is 'élite graduates have higher intelligence' (higher
intelligence). The distribution of the respondents for the second item is
5.9 per cent for 'I definitely agree', 54.8 per cent for 'If anything, I agree',
32.9 per cent for 'I cannot give a definite answer and 6 per cent for the
negative answers. The third item is 'élite graduates do everything with
confidence' (strong confidence), which has its basis in their feelings of
superiority because they passed a difficult examination.

The fourth item is 'élite graduates have much technical knowledge'
(technical knowledge). This item inquires how they can accumulate

Table 8.5 Evaluation of élite university graduates (average score)

Ability item	Total	Case A			Case B	
		Elite	Non-élite	Other	Total	Order
Networking	0.839	0.915	0.755	0.845	1.044	1
Higher intelligence	0.579	0.690	0.473	0.518	0.823	2
Strong confidence	0.345	0.476	0.249	0.136	0.509	3
Technical knowledge	0.167	0.261	0.065	0.164	0.316	4
Good presentation	0.160	0.181	0.116	0.259	0.263	5
Work hard	0.046	0.169	−0.045	−0.141	0.122	6
Manage organization	−0.002	0.064	−0.059	−0.073	0.048	7
Mental strength	−0.115	−0.005	−0.211	−0.218	−0.095	8
Sociability	−0.203	−0.098	−0.311	−0.232	−0.227	9

human capital in élite universities. The table shows that the average score is positive, but much lower than that of the previous item. More specifically, the distribution of its respondents is such that only 2 per cent say 'I definitely agree', 31.7 per cent say 'If anything, I agree' and more than 50 per cent say 'I cannot give a definite answer'. A similar tendency applies with the item 'élite graduates present themselves well' (good presentation).

The average score of the item of 'élite graduates work hard' (work hard) is positive although very small, that is 0.046. Interestingly, as shown in Table 8.5, the respondents who graduated from non-élite universities or other schools are rather negative to this item. Similarly, the average score of the item 'élite graduates have excellent skills to manage an organization' (manage organization) is positive in case B, but negative in case A. This implies that most respondents cannot give a definite answer to this item, and 72.4 per cent of all respondents did not.

The average scores for 'élite graduates have mental strength' (mental strength) and 'élite graduates are sociable and cooperative' (sociability), are negative, and are lower for non-élite graduates than for élite ones. Thus executives give lower evaluation to élite graduates regarding their mental strength, sociability and spirit of cooperation compared to non-élite graduates. But these evaluations are not decisive because more than 65 per cent of the respondents say 'I cannot give a definite answer' to both questions.

To sum up, élite graduates are assessed relatively highly in information gathering, intelligence, aggressiveness and technical knowledge, but not in mental strength and sociability. However, it should be stressed here that the accumulation of human capital, which is assumed to be a major purpose of education, does not have an important effect on the assessment of élite graduates in organizations. Rather, graduates are assessed largely according to acquisitions incidental to schooling, that is, good networking and confidence, or innate abilities such as high intelligence.[3]

Next, in order to know which attributes and qualifications affect evaluations of the ability of élite graduates, we conducted an ordered probit analysis, using the following dummy variables.

ELITE = 1 if the respondent graduated from an élite university.
= 0 otherwise.

NONEL = 1 if the respondent graduated from a non-élite university.
= 0 otherwise.

POST = 1 if the respondent is in a position equal to or higher than chief executive.
= 0 otherwise.

SIZE = 1 if the respondent works at a company with 5,000 employees or more.
= 0 otherwise.

INDUS = 1 if the company at which the respondent works belongs to a service industry such as transportation, wholesale, retail, finance and insurance.
= 0 otherwise.

ACHIEV = 1 if the respondent answered positively to the question 'Have you done well in your specialized field to get your current position?'.
= 0 otherwise.

COMPET = 1 if the respondent answered positively to the question 'Have you worked hard not to be behind your rivals until now?'.
= 0 otherwise.

SCIENCE = 1 if the respondent graduated from a science course such as engineering, agriculture and medicine.
= 0 otherwise.

The results are shown in Table 8.6 and indicate some interesting facts. First, élite graduates tend to evaluate themselves more highly than do the non-élite. That is, the effect of *ELITE* is positive and statistically significant in six estimation equations out of nine, and that of *NONEL* is negative in six equations although it is statistically significant in only two equations. It should be stressed here that the negative sign does not imply that non-élite graduates evaluate the ability of élite graduates 'negatively', but that they evaluate them less highly than other school graduates do. For example, take the item 'élite graduates know a wide range of helpful people', many of the élite graduates answered 'I definitely agree', while many of the non-élite answered 'If anything, I agree to it', or 'I cannot give a definite answer'. If the non-élite graduates evaluate the élite negatively, then the average score for this item should be negative, but actually it is positive at 0.755, as shown in Table 8.5.

Second, older executives evaluate élite graduates higher in human relationships, intellectual faculties, confidence, technical knowledge and presentation. This may be because older executives have based their evaluations on opinions which were formed when the number of élite graduates was small and they were given preferential treatment in the assignment of jobs and promotion.

Third, as shown in Table 8.5, it is interesting that the negative effect of *INDUS* on technical knowledge is statistically significant at the 1 per cent level of confidence in finance, insurance, transportation and the service industries. Why are élite graduates rated lower in these industries? We may conjecture that the technical knowledge which they have learned in the universities has no close and direct relevance to the jobs in these industries.

Fourth, since the effect of *COMPET* is positive and statistically significant at the 1 per cent level of confidence in seven equations, we can say that graduates who have a strong sense of rivalry assess élite graduates higher on all factors. One of the main reasons is that executives who have worked hard not to fall behind rivals have paid special attention to élite graduates as their main rivals, since élite graduates are likely to be promoted faster.

Finally, it is interesting to note that both 'élite graduates know a wide range of helpful people', which obtained the highest score, and 'élite graduates are sociable and cooperative', which obtained the lowest score, are significantly affected by only one dummy. This implies that these items are generally agreed to be true regardless of age, industry, firm size, position, a sense of rivalry and academic speciality.

Table 8.6 Ordered probit analysis on the evaluation of élite graduates

Ability	ELITE	NONEL	AGE	POST	SIZE	INDUS	ACHIEV	COMPET	SCIENCE	Log L	χ^2
Networking	0.068	-0.139*	0.010*	0.021	0.007	0.009	-0.028	0.085	0.043	-2339.0	101.2
	(0.08)	(1.65)	(1.91)	(0.32)	(0.12)	(0.16)	(-0.47)	(0.05)	(0.82)		
Higher intelligence	0.179**	-0.091	0.011**	0.070	0.084	-0.040	0.042	0.219***	0.044	-2332.9	146.2
	(2.09)	(1.07)	(2.18)	(1.07)	(1.41)	(0.72)	(0.70)	(4.37)	(0.82)		
Strong confidence	0.538***	0.196**	0.027***	-0.148**	-0.001	-0.047	0.013	0.225***	-0.015	-2204.9	213.2
	(5.86)	(2.16)	(4.95)	(2.12)	(0.01)	(0.79)	(0.21)	(4.24)	(0.27)		
Technical knowledge	0.078	-0.126	0.023***	0.179***	-0.039	-0.155***	0.087	0.133***	0.058	-2441.2	174.2
	(0.90)	(1.47)	(4.47)	(2.70)	(0.65)	(2.74)	(1.46)	(2.65)	(1.08)		
Good presentation	-0.145	-0.224**	0.016***	-0.026	-0.029	0.070	-0.025	0.176***	0.004	-2022.8	97.8
	(1.62)	(2.53)	(2.91)	(0.37)	(0.46)	(1.19)	(-0.40)	(3.37)	(0.06)		
Work hard	0.423***	0.140*	0.003	0.085	0.064	-0.005	-0.112*	0.138***	0.017	-2362.2	148.2
	(4.96)	(1.67)	(0.57)	(1.30)	(1.09)	(-0.09)	(-1.91)	(2.82)	(0.33)		
Manage organization	0.228**	-0.009	0.005	0.017	-0.020	0.028	-0.026	0.180***	-0.027	-1942.2	86.4
	(2.45)	(-0.10)	(0.93)	(0.24)	(-0.31)	(0.47)	(-0.41)	(3.40)	(-0.48)		
Mental strength	0.329***	0.006	0.007	-0.099	0.048	-0.046	-0.077	0.158***	-0.035	-2152.4	130.4
	(3.68)	(0.07)	(1.33)	(-1.46)	(0.77)	(-0.79)	(-1.25)	(3.05)	(-0.64)		
Sociability	0.204**	-0.136	0.001	-0.026	0.001	-0.039	0.056	0.080	-0.064	-2197.0	118.6
	(2.36)	(-1.59)	(0.20)	(-0.40)	(0.02)	(-0.68)	(0.93)	(1.58)	(-0.19)		

Notes: The values in parentheses are asymptotic *t*-values. *** means significant at the 1 per cent level of confidence, ** at the 5 per cent level, and * at the 10 per cent level, respectively. The value of χ^2 is given by $-2(\log L - \log L_0)$ and in distribution to a chi-squared variate with 9 degrees of freedom. $-2 \log L_0$ is the restricted ML estimate which was obtained by assuming that the coefficients of all dependent variables except the intercept are equal to zero.

8.4 WHY ARE THE ELITE UNIVERSITY GRADUATES AT AN ADVANTAGE IN THE ORGANIZATION?

In the questionnaire we asked the reasons why élite graduates are more likely to be promoted in the organization even when their ability to do the job is comparable to the non-élite. More specifically, our aim is to analyse whether there are any organizational factors which give the élite graduates an advantage in promotion, assuming that their individual ability, personality and mental strength are the same as other graduates. The respondents answered each question by choosing one of the same responses which were listed in the previous section. We also assigned the same score to each response in both case A and case B.

Table 8.7 shows the average score on each factor of ability or personality according to academic career. The factors are in the same order for case A and case B, and the factor which has the highest average score (0.786), is 'since élite graduates have many friends who play an active part in government offices and other companies, this is an advantage in getting good jobs' (many active friends). Thus we again recognize that a by-product of education works crucially to promote élite graduates to higher positions. This also applies to the factor 'there are many superiors who graduated from the same university' (senior superiors), which has the third highest score. In turn, the average score of the factor 'there are many colleagues who graduated from the same university in the same year' (many colleagues), is nearly zero, and negative for élite graduates. This is because colleagues can be rivals rather than supporters.

The factor which has the second highest score is 'élite graduates are likely to be allocated to favourable places of work' (favourable transfer). Why do élite graduates receive preferential treatment even if they have the same abilities and personality as the other graduates? This problem seems to be closely related with other factors such as 'there are many superiors who graduated from the same university' (0.431), 'many friends who play an active part in government offices and other companies' (0786) and 'élite graduates perform jobs with confidence' (with confidence) (0.432). These factors can ensure that élite graduates are received favourably or encouraged into many sections.

It should also be noted that the factor 'élite graduates do their best to comply with the expectation held by those around them' (compliance) obtained a positive and high score (0.388). This expectation is likely to put mental pressure on élite graduates and at the same time makes them seek favourable treatment from the company. That is, if they are not treated as they expect, then they will be discouraged and become less

Table 8.7 Why do élite university graduates have an advantage? (average score)

Advantage factor	Case A				Case B	
	Total	Elite	Non-élite	Other	Total	Order
Many active friends	0.786	0.796	0.770	0.814	1.015	1
Favourable transfer	0.596	0.564	0.603	0.723	0.839	2
Senior superiors	0.431	0.480	0.419	0.250	0.618	3
With confidence	0.423	0.550	0.316	0.286	0.606	4
Compliance	0.388	0.492	0.298	0.282	0.569	5
Appealing presence	0.238	0.213	0.257	0.277	0.369	6
Many colleagues	0.028	0.079	–0.015	–0.032	0.101	7
Little resistance	–0.168	–0.207	–0.134	–0.136	–0.138	8

loyal to the company. Therefore, it is quite possible that the company will treat élite graduates more favourably than non-élite, even if it causes some dissatisfaction within the company.

Another reason why élite graduates are likely to be allocated to favourable places of work is that since companies do not have enough information about the ability of employees in the early stages of employment, they use their knowledge of the academic career to make an informed guess. For example, companies may hold the opinion that élite graduates have a higher ability and that the range of variation in their ability is smaller. Thus, academic career functions as a signal of ability and élite graduates can receive favourable treatment in the early stages of employment even if their ability is actually the same as that of the non-élite.

It is interesting to note in Table 8.7 that the factor 'there is only little resistance to the favourable treatment of élite graduates within the company' (little resistance) has a negative average score (–0.168). From this result companies must be careful not to show differences in treatment among the graduates, but in reality they are likely to allocate better jobs to élite graduates. This gap between principle and practice shows that the three positive effects of favourable treatment which were discussed above are greater than the negative effect of dissatisfaction felt by the non-élite graduates.

It should be stressed here that a favourable allocation of jobs has a positive effect on skill formation and hence on the fast promotion of élite graduates, since it gives them a good opportunity to develop and demonstrate their ability. Ushiogi (1978) insisted that in modern organizations it does not matter so much who has the right ability for that position, but rather what post is assigned to each individual. This is because individual ability and achievement depend crucially on the position where one works. In other words, a person is formed by the position he or she is in.

8.5   REQUIREMENTS FOR EXECUTIVES

In previous sections we analysed how élite graduates differ in their ability and characteristics from other school graduates and what mechanisms make them more likely to be promoted in companies even when their ability and characteristics are comparable. In this section we attempt to test if the results obtained in the previous sections actually hold, using the data obtained from the question concerning reasons for the appointment to executive status in the present company.

For each of the reasons we calculate the average score according to academic career, based on the allotment of scores as indicated by case A. The results are shown in Table 8.8. From this table we know that the reason which obtained the biggest average score overall is 'I was trusted and supported by my workers' (trusted by workers), and the second is 'I had experienced a wide range of jobs and could look at the company from the whole perspective' (wide range of jobs). If we look only at the average scores of the élite graduates, then the order of importance is reversed. We should note here that the experience of a wide range of jobs is one of the

Table 8.8 Reasons for appointment to executive status (average score)

Reason	Total	Elite	*t*-test
Trusted by workers	0.89	0.89	No
Wide range of jobs	0.88	0.92	Yes (+)**
Company wanted me	0.86	0.90	Yes (+)**
Achieved results	0.80	0.80	No
Simply lucky	0.79	0.67	Yes(–)**
Good superiors	0.73	0.74	No
Persistent effort	0.55	0.44	Yes(–)**
Expectations justified	0.10	0.15	Yes(+)*
No other suitable person	–0.07	–0.13	Yes(–)**

Notes: The ordered probit analysis was conducted to test if there exists any significant difference between the response of élite graduates and those of other graduates, using the dummy variable, *ELITE*. When *ELITE* is significant at the 5 per cent level of confidence positively, it is indicated as Yes(+)**, and when at the 10 per cent level negatively, it is indicated as Yes(–)*.

most important requirements for executives and remember that many executives are positive to the factor that 'élite graduates are likely to be allocated to favourable places of work'. If this factor includes the experience of a wide range of jobs as one of its implications, then élite graduates are at an advantage in the matter of promotion. But this does not lead us to conclude that there are fast tracks in Japanese companies. The average score for 'I had justified early expectations' (expectations justified) is almost zero. This is consistent with the traditional view that in the early stages of employment, equal treatment of workers who graduated in the same year is a characteristic of the Japanese employment system.

It is natural that both 'the company wanted a talented person such as me' (company wanted me), and 'I achieved good results in my specialized field' (achieved results), are supported by many executives and get high scores. But note that the former reason may include promotions associated with transfers from parent companies.

There are also many executives who are positive to 'I was simply lucky' (simply lucky). Interestingly, according to the *t*-test, there is a significant difference here between élite and non-élite graduates. That is, since non-élite graduates feel that they are less likely to be promoted, they therefore feel very strongly that any promotion they do get will be based more on luck. We can also find a similar result concerning the reason 'I had made steady and persistent effort without any serious failure' (persistent effort). That is, non-élite graduates support this reason more strongly than élite graduates. Thus non-élite executives tend to consider somewhat modestly that they were fortunate to be appointed to the present position as a consequence of steady and persistent effort.

As discussed above, managers are required to experience a wide range of jobs in order to be appointed to executive posts. We can ascertain that this is actually true by using the data relating to experiences of transfer among different functions. That is, we asked how many functions the executives had experienced in each position.[4] The average number of different functional experiences that the respondents had in each position are 1.51 (rank-and-file staff), 1.53 (section heads), 1.86 (department heads) and 2.19 (directors). The number of different functional experiences increases as the person's position in the firm becomes more senior.

In conducting an ordered probit analysis we defined the dependent variables as the six ordered variables based on the number of experiences which each respondent had, and the independent variables as the dummy variables concerning academic career, present position, firm size and industry, which were explained in the previous section. If the number experienced is more than six, then we regarded it as six. This is because there are only a small number of respondents who had experienced more than six functions in a position and because the continuity of the variable would be lost.[5]

The results are shown in Table 8.9, where we find some interesting facts. First, the positive effect of the dummy variable of élite graduates is statistically significant at the ordinary level of confidence in all the estimations, excluding that of department head in which the level of confidence is 10 per cent. This supports the notion that the élite are more likely to be promoted because they are more likely to experience a wide range of jobs than the non-élite as a whole.

Second, it is interesting that the effect of *SCIENCE* is positive and statistically significant in positions higher than section head, while it is negative among the rank and file although not significant. From these results we know that in the process of promotion to upper manager, the graduates who majored in science and technology at university experience a wider range of jobs than those who majored in humanities and social science, because they were transferred fewer times while they were still among the rank and file. Note that the coefficient and the asymptotic *t*-value of *SCIENCE* increase as the position becomes higher.

Third, the current executive position defined by *POST* has a positive and significant effect on the experience of intra-transfers. That is, upper executives, such as chief executive and president, experience more intra-transfers than lower ones, particularly at the level of section head and director. Thus we can ascertain that the experience of a wide range of jobs and the ability to see the company from a broad perspective are important requirements for executives.

Table 8.9 Analysis of functional experiences

Position	*SCIENCE*	*ELITE*	*POST*	*SCALE*	*INDUS*	Log L	χ^2
Rank and file	−0.084	0.138**	0.022	−0.012	−0.139**	−2027.3	13.2
	(1.44)	(2.52)	(0.32)	(0.19)	(2.24)		
Section head	0.103*	0.172***	0.179***	−0.100	−0.026	−2063.8	25.5
	(1.77)	(3.14)	(2.62)	(1.55)	(0.42)		
Department head	0.122**	0.091*	0.022	−0.092	−0.071	−2660.3	15.5
	(2.25)	(1.77)	(0.33)	(1.55)	(1.23)		
Director	0.188***	0.175***	0.176***	−0.031	−0.091	−3025.9	49.9
	(3.58)	(3.54)	(2.81)	(0.53)	(1.63)		

Note: See notes in Table 8.6. But note here that the value χ^2 is in distribution to a chi-squared variate with 9 degrees of freedom.

Fourth, the effect of the industry dummy on intra-transfers is negative although it is statistically significant at the 5 per cent level of confidence only at the level of rank-and-file staff. It is possible that the organizational structure of a company in the service industry is different from those in the manufacturing and primary industries. More specifically, in the companies of transportation, finance, business and retail, the sales department shares a large weight relative to other departments and hence most staff are likely to be transferred within that department. In addition, since our questionnaire was designed mainly for the manufacturing industry, there may be some departments which are important in the service industry, but which are not defined here, for example, the inspection department.

Finally, it should be noted that élite graduates experience different functions more than the non-élite even at the level of rank-and-file staff. As discussed above, this does not imply that there is an early selection of stars in Japanese companies, but that although crucial and clear selection comes later, for example, 10 to 15 years after entering the company, employees are given important signals on promotion prospects through differentiating transfers and the number of different jobs held even during the early stages of employment. This is an elaborate scheme to motivate employees through a system of equal treatment.[6]

8.6 HOW DO EXECUTIVES RELATE TO THEIR JUNIORS IN THE COMPANY?

According to Table 8.7, élite graduates are more likely to be promoted for the reason that they have many superiors who graduated from the same university. This favourable factor is ranked third in the approval measured by the average score. In order to analyse why this factor is important in the company, we asked 'How do you feel when you hear that there is an excellent junior in your company?' and suggested four answers: 'I feel delighted', 'I shall pay attention to him/her', 'I hope to move him/her near me' and 'I feel inclined to support him/her in various ways'. To each of these answers the respondents expressed their feelings by choosing one of the following: 'Yes, I do (shall)', 'No, I do not (shall not)', and 'I cannot give a definite answer'. The percentage of respondents who expressed their feelings positively, that is, chose 'Yes, I do' are shown in Table 8.10, according to university.

It is natural as a human being to answer 'I feel delighted', or 'I shall pay attention to him/her'. The percentage for the former is high, at 80.4 per cent on average, and so is that for the latter, at 72.4 per cent. By contrast, the average percentage of respondents who answer 'I hope to move him/her near me' is low at 8.8 per cent as can be expected, but it is surprising that almost half of the respondents, that is, 48.1 per cent, feel

Table 8.10 How executives relate to their juniors (percentage ranking)

University	Number	I feel delighted		I shall pay attention to him/her		I hope to move him/her near me		I support him/her in various ways	
Hokaido U.	30	86.67	(4)	86.67	(1)	0.00	(18)	56.67	(2)
Tohoku U.	53	79.25	(11)	64.15	(17)	11.32	(4)	32.08	(18)
Tokyo U.	184	70.65	(18)	67.93	(12)	8.70	(10)	37.50	(16)
Nagoya U.	40	85.00	(6)	82.50	(3)	7.50	(12)	40.00	(15)
Osaka U.	50	76.00	(12)	80.00	(6)	6.00	(16)	48.00	(11)
Kyoto U.	177	85.88	(5)	80.90	(5)	10.11	(7)	59.32	(1)
Kyushu U.	57	91.23	(1)	77.19	(8)	8.77	(9)	50.88	(5)
Hitotubashi	67	86.57	(3)	82.09	(4)	5.97	(17)	50.75	(7)
Kobe U.	67	88.06	(2)	83.58	(2)	8.96	(8)	53.75	(4)
Other N & M	400	81.25	(10)	73.25	(9)	7.50	(12)	49.50	(10)
Waseda U.	164	82.32	(7)	67.68	(14)	6.71	(14)	42.68	(14)
Keio U.	138	81.88	(8)	69.57	(11)	10.14	(6)	44.93	(13)
Meiji U.	53	75.47	(13)	60.38	(18)	15.09	(2)	47.17	(12)
Chuo U.	72	75.00	(14)	70.83	(10)	15.28	(1)	50.00	(9)
Nihon U.	65	72.31	(15)	67.69	(13)	12.31	(3)	50.77	(6)
Doshisha U.	65	72.31	(15)	78.46	(7)	10.77	(5)	53.85	(3)
Kanseigakuin	32	71.88	(17)	65.63	(16)	6.25	(15)	34.38	(17)
Other P	276	81.52	(9)	67.03	(15)	8.70	(10)	50.54	(8)
Average (%)		80.40		72.38		8.84		48.07	

Note: 'Other N & M' means the other national and municipal universities, and 'Other P' stands for the other private universities. 'Number' is the number of executive respondents.

'inclined to support him/her in various ways'. Therefore, élite graduates may be more likely to be promoted if they have many superiors who graduated from the same university.

There are large differences among the listed universities in the percentage of respondents who have positive feelings of support for their juniors. These differences seem to be closely related to culture in the area around the university, the number of the graduates, history and some social background. Analysing these differences would be an interesting task, but beyond the scope of economics.

8.7 CONCLUSIONS

Based on data concerning the percentage of graduates from different universities who are promoted to section head, Koike and Watanabe (1979) maintain that graduates from élite universities such as Tokyo and Kyoto, are as likely to be promoted as graduates from non-élite universities such as Nanzan and Yokohama National University. Their main aims are to show that people can be allocated better places of work even if they are not graduates of famous universities and to warn against giving preference to graduates of universities which have been ranked highly. We can understand their desire to be rational, but unfortunately, as shown in Higuchi (1994) and in this chapter, élite graduates are more likely to be promoted to positions, such as directors and executives which are higher than section heads and to obtain jobs which are more stable and command higher salaries. Therefore, we have to analyse the functions of education under the assumption that the name of the university does matter in our society.

According to our analysis the basic reasons why élite graduates are more likely to be promoted to executive status are the following. First, élite graduates have a wider network of contacts with other companies and government offices and higher innate ability than the non-élite, and place less importance on human capital and technical knowledge. Second, because of these characteristics élite graduates are likely to be appointed to good jobs which allow them to view the company from a wide perspective. Third, there are many seniors in the firm who are themselves graduates of élite universities, and who are happy to promote the interests of the younger generation.

NOTES

1. See Table 8.10 in which the numbers of respondents by university are reported.
2. Higuchi (1994) surveyed the number of the graduates by directly questioning each university although the number of the universities from which the data was obtained is very limited, that is, 23.

3. The average scores by academic career are also reported in Table 8.5. Interestingly, the results show that élite university graduates generally assess themselves highly compared with the non-élite and other school graduates. With the latter we shall test to see if this difference is statistically significant.
4. The functions are defined as ① Accounting/Finance, ② Personnel/Labour, ③ General Affairs/Public Relations, ④ Management Planning, ⑤ Information Processing, ⑥ Sales, ⑦ Purchasing, ⑧ Distribution, ⑨ Manufacturing, ⑩ Technology, ⑪ R&D, ⑫ International/Trade, ⑬ Outside Transfer, ⑭ Overseas Work and ⑮ Others.
5. For example, concerning the position of rank-and-file workers, 1,361 responded 'I have been transferred once'; 511: 'twice'; 168: 'three times'; 50: 'four times'; 13: 'five times'; 3: 'six times'; 2: 'seven times'; and 1: 'ten times', respectively.
6. See Ohashi and Teruyama (1998) on this issue.

REFERENCES

Higuchi, Yoshio (1994), 'Education in Universities and Income distribution', in Tuneo Ishikawa (ed.), *Japanese Incomes and the Distribution of Wealth*, Tokyo: Tokyo University Press, pp. 245–78.

Koike, Kazuo and Yukiro Watanabe (1979), *The Falseness of Diplomaism*, Tokyo: Toyokeizai Shinposha.

Ohashi, Isao and Hiroshi Teruyama (1998), 'Intra-firm Mobility, Wages and Promotions in the Japanese Employment System', in I. Ohashi and T. Tachibanaki (eds), *Internal Labour Market, Incentives and Employment*, London: Macmillan.

Spence, A.M. (1974), *Market Signaling: Informational Transfer in Hiring and Related Screening Process*, Cambridge, MA: Harvard University Press.

Takeuchi, Hiroshi (1988), *Screening Society*, Tokyo: Recruit Press.

Thurow, Lester C. (1975), *Generating Inequality*, New York: Basic Books.

Ushiogi, Morikazu (1978), *Changes in Diplomaism*, Tokyo: Tokyo University Press.

9. Careers and work attitudes of engineers

Yasunobu Tomita

9.1 INTRODUCTION

One of the factors which contributes to the high productivity of Japanese manufacturing industries is the development of efficient production technology. In large firms, employees who are engaged in the development of production technology as engineers are graduates who studied science and technology at university. I shall investigate how they have acquired high skills which enable them to develop efficient production technology. According to research findings on skill formation practices of blue-collar workers, whose high skills are another factor which contributes to the high productivity of Japanese manufacturing industries, they acquire the skill required for their job by experiencing a wide range of jobs which are related to each other in the workplace. I shall investigate whether the above findings on skill formation practices of blue-collar workers are also applicable to engineers.

Recently in Japan, it has often been said that young people are not so attracted to manufacturing industries, that they are now less interested in studying science and technology at university than before, and even graduates in those majors do not necessarily seek jobs in manufacturing industries. Some are very worried that if this tendency were to last for a long time, it would gradually erode the high productivity of Japanese manufacturing industries. Various proposals have been put forward for more young people to be attracted to manufacturing industries. However, they have often been made without investigating the work attitudes of employees in manufacturing industries. Here I shall analyse the work attitudes of employees who graduated in science and technology and now work in manufacturing industries, and I shall investigate why they are dissatisfied with their work. From this investigation, I shall derive the implications for manufacturing industries if these industries are to become more attractive to the graduates.

In Section 9.2, I shall explain the data which I use here. Then in Section 9.3, I shall investigate how wide a range of jobs graduates in science and technology, in particular engineers, have experienced in the workplace. In Section 9.4, I shall investigate whether there are incentives in promotion and salary systems for them to experience a wide range of jobs by transfer in the workplace. In Section 9.5, I shall investigate their work attitudes, in comparison with graduates in humanities and social science. In the last section, I shall summarize my findings.

9.2 THE DATA

I shall analyse 349 male graduates in science and technology at university, from the survey on white-collar employees conducted by the RIALS in 1993. I shall describe briefly the basic characteristics of my sample. Each of the graduates works for one of four very large manufacturing companies, which are electronics, automotive, chemical and electric power companies. As to their length of service, 28 per cent have worked for five years or less, 36 per cent have worked for 6–10 years, 25 per cent have worked for 11–15 years, and 11 per cent have worked for 15 years or more. As to functions which they are engaged in, 40 per cent are engaged in technology, and 28 per cent are engaged in research. Therefore 68 per cent of the graduates in science and technology work as engineers.

9.3 CAREERS OF ENGINEERS

9.3.1 Previous Research Findings

Koike and Inoki (1990) have developed the theory of skill formation practices of blue-collar workers, and Koike (1990) has also been doing research on the careers of white-collar workers. According to him, white-collar workers have experienced a wide range of jobs, but many have been transferred within each function. Therefore, they are trained on the various jobs to acquire the knowledge required for each function as blue-collar workers. That white-collar workers who graduated from universities are trained as generalists without any function-specific knowledge is a misleading concept. Moreover, he demonstrates that there are a few differences in the careers of white-collar workers between Japan and other industrialized countries. Japanese white-collar workers have experienced a wider range of jobs within each function than their counterparts in other industrialized countries. Moreover, it takes much longer

(15–20 years) for Japanese white-collar workers to be promoted to a management position (section manager) than their counterparts in other industrialized countries. Therefore, Japanese white-collar workers have acquired the full knowledge of their functions with long experience of a wide range of jobs before they are promoted to a management position.

Before I describe my own research, I shall survey a few previous research findings on careers of engineers in Japan. Lam (1996) compared the work content of engineers in Japan and the UK. According to her findings on Japanese engineers, most engineers have experienced working in production in the early stage of their career. Moreover, they often exchange information on their projects with other engineers and employees in charge of production and marketing, and coordinate their projects with them. This means that they are involved in a managerial role, although they are not yet promoted to a management position. In contrast, jobs of English engineers are very compartmentalized, and they seldom exchange information on their projects with others. Project managers and higher management exclusively collect information on the projects and coordinate them. In addition, because the jobs of English engineers are very compartmentalized and narrowly specialized, they feel that their potential abilities are not fully utilized in their present job. This is one of the reasons why English engineers feel that their jobs are unattractive, and they want to be promoted to a management position as early as possible. Ito (1993) referred to a paper which compared the careers of engineers in Japan and France. According to this paper (LEST and Japan Institute of Labour 1992), French engineers are promoted to management positions faster than their counterparts in Japan, and thereafter they are involved exclusively in a managerial role, so they will not have fully experienced a wide range of projects as engineers. Imano (1990) investigated careers of engineers in detail, with data of the careers of 120 engineers in 13 firms. According to him, about 20 per cent of engineers have experienced working in functions other than technology and research. Engineers have been transferred not only to production, technology and research, but also to sales and marketing, and management planning, which are not usually included in the career paths of engineers. Moreover, engineers who have experienced transfer between functions in the early stage of their career tend to be promoted to section manager faster than other engineers.

9.3.2   Wide Range of Job Experience

One of the factors which contributes to the high productivity of Japanese manufacturing industries, is the high skills which blue-collar workers have acquired through on-the-job training. Moreover, we should emphasize the importance of the development of efficient production technology as another factor. In large firms, employees who are engaged in the development of production technology are graduates who have studied science and technology at university. I shall investigate how they have acquired these high skills, which enable them to develop efficient production technology. According to research findings on skill formation practices of blue-collar workers, they have acquired skills required for their job, through experiencing a wide range of jobs which are related to each other in the workplace. If we can apply the findings on the skill formation of blue-collar workers to careers of engineers, we would say that engineers also experience a wide range of jobs within each of the technology and research functions, and some are transferred between research, technology and production functions. Work experience in production may be very important for engineers to develop efficient production technology.

From the data which I use here, I do not know how often employees have changed their jobs within a section, but I do know whether they have experienced transfers between sections within their functions, and transfers between functions. Therefore, looking at these transfers, I can investigate how wide a range of jobs engineers have experienced (Figure 9.1).

First, I analyse the careers of 138 engineers who now work in technology. Eighteen per cent (25 employees) have experienced working in functions other than technology. Most of them (11 employees) worked in production, and eight worked in research. Both functions are closely related to technology. Thirty-five per cent have experienced transfers

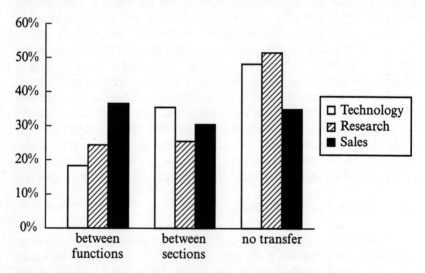

Figure 9.1 Types of transfer experienced, by major functions

between sections, although they have never worked outside technology. The rest (47 per cent) have been working in the same section of technology since they joined their company. Second, I analyse the careers of 99 engineers who now work in research. Twenty-four per cent (24 people) have experienced working in functions other than research. Most of them (11 employees) have worked in technology, but only three persons have worked in production. Twenty-five per cent have experienced transfers between sections, although they have never worked outside research. The rest (51 per cent) have been working in the same section of research since they joined their company. According to the above results, 20 per cent of engineers in technology and research have experienced transfers between functions. Engineers in technology tend to have experienced working in production and research, and engineers in research tend to have experienced working in technology. It means that not so many engineers have been transferred between functions, but transferred engineers have experienced working in other functions which were closely related to their present function.

Of course, I shall establish how wide a range of jobs engineers have experienced only after I have compared their careers with careers of employees in other functions. Here I take as a reference group employees who graduated in humanities and social science and now work in sales and marketing. The data for those employees are also available from the same questionnaire survey which was used for engineers. I shall analyse the careers of 191 of those employees.

Thirty-nine per cent have experienced working in functions other than sales and marketing, and 30 per cent have experienced transfers between sections, although they have never worked outside sales and marketing. The rest (34 per cent) have been working in the same section of the sales and marketing function since they joined their company. It is often alleged that graduates in humanities and social science are trained as generalists, and experience working in many functions by transfer. However, according to the results of employees in sales and marketing, about a third of them have never experienced any transfer outside their section. On the other hand, as I showed in the previous paragraph, about half of the engineers have experienced transfers outside their section. We can conclude that quite a few engineers have experienced a wide range of jobs in the workplace.

9.3.3 Long-term Career of Engineers

So far, I have investigated the careers of engineers who now work in technology and research. Now I shall investigate the careers of employees who have experienced working as engineers in those two functions, but now work in other functions.

There are two reasons why I shall investigate the careers of those employees. First, there are a number of jobs in other functions which require the knowledge of production, technology and research. For example, salespersons often have to talk with their clients about highly technological aspects of their products. If they have experienced working as engineers and can understand highly technical matters very well, they can reply accurately to questions, and put forward proper proposals to their clients. In order to train salespersons with highly technological knowledge, the best way is for firms to transfer engineers who have had several years' experience in technology and research to sales and marketing, where they will acquire the skills required for those functions. Another example is that manufacturing firms cannot devise proper management strategies if they do not have any employees in management planning who can understand the future development of technology and science very well. Therefore, firms will transfer some engineers to management planning. I would expect to find this type of transfer in the early stage of an engineer's career.

Second, there is also a negative reason for transferring engineers. Some of their knowledge becomes out of date because of the rapid progress made in technology and science. Many engineers supplement their outdated knowledge by acquiring new knowledge, and can continue to work as engineers. However, some engineers would no longer be expected to perform so well, so they are transferred to other functions. I would expect to find this type of transfer in the later stage of an engineer's career. In particular, it would be easy to find this type of transfer of engineers in large manufacturing firms which have had to restructure in the face of changing economic conditions.

In my sample, there are 182 employees who have experienced working in technology, and 44 of them are now working in functions other than technology. Most of them were transferred to research (11 employees), and six are now working in information processing. They were transferred to functions which were related to technology. However, nine are now working in sales and marketing, and five in management planning. On the other hand, there are 135 employees who have experienced research, and 36 of them are now working in functions other than research. Most of them were transferred to technology (eight employees). However, six are now working in international business, six in sales and marketing, and five in management planning. I find that quite a few engineers were transferred to functions which are not generally part of the typical career of an engineer. Some engineers have experienced a wide range of jobs outside technology and research.

Moreover, it is important to investigate when they were transferred. Here, I analyse 22 engineers who used to work in technology and research, but were transferred to sales and marketing and management planning, which were not generally part of the typical career of an engineer.[1] Fifteen of the 22 employees were transferred during the first 5 years of service, On the contrary, only three were transferred after 16 years of service. Many were transferred in the early stage of their career, and are now working in functions other than technology and research, having the advantage of experience as engineers. To date, there are only a few engineers who had worked in technology and research for a long time, and were then transferred to other functions.

9.4   INCENTIVES FOR ENGINEERS TO BE TRANSFERRED

9.4.1   The Effect of Transfer on Salary

A wide range of job experience for graduates in technology and science will increase the productivity of manufacturing firms. However, unless employees who have experienced transfer are promoted faster and gain more salary increases than employees who have never been transferred, then employees will be reluctant to be transferred, which will impair management efficiency. Therefore I shall investigate whether there exist incentives in the promotion and salary system which will encourage them to be transferred.

First, I shall analyse econometrically the effect of experiencing transfer on the salary of graduates in technology and science, by using OLS. The dependent variable is annual income. The independent variables are age, length of service, the number of transfers between establishments, the number of transfers between sections within establishments, whether they are now working in technology and research, whether they have experienced working in production, technology and research, and dummy variables of firms which they work for. In the Japanese salary system, salaries are expected to increase with age and length of service. So coefficients of these two variables are expected to be positive. If the salary system incorporates incentives for them to be transferred, the coefficients of two transfer variables are expected to be positive. If experience of working in each of production, technology and research is useful to jobs in other functions and it is assessed in the salary system, employees who have worked in these three functions will have higher salaries than other employees. So the coefficients of experience of working in production, technology and research are expected to be positive. Moreover, I shall investigate whether employees in technology and research have higher salaries than employees in other functions.

Table 9.1 shows the estimation result. The coefficients of age and length of service are positive, as I expected, and statistically significant. This suggests that salary will increase by 5.3 per cent if employees work for the current firm for one year. All firm dummies are significant. It means that salaries of graduates in technology and science differ widely between firms. According to the results from these four firms, salary differentials between firms are 15 per cent at the maximum, even if other things are the same. I do not find any significant effect on their salary of experiencing transfers between establishments or between sections. As to functions where they are now working or they have worked, I find a significant coefficient only in the case of research, but it is a very interesting finding. The coefficient of the dummy indicating that they are now working in research is positive (0.103), but the coefficient of the dummy indicating that they have worked in research is negative (−0.058). According to this result, employees who are now working in research have salaries 4.5 per cent higher than employees in other functions. On the contrary, employees who have worked in

Table 9.1 Effects on salary of experiencing transfer and functions

	Coefficient	*t*-value
Age	0.039	7.391**
Length of service	0.014	2.703**
Number of transfers between establishments	−0.012	−1.384
Number of transfers between sections	0.002	0.264
Working now in technology	0.043	1.430
Working now in research	0.103	3.038**
Experiencing production	0.013	0.381
Experiencing technology	−0.039	−1.265
Experiencing research	−0.058	−1.753**
Firm 1	−0.053	−1.842*
Firm 2	0.112	3.581**
Firm 4	0.137	3.695**
Constant	4.916	35.896**
R^2	0.793	
Number in sample	344	

Notes: ** Significant at the 5 per cent level. * Significant at the 10 per cent level.

research but are now working in other functions have salaries 5.8 per cent lower than other employees. Therefore, there is a large salary differential (10.3 per cent) between engineers who continue to work in research and engineers who have been transferred from research to other functions.

9.4.2   The Effect of Transfer on Promotion

Next, I shall investigate the effect of transfer on the promotion of graduates in technology and science. In many Japanese firms, in particular, almost all large firms, salary increases and promotion to management positions are largely determined on the basis of the job grade system. Salaries depend on job grades. If employees are not promoted to higher job grades, they can gain only slight salary increases. Moreover, in many firms, a necessary condition of promotion to each of the management positions is that employees should already have a given job grade. If they are not promoted to higher job grades, employees cannot be promoted to higher management positions either. Promotion in the job grade system depends not only on length of service, but also on an assessment of their job performance. In the middle and late stage of their career, the latter is a decisive factor for promotion. If a wide range of job experience is positively appraised in the assessment of the job performance, then employees who have experienced transfers will be promoted to higher job grades faster than other employees without transfers. In this case, we can say that there is an incentive in the job grade system for employees to be transferred.

Here, I shall analyse econometrically how quickly employees have been promoted to higher job grades. However, first I shall explain in detail the promotion variable classification. From the data used here, I not only know the job grade, but also when promotion to their present job grade occurred. Here I allocate promotion variable 1 to employees who were the last to be promoted to the lowest job grade. Promotion variable 2 is allocated to employees who were the second to last to be promoted to the lowest job grade. If employees who were the quickest to be promoted to the lowest job grade have stayed in this grade for, for example, five years, they are given the number 5, and number 6 is allocated to employees who were promoted this year to the second lowest job grade. In this way all employees are allocated a promotion variable number. Using OLS, I shall analyse this promotion variable with the same independent variables as for salary in the previous subsection. Moreover, the job grade systems differ widely between firms, so I shall estimate this promotion function for each firm separately, although each sample size becomes smaller.

Table 9.2 shows the estimation results. The results for firm 1 show that coefficients of age and length of service are positive and statistically significant. This means that the older employees are, and the longer they work for the current firm, the higher grade they will have, and the faster they will be promoted to the same job grade. Moreover the coefficient of transfer between establishments is positive and statistically significant. This means that employees who have experienced transfer between establishments were promoted faster than employees without such transfer. It can be concluded that there is an incentive in the job grade system of firm 1 for graduates in science and technology to be transferred between establishments. As to the functions which they have experienced working in or are now working in, there are significant coefficients only for research. The coefficient of the dummy indicating that they are now working in research is positive, but the coefficient of experience of working in research is negative. Both effects on promotion are almost cancelled out for employees who are now working in research. Employees who have experienced working in research but are now working in other functions, do not have any disadvantage, because they have the positive effect of transfer on their promotion. The results for firm 3 show that the coefficient of transfer between establishments is positive, and statistically significant. Employees who have experienced this kind of transfer were promoted faster than other employees without transfer, even if all other things, for example, age and length of service, were the same. However, functions do not have any significant effect on their promotion. The results for firms 2 and 4 show that neither transfers nor functions have any significant effect on their promotion. However, the coefficient of transfer between establishments of firm 4 is positive, although it is not significant at the 10 per cent level. Therefore, the results for these four firms show that in two (or three, in the broader criteria) of the four firms there are incentives in the job grade system for graduates in science and technology to be transferred between establishments.

9.5 WORK ATTITUDES OF GRADUATES IN SCIENCE AND TECHNOLOGY

9.5.1 Factors of Work Satisfaction

Recently in Japan, it has often been said that young people are less interested in studying science and technology at university than before, and even some graduates in those majors do not get jobs in manufacturing

Table 9.2 Effects on job grade promotion of transfer and functions, by firms

	Firm 1		Firm 2	
	Coefficient	*t*-value	Coefficient	*t*-value
Age	0.810	8.675**	0.448	1.282
Length of service	0.422	4.706**	1.158	3.325**
Number of transfers between establishments	0.675	3.757**	−0.558	−1.582
Number of transfers between sections	−0.082	−0.571	0.171	0.505
Working now in technology	0.389	0.674	−1.190	−1.057
Working now in research	5.440	4.771**	4.101	1.394
Experiencing production	0.037	0.068	−0.608	−0.322
Experiencing technology	−0.253	−0.468	1.063	0.802
Experiencing research	−5.570	−5.099**	−0.285	−0.220
Constant	−18.439	−7.811**	−14.354	−1.692*
R^2	0.957		0.834	
Number of sample	124		65	

	Firm 1		Firm 2	
	Coefficient	*t*-value	Coefficient	*t*-value
Age	0.838	6.203**	1.198	7.460**
Length of service	−0.061	−0.400	−0.273	−1.760*
Number of transfers between establishments	0.567	2.311**	0.355	1.387
Number of transfers between sections	0.290	1.222	0.260	0.996
Working now in technology	1.220	1.618		
Working now in research	3.140	1.604	−0.242	−0.372
Experiencing production	−0.209	−0.247	1.698	0.746
Experiencing technology	−1.030	−1.229	−0.312	−0.297
Experiencing research	0.405	0.471	1.561	0.110
Constant	−18.851	−5.835**	−30.129	−7.459**
R^2	0.952		0.783	
Number in sample	44		75	

Notes: ** Significant at the 5 per cent level. * Significant at the 10 per cent level.

industries. Some are very worried that if this tendency were to last for a long time, it would erode the high productivity of Japanese manufacturing industries. Many proposals have been put forward for manufacturing industries to become more attractive as a workplace for young people. However, these proposals often lack an analysis of work attitudes of graduates who have studied science and technology and are now working in manufacturing industries.

Generally speaking, salary increases and promotion to a management position are major incentives for employees to work hard and acquire skills. I shall investigate whether these incentives are sufficient for graduates in science and technology, by analysing their work attitudes. I shall investigate the fact that although promotion is a sufficient incentive for graduates in humanities and social science, it is not for graduates in science and technology.

In the questionnaire survey, respondents were asked how well they are satisfied with fourteen factors which seem to be related to their job satisfaction (see Table 9.3). According to the statistical criteria, graduates in science and technology are more dissatisfied with five of the fourteen fac-

Table 9.3 *Percentage of employees who are dissatisfied with each factor which is important for job satisfaction*

	Graduates in science and technology	Graduates in humanities and social science
To be given a job with responsibility	26.44**	18.98
To be a given a job suited to my personality	23.28	20.55
My proposal to be adopted	19.25	17.61
To do a given job perfectly	17.82*	13.89
My work to be recognized by others	24.43**	15.88
To have a higher salary	57.47	59.02
To be promoted to a higher position	30.75	32.02
To take all holiday entitlements	35.45**	29.22
To have hobbies besides work	31.12	30.53
To work in cooperation with colleagues	25.00**	16.27
To do a job at my discretion	23.85	20.20
To improve knowledge and skills	38.79	35.62
To foster skills of younger colleagues	41.91	37.62
To manage the workplace	43.19	39.19

Notes
** The difference between graduates in two majors is significant at the 5 per cent level.
* The difference between graduates in two majors is significant at the 10 per cent level.

tors compared to their counterparts. In contrast, there is no factor which graduates in humanities and social science are more dissatisfied with compared to their counterparts. With the data, I shall ascertain that graduates in science and technology are more dissatisfied with their work than are their counterparts.

Moreover, respondents were asked how important each factor was for their job satisfaction, and they chose one of three alternatives: 'very important', 'quite important', and 'not important'. Figure 9.2 shows the percentage of employees who answered 'not important' subtracted from the percentage of employees who answered 'very important' with regard to all fourteen factors. I regard them as indicators of how important each factor is to job satisfaction. As for graduates in science and technology, 'to be given a proper job well suited to my personality' is the most important factor for job satisfaction. 'To improve my knowledge and skill' ranks second, and 'my work to be recognized by my boss and colleagues' is third. In order to investigate the difference in work attitudes between graduates in science and technology and graduates in humanities and social science, Figure 9.2 also shows the difference of the importance of each factor for job satisfaction between graduates in science and technology and their counterparts. In comparison with graduates in humanities and social science, very important factors for graduates in science and technology are 'to improve my knowledge and skills', 'to take all holiday entitlement', and 'to have hobbies besides work'. On the contrary, relatively unimportant factors for them are 'to be promoted to a higher position', 'to be given a job with more authority', and 'to manage the workplace'.

Although I cannot explain the full result of the analysis because of limited space, I shall obtain a few common factors from those fourteen for graduates in science and technology, by performing factor analysis. The first common factor is closely related to the following: 'to be given a job suited to my personality', 'to take all holiday entitlement' and 'to have a higher salary'. It could be interpreted as being the factor which is related to the value of private life, independent from the workplace. Therefore, this factor will be called the individual factor. On the other hand, the second factor is closely related to the following: 'to be given a job with more responsibility', 'to manage the workplace' and 'to be promoted to a higher position'. This could be interpreted as being the factor which is related to promotion to management positions. Therefore, this factor will be called the promotion factor. As shown in the previous analysis of job satisfaction, this promotion factor is a relatively unimportant factor for job satisfaction of graduates in science and technology. Therefore, it can be concluded that promotion is not a real incentive for graduates in science and technology, although it is a real incentive for graduates in humanities and social science.

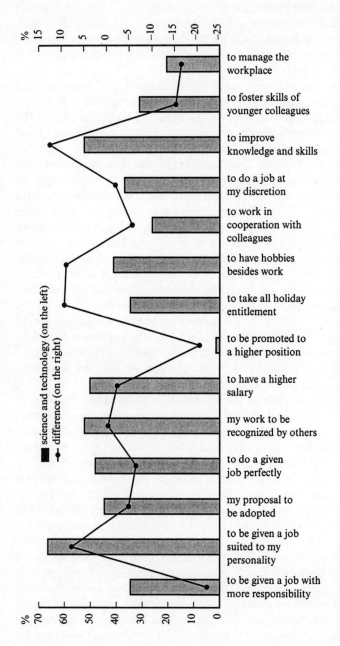

Notes: Science and technology is the percentage of graduates in science and technology who answered 'not important' subtracted from the percentage of those who answered 'very important'. Difference is the above percentage of graduates in humanities and social science subtracted from the percentage of graduates in science and technology.

Figure 9.2 Importance of different factors for job satisfaction

9.5.2 Orientation for Promotion

In the previous subsection, I ascertained that the promotion factor is not important for job satisfaction of graduates in science and technology. Their work attitudes are greatly reflected by their desire for future careers, that is whether they want to work as managers or specialists in the future. As Figure 9.3 shows, 52 per cent of graduates in humanities and social science want to be managers. In contrast, only 30 per cent of graduates in science and technology want to be managers, but 46 per cent want to be specialists.

Whether they want to work as managers or specialists depends to a large extent on how attractive they feel that working as managers would be. In the questionnaire survey, respondents were asked how attractive or unattractive they feel that working as managers would be in terms of twelve factors. They chose one of the three alternatives, 'very attractive (unattractive)', 'quite attractive (unattractive)', and 'not attractive (unattractive)'. Figures 9.4 and 9.5 show the percentage of employees who answered 'not attractive (unattractive)' subtracted from that of employees who answered 'very attractive (unattractive)'. Moreover, Figures 9.4 and 9.5 also show the differences in the attractiveness of working as a manager between graduates in science and technology and their counterparts. For many graduates in science and technology, 'to do a job with more authority', and 'to be involved directly in the management' are not attrac-

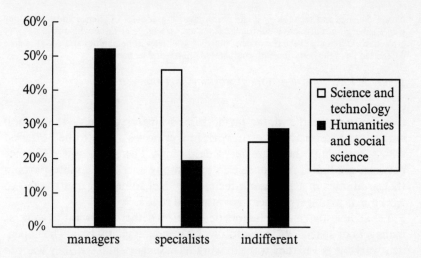

Figure 9.3 Percentage of employees who want to work as managers or specialists

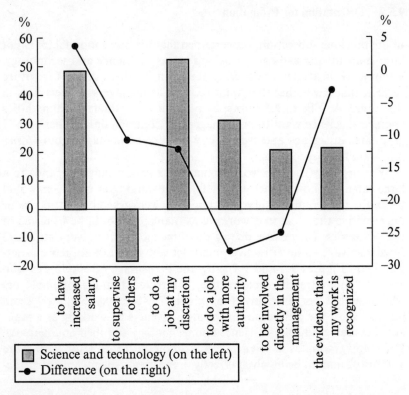

Notes: Science and technology is the percentage of graduates in science and technology who answered 'not attractive' subtracted from the percentage of those who answered 'very attractive'. Difference is the above percentage of graduates in humanities and social science subtracted from the percentage of graduates in science and technology.

Figure 9.4 Attractive factors of working as a manager

tive. On the other hand, for them, 'to be transferred often', 'to do a job with more responsibility', 'to work longer hours', and 'to be bothered with supervising others' are very unattractive. There is a large difference between graduates in science and technology and their counterparts in that graduates in science and technology feel somewhat unattracted to working as managers rather than attracted to it.

I shall investigate what factors determine whether they want to work as managers or specialists in the future, by using a logit analysis. The dependent variable is 1 if they want to work as managers, and 0 if they want to work as specialists. The independent variables are, first, twelve attractive and unattractive aspects of working as managers. Each variable of attrac-

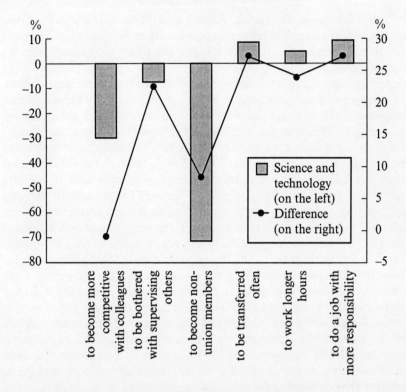

Notes: Science and technology is the percentage of graduates in science and technology who answered 'not unattractive' subtracted from the percentage of those who answered 'very unattractive'. Difference is the above percentage of graduates in humanities and social science subtracted from the percentage of graduates in science and technology.

Figure 9.5 Unattractive factors of working as a manager

tive factors is 0, if respondents chose 'quite attractive', 1 for 'very attractive' and –1 for 'not attractive'. Likewise, each variable of unattractive factor is 0, if they chose 'a little attractive', 1 for 'very unattractive', and –1 for 'not unattractive'. Coefficients of attractive factors are expected to be positive, and coefficients of unattractive factors are expected to be negative. Moreover, there are age and firm dummies in independent variables. In most Japanese firms, as employees grow older, many colleagues of the same age are promoted to manager. Therefore, as they get older, they are obliged to aim at being promoted to manager, even if the attractions of working as a manager do not change. Likewise, in firms where more colleagues are promoted to manager than in other firms, they are obliged to aim at being promoted to manager, even if they are not as attracted to the position of manager as employees in other firms.

Table 9.4 shows the result. First, I shall look at the effects of the attractiveness and unattractiveness of working as managers on the orientation to management positions, using the result for graduates in all specialities combined. Among attractive factors, the coefficients of 'to supervise others', 'to work at my discretion', and 'to participate directly in management' are positive and statistically significant. This means that employees who feel that those factors are more attractive, want to work as managers. However, the coefficient of 'evidence that my work is recognized' is negative and statistically significant. This means that employees who want to work as specialists regard promotion as the evidence that their work is recognized, more than employees who want to become managers. It reflects their ambivalent feelings for promotion. Among unattractive factors, the coefficients of 'to be bothered with supervising others', 'to become non-union members', 'to work longer hours' and 'to have a job with more responsibility' are negative and statistically significant. It is worth noting that 'to become non-union members' has a negative effect on orientation to work as managers. Recently many large firms have been restructuring and downsizing their labour force. Union members have security in their jobs because of the trade union, which negotiates conditions of transfer and redundancy with the firm on behalf of union members. However, because managers are not union members, they do not have the support of the trade union. Given recent economic circumstances, some employees do not want to work as managers, because they would lose the job security guaranteed by the trade union, if they are promoted to management positions and become non-union members. Judging from the absolute values of the coefficients of attractive and unattractive factors, whether employees feel 'to be involved directly in management' is attractive or not, and 'to be bothered with supervising others' is unattractive or not, are the most influential factors in the orientation to management positions.

Next, I shall look at the effects of age and firm dummies on the orientation to management positions of graduates in science and technology, in comparison with their counterparts. As far as graduates in the humanities and social science are concerned, the coefficients of age and all firm dummies (except for firm 2) are not statistically significant. This means that regardless of their age and the firms where they are working, many want to be a manager. In contrast, for graduates in technology and science, the coefficient of age is positive and statistically significant. This means that even if the attractiveness of working as a manager does not change with their age, the older they grow, the more they want to be a manager. Moreover, all coefficients of firm dummies are statistically significant, and the order of the coefficients of firm dummies is equal to the order of the

Table 9.4 Effects of the attractiveness of working as a manager on the orientation to managers

	All	Graduates in science and technology	Graduates in humanities and social science
To have increased salary	0.118	0.217	0.123
To supervise others	0.321**	0.367	0.297
To do a job at my discretion	0.389*	0.247	0.338
To do a job with more authority	-0.113	-0.452	-0.024
To be involved directly in the management	0.698**	0.764**	0.619**
Evidence that my work is recognized	-0.294*	-0.221	-0.256
To become more competitive with colleagues	0.118	-0.195	0.208
To be bothered with supervising others	-0.697**	-0.176	-0.993**
To become non-union members	-0.396**	-0.800**	-0.233
To be transferred often	-0.114	0.096	-0.179
To work longer hours	-0.352**	-0.354	-0.268
To do a job with more responsibility	-0.285*	-0.561*	-0.034
Age	0.036**	0.057*	0.036
Firm 2	1.341**	1.424**	1.069**
Firm 3	-0.046	-1.135**	-0.460
Firm 4	0.886**	1.297**	0.619
Constant	-2.130**	-3.621**	-1.218
Number of sample	612	257	355
Log likelihood	-328.12	-133.87	-168.48

Notes: ** Significant at the 5 per cent level. * Significant at the 10 per cent level.

percentage of graduates in the humanities and social science who want to work as a manager in each firm.[2] Graduates in science and technology in firms where more colleagues want to work as a manager are obliged to seek promotion to manager, even if they feel less attracted to the idea of becoming a manager than employees in other firms do. Graduates in science and technology who want to work as specialists, are obliged to aim at being promoted to manager, as they grow older, and in the atmosphere of a workplace where more colleagues want to be a manager.

9.5.3   Satisfaction with Salary

In addition to promotion, salary increases are important incentives for employees to work hard and acquire skills. Now, it is often said that even if employees make considerable contributions to their firm, they cannot immediately get great salary increases which correspond to this contribution, in a salary system where salary increases depend not only on the assessment of job performance, but also on age and length of service. In order that Japanese manufacturing industries should maintain their competitiveness in future world markets, they will have to encourage engineers to do creative research and development which involves a high degree of risk but is difficult for other firms to match. Therefore, it is often said that they will have to introduce a new salary system where engineers who make large contributions to their firm can immediately get large salary increases which correspond to their contribution. This would result in wider salary differentials between employees of the same age, depending on their job performance. I shall consider the implications for a salary system well suited to graduates in science and technology, by analysing how satisfied they are with salary levels and the existing salary system.

From the data which I use here, as far as graduates in science and technology are concerned, 43 per cent are satisfied with their salary, but 57 per cent are dissatisfied. Satisfaction with salaries depends largely on whether they feel that their salary reflects their contribution to the firm. Figure 9.6 shows the relationship between salary and contribution. Sixty-one per cent feel that their salary is less than their contribution to the firm, and 75 per cent of them are dissatisfied with their salary. In contrast, 34 per cent feel that their salary almost corresponds to their contribution to the firm, and only 31 per cent of them are dissatisfied with their salary.

There are three reasons why they might feel that their salary is less than their contribution, and which would cause dissatisfaction with their salary level. First, even if employees have a similar career or education and work experience which may determine their contribution, their

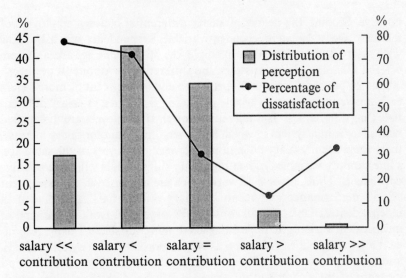

Figure 9.6 Perception of the relationship between salary and contribution to the firm, and percentage of employees who are dissatisfied with salary

salary differs widely between firms where they are now working, as shown in the previous section on salary estimation. Therefore, employees who are working for firms who pay their employees lower salaries than other firms, feel their salary does not reflect the contribution level, and feel dissatisfied with their salary. Second, if they work for the firms where age is very important for salary increases and salary differentials between employees of the same age are very small, they feel that their salary is less than their contribution and are dissatisfied with their salary, because their contribution is not fully reflected. Third, if employees regard the aspects of work to which their boss attaches importance in the assessment of job performance as a good measure of their contribution, they would think salary differentials on those assessments are acceptable, and would be satisfied with their salary.

I shall investigate how those factors influence satisfaction with salaries, by using a logit analysis. The dependent variable is 1 if employees are satisfied with their salary, and it is 0 if employees are dissatisfied. Independent variables are the following: first, the firm variable reflects salary differentials between firms, and it equals each of the coefficients of firm dummies obtained by the salary estimation in Section 9.4.1. Employees who work for firms which pay higher salaries are more satisfied with their salary, so the coefficient of the firm variable is expected to be positive. Second, the degree of salary differential between employees of the same age is also an independent variable. Respondents were asked how wide salary differentials between employees of the same age are, and were offered a choice of five answers, 'no differentials', 'about 10 per cent', 'about 20 per cent', 'about 30 per cent', and '40 per cent or more'. Here each answer is a dummy variable indicating the degree of salary differentials ('no differentials' is a reference group). If employees are dissatisfied with salaries in a system in which age is very important for salary increase, then, there are no salary differentials between employees of the same age, some dummy variables indicating salary differentials will have positive coefficients. Third, aspects of work which are appraised in the assessment of job performance and result in salary differentials are included in independent variables. I shall consider five aspects of work as this kind of independent variable in Table 9.5; each dummy variable is 1 if the respondent answered that each factor was very important for salary differentials, and 0 otherwise. If employees regard the aspect of work as a good measure of their contribution, they are satisfied with their salary which is determined by that aspect of work. Therefore, the coefficient of the variable is expected to be positive.

Table 9.5 shows the results. First, the coefficient of the firm variable is positive, as expected, and statistically significant. This means that employees who work for firms which pay higher salaries are more satisfied with their salary. Second, there is no significant result concerning variables indicating the degree of salary differentials. However, employees who feel that their job performance is better than or as good as their bosses expected may be satisfied with a salary system which allows wider salary differentials according to their job performance. Therefore, I estimated the salary satisfaction, by restricting the sample to employees who feel that their job performance is better than or as good as their boss expected.[3] The result can be seen in (2) of Table 9.5. However, the results do not show that there are more employees who are satisfied with their salary in firms which have wider salary differentials. Third, as to the aspects of work which cause salary differentials, the coefficient of 'to work conscientiously' is positive, and statistically significant. This means that employees are satisfied with their salary in a system where working conscientiously is appraised in the assessment of job performance and therefore results in salary increases. Moreover, the coefficient of 'to work more than others' is negative, and statistically significant. This means that employees are dissatisfied with their salary in a system where working conscientiously is appraised in the assessment of job performance and therefore results in salary increases. Moreover, the coefficient of 'to work more than others' is negative, and statistically significant. This means that

Table 9.5 Analysis of factors which influence satisfaction with salary

	(1)	(2)
Firm	1.631**	1.623**
Salary differentials		
10%	0.025	–0.150
20%	–0.151	–0.106
30%	0.136	–0.785
40% or more	–1.322	–1.326
Causes of salary differentials		
To work conscientiously	1.155**	1.134**
To work more than others	–0.552*	–0.385
To improve knowledge	–0.118	–0.047
To have better job performance	–0.143	–0.239
To foster skills of younger colleagues	–0.129	–0.195
Constant	0.008	0.059
Number in sample	348	299
Log likelihood	–217.986	–186.068

Notes: ** Significant at the 5 per cent level. * Significant at the 10 per cent level. (1) Estimated for the whole sample. (2) Estimated for those who feel their job performance is as good as, or better than, expected by the boss.

employees are dissatisfied with their salary in a system where working longer and more than others is appraised.

9.6 SUMMARY

Here I shall summarize my findings of careers and work attitudes of graduates in science and technology, and in particular of engineers.

Regarding engineers now working in technology and research, about 20 per cent have experienced working in other functions which are closely related to their present one. Engineers in technology have experienced production and research, and engineers in research have experienced technology. About 30 per cent have experienced transfer between sections, although they have never been transferred between functions. About 50 per cent have been working within the same section since they joined the firm. It can be concluded that quite a number of engineers have experienced a wide range of jobs. sometimes outside functions, which develop efficient production technology.

I have investigated whether there are incentives in salary and promotion systems to encourage engineers to be transferred. However, I could not find any such incentives in the salary system. Regarding promotion in the job grade system, in two (or three, in a broader criterion) of the four firms which I have investigated here, engineers who have experienced transfer between establishments were promoted to higher job grades faster then other employees without such experience, even if other things were equal. However, I could not find any significant effect on promotion of the different functions which they have experienced.

Among factors which seem to be important for job satisfaction, 'to be promoted to a higher position', 'to be given a job with more authority' and 'to manage the workplace' are not important for job satisfaction of graduates in science and technology, in comparison with graduates in humanities and social science. This is the reason why more graduates in science and technology want to work as specialists, in comparison with their counterparts. Therefore promotion to management positions is not a good incentive for them to work hard and acquire skills. One of the important findings here is that many graduates in humanities and social science want to work as a manager, regardless of their age and the firms where they are working. In contrast, graduates in science and technology, as they grow older, and in an atmosphere where more colleagues are promoted, are obliged to aim at being promoted, even if they are not attracted to working as managers.

With respect to salary satisfaction, the results indicate that graduates in science and technology are dissatisfied with their salary in a system where working longer and more than others is appraised in the assessment of job performance and is a contributory factor in salary differentials. Moreover, they are satisfied with their salary in a system where working conscientiously is appraised and causes salary differentials. They do not reject a new salary system in which job performance is more important for their salary increases than before. However, if the new salary system destroys an important aspect of the existing Japanese salary system where not only greater contribution to the firm, but also working conscientiously, are assessed in the job performance, then salary satisfaction for graduates in science and technology will be reduced.

NOTES

1. In the previous paragraph, I noted that there were 14 employees who had been transferred from technology to sales and management planning, and 11 who had been transferred from research to sales and management planning. However, because there are three employees who have experienced working in technology and research, I analyse the careers of 23 employees in all.

2. The percentage of graduates in the humanities and social science who want to work as a manager are 51 per cent in firm 1, 65 per cent in firm 2, 45 per cent in firm 3, and 51 per cent in firm 4. The order of these percentages corresponds to the order of coefficients of firm dummies.
3. Respondents were asked how well they have contributed to their firms, and they chose the following alternatives: 'have contributed more than expected', 'have contributed as much as expected, and 'have contributed less than expected'. Here I estimate the salary satisfaction with the sample, except for those employees who answered 'have contributed less than expected'.

REFERENCES

Imano, K. (1991), 'Gijutsusha no kyaria' (Careers of engineers), in K. Koike (ed.), *Daisotu Howaitokara no Jinzaikaihatsu* (Skill Formation of University Graduates), Tokyo: Toyokeizaisinposha, pp. 29–62.

Ito, M. (1993), 'Kenkyukaihatsu gijutsusha no kigyonai ikusei no genjo' (In-house skill formation of R&D engineers), in *Nihon Rodo Kenkyu Zassi*, June, pp. 22–8.

Koike, K. (ed.) (1990), *Daisotu Howaitokara no Jinzaikaihatsu* (Skill Formation of Graduates), Tokyo: Toyokeizaisinposha.

Koike, K. and T. Inoki (1990), *Skill Formation: Japan and South Asia*, Tokyo: University of Tokyo Press.

Lam, A. (1996), 'Work Organization, Skill Development and Utilisation of Engineers', in R. Crompton, D. Gallie and K. Purcell (eds), *Changing Forms of Employment*, London: Routledge, pp. 182–203.

LEST and Japan Institute of Labour (1992), *Innovation: Actors and Organisations,* Aix-en-Provence: LEST.

10. White-collar careers and trade unions

Fujikazu Suzuki

10.1 INTRODUCTION

One of the psychological conflicts that potentially conditions the behaviour of today's white-collar workers is the conflict between their position as 'labourer, employee' and that as 'management, delegation of authority'. This is a problem that many white-collar workers face during the course of their career. While the labour issue of white-collar workers is becoming serious, this reason explains why labour unions cannot be directly involved. However, the development of situations such as the 'crisis of the white-collar workers' emerged in the recession after the bursting of the so-called 'bubble economy' in the early 1990s, reinforcing the 'voice' of the labour union concerning security of employment and rules for labour conditions.

In this chapter we shall examine white-collar workers and the labour union, based on the analysis in the 'Survey on white-collar employees'. This chapter is an attempt to shed light on a problematic field continuing the investigations of 'Path to becoming a top executive' (Chapter 1) and 'Path to becoming a manager' (Chapter 4).

Section 10.2 will examine the relationship between white-collar workers and the labour union, focusing on the general trend that Japanese white-collar workers leave the labour union at a certain point in their career. Section 10.3 will analyse the position of promotion in various factors that contribute to contentment in professional life. Section 10.4 will define the influence of the speed of promotion on professional life, and the reason why promotion is sought after. Section 10.5 will analyse the current conditions of work attitude, considering the limits of seeking a single target in a career. Finally, Section 10.6 will consider the attitude of the labour union to the white-collar labour issue.

10.2 JAPANESE WHITE-COLLAR LABOUR UNION MEMBERS

Japanese white-collar labour union members have two main features. The first is that they belong to the same union as the blue-collar workers. Many labour unions in the United States and Europe are separated into those for white-collar and those for blue-collar workers, even with different national centres. The conflict of interest between the two groups is deeply rooted in the historical background. In contrast, Japan today rarely sees acute conflicts of interest between blue-collar and white-collar workers, and the labour union is based on the concept of 'employees belonging to the same company' as common ground. In the union shop system adopted in the labour unions of many private enterprises, all employees automatically become union members upon employment. This mechanism helped working Japanese labour unions to adapt fairly well to the shift of the working population to white-collar workers. In fact, the unions have a large number of white-collar members.

The second main feature is that the Japanese white-collar union members more or less consider membership in the union as a 'transition'. This is because they are excluded from the union when they are promoted to a managing position, as they are considered to be 'representatives of the employer'. Employees climbing up the corporate ladder are considered to have 'graduated' from the union when they cross the border into a managing position, and become representatives of the management. This trend is especially notable for university-graduate white-collar union members, who consider that being a member of a union is just one step in their career. This is completely different from union members in the United States and Europe who usually maintain their union member status throughout their career. And herein lies the reason why the involvement of Japanese white-collar workers with their union is so different. They tend to view the union only as a step in their career, while a large part of the union comprises white-collar workers. This may explain the reason why the union has little influence in their career.

The border in the corporate ladder between union and non-union member differs according to the organization. Generally the distinction is made from the time the employee becomes a manager. Historically, this was a product of compromise between the union, which wants to have as wide a range of members as possible, and the management, which wants to secure middle managers on the side of management. The administrative interpretation of the labour union law clause 2 is influenced by the fact that employees are non-members once they become a manager. However, this interpretation is a relic of the mid-1940s to 1950s, when the position of manager was quite different from what it is today. The domination of the qualification systems today has also produced a large number of 'qualified' middle management without subordinates, pressing for the need to reevaluate the 'range of union members' (see RIALS, 1994a). This research shows that white-collar workers do consider membership in a union as an initial step in their career.

Most people are attracted to promotion to a management post, but they also foresee some burden. Six questions were given in this study, about the attractions and burdens of being promoted to a managing position, are shown in Table 10.1. Most people (53.8 per cent) answered that all the given six items are attractive (very attractive + somewhat attractive), while 89.4 per cent thought that more than four items are attractive; only 1.7 per cent found none of the items attractive. The burdens of being promoted to the position of manager, on the other hand, saw only 11.8 per cent who considered all six items as burdens (very burdensome + somewhat burdensome), but there were some 57.2 per cent who considered more than four items as burdens; only 7 per cent considered no items burdensome. Promotion is indeed attractive to anyone, but most people feel that there is also a need to face certain burdens. However, only 23.5 per cent found 'leaving the union' a burden. This percentage is very low compared to other items which 60 to 70 per cent consider burdensome. It seems to be readily understood that climbing up the corporate ladder means having to leave the labour union at some stage.

10.3 PROMOTION AND CAREER SATISFACTION

The character of Japanese white-collar union members as temporary members will continue into the future. However, this does not always mean that a union with many white-collar members does not make a positive contribution to the future of their careers. In this section, we shall study the meaning of promotion for white-collar workers.

First, we view the relationship of satisfaction in career and promotion. The following analysis considers male university graduates only, so as to remove factors concerning academic background and gender difference.

The following 14 items concerning satisfaction in work were studied, and three alternative responses were given: 'very satisfied', 'satisfied' and 'not satisfied'.

1. More authority and responsibility is given.
2. More apt work is given.
3. Plans and proposals are adopted.

Table 10.1 Attractions and burdens of being promoted to a management post (gender, academic background, total)

Attraction of being promoted ('very attractive' + 'somewhat attractive')

		Burden of 'leaving the labour union'	
	Total	Burdensome	Not burdensome
Higher income	94.9	96.9	94.3
Can control people	67.7	66.6	68.1
Can work at own discretion	96.2	95.3	96.5
Can work with more authority	90.1	86.6	91.1
Can participate directly in corporate management	84.3	82.4	84.8
Can be recognized for results and skills	86.4	86.4	86.4

Burden of being promoted ('very burdensome' + 'somewhat burdensome')

		Burden of 'leaving the labour union'	
	Total	Burdensome	Not burdensome
Competition between peers becomes intense	57.6	74.6	52.4
Troublesome management of subordinates	67.4	81.8	63.0
Have to leave the union	23.5	–	–
More transfers of positions and workplace	70.2	89.1	64.4
Longer work hours	71.5	87.7	66.6
More responsibility	72.5	83.8	69.0

4. Can complete given work.
5. Result of work is recognized by superiors and peers.
6. Higher salary.
7. Higher position.
8. Taking regular holidays and getting refreshed.
9. Having pleasures in life other than work, such as hobbies.
10. Cooperating with peers to complete work.

11. Can decide how to process work.
12. Can acquire special knowledge and skill.
13. Training subordinates.
14. Leading subordinates and directing the entire project.

To measure the total career satisfaction, points were given ('very satisfied' = 2, 'satisfied' = 1, 'not satisfied' = 0) to each answer and the arithmetic average of the 14 items was defined as the 'Total Satisfaction Index'. The range of this Total Satisfaction Index is between 0 and 2; the lower the index (less than 1), the lower the satisfaction, and the higher the index (1 or more), the higher the satisfaction.[1]

The average Total Satisfaction Index of all the male university graduates was 0.84, which shows that people are not very satisfied. Approximately two-thirds was less than 1.0. The index naturally changes according to attributes such as age, position, or whether the person is career-orientated (promotion- or specialist-orientated), or what their view of promotion is. Then, what factor decides the Total Satisfaction Index? We tried statistical analysis by quantification type I, to identify this point.

Quantification type I is a statistical method to explain measured values, with information on qualification factors such as sex, profession and trends, defined as explanatory variables. For example, when other conditions are constant and the position is 'manager', or when the annual income is ¥8 million, the increase/decrease of the Total Satisfaction Index can be assumed.

The following eight factors are the explanatory variables: (1) age, (2) current position, (3) future prospect for promotion, (4) future career orientation, (5) reflection on difference in salary, (6) reflection on contribution and salary, (7) annual salary of last year, and (8) company name.

Table 10.2 is the result of stochastic analysis.[2] As the analysis is based on individual samples, the coefficient of determination is as low as 0.129, but the results show a very interesting trend. The category score of this table shows the increase and decrease of the Total Satisfaction Index of each category of the explanatory variables. For example, when other conditions are constant and the age is 29 years or less, the Total Satisfaction Index decreases by 0.001545.

The constant term 0.852810 is the average Total Satisfaction Index of the entire sample, but the sample that was used in the stochastic analysis was 989, and is somewhat different from the average of the university-graduate male sample mentioned above.

The marginal sum of squares[3] is used as an index to judge the degree of effect of each explanatory variable in the figure shown in the 'effect of explanatory variable' field. The figures of the 'effect of explanatory variable' show that more than 40 per cent can be explained by the 'current position'.

Table 10.2 Career satisfaction by quantification 1 (university graduates, 989 samples)

Explanatory variable, category	Frequency	Category score	(Marginal sum of squares)
(1) Age			
1 : Below 30	273	–0.001545	1.20
2 : 30 to 34	410	0.006193	
3 : 35 to 39	171	–0.018591	
4 : 40 to 44	83	–0.015861	
5 : Over 45	52	0.045733	
(2) Current position			
1 : General	604	–0.047109	41.69
2 : Section head class	217	–0.001710	
3 : Manager without subordinate	38	0.050469	
4 : Manager with subordinate	102	0.194678	
5 : Senior manager	10	0.207811	
6 : Director	18	0.276218	
(3) Future prospects for promotion (where will you end up?)			
1 : Section head class	57	–0.086494	12.96
2 : Manager	332	–0.040667	
3 : Senior manager	194	–0.000364	
4 : Director	350	0.033158	
5 : Director or above	56	0.123157	
(4) Career orientation			
1 : Management-post-orientated	410	0.018268	1.39
2 : Specialist-orientated	323	–0.015145	
3 : Either	256	–0.010148	
(5) Difference of salary (difference between the highest and lowest)			
1 : Almost none	493	0.022794	8.96
2 : Approx. 10%	312	–0.012569	
3 : Approx.20%	130	–0.001230	
4 : Approx. 30%	41	–0.092436	
5 : More than 40%	1 3	–0.258924	

Explanatory variable, category	Frequency	Category score	(Marginal sum of squares)
(6) Your contribution and salary (is your current salary sufficient compared to your contribution?)			
1 : Very low	173	−0.026301	17.30
2 : Low	443	−0.041598	
3 : Equivalent	336	0.074240	
4 : High	29	−0.081475	
5 : Too high	8	0.049488	
(7) Annual income of previous year			
1 : Less than 4 million (yen)	122	0.015598	12.38
2 : 4 million	127	0.007293	
3 : 5 million	180	−0.022330	
4 : 6 million	179	−0.002109	
5 : 7 million	164	0.037908	
6 : 8 million	82	0.017677	
7 : 9 million	64	0.063841	
8 : 10 million or more	71	−0.143444	
(8) Company type			
1 : Electronics company B	230	−0.019021	4.12
2 : Automotive company A	195	0.031688	
3 : Chemical company C	263	−0.022140	
4 : Electric power company D	199	−0.006868	
5 : Department store E	102	0.052796	
Constant term		0.852810	

Notes: Multiple correlation coefficient 0.359; Coefficient of determination 0.12904.

The next is 'contribution and salary', which is only half the 'current position' (approximately 17 per cent). Then, comes 'prospects for promotion', 'annual income of previous year' which are 12 to 13 per cent of the total variance. When the factors are constant, 'age' 'career orientation' and 'company type' did not have much influence. The variable 'position', including future prospects, explains most of the variances of the satisfaction factor.

Next, we shall study what kind of change each variable makes to satisfaction. Reading satisfaction with the 'current position' it is clear that, the higher in the hierarchy, from general, section head, manager (without subordinates), manager (with subordinates), senior manager to director, the higher the general satisfaction index. The effect is relatively high from the category score. A similar trend is seen in 'prospects for promotion'; the higher the future prospect, the higher the 'general satisfaction index'. However, the degree of the effect is not as large as for the current position. The fact that a higher position brings higher satisfaction results from the fact that many people are attracted to promotion. Why is this? And what can they gain by promotion to a higher position? We shall study this in the next section.

The recognition related to 'contribution and salary' (whether the salary is equivalent to one's contribution to the company) had the second largest effect on satisfaction, after the current position, but did not show a clear relationship with each category. The dissatisfaction is estimated to be large when people think that their current salary is low compared to their contribution to the company, while satisfaction is estimated to be high for those who think their salary 'equivalent' or 'high'. The category score as result of calculation had higher minus values for 'high', 'low' and 'very low' salary compared to the worker's contribution, and higher plus values for 'equivalent' and 'very high', in this order. Although the satisfaction of people who think that their salary is 'equivalent' to their contribution is somewhat high, the satisfaction of those who think it 'high' and 'low' has no clear relationship. However, there is a limited number who consider their contribution 'low' compared to their salary (37 cases, 37 per cent), so a general trend shows that satisfaction is high when a worker's salary is 'equivalent' to his/her contribution, while the satisfaction decreases when it is 'low'. This means that it is important to evaluate appropriately the contribution of employees and to pay their salary accordingly. This has special significance when evaluating specialists; the valuable point is to examine their contribution from all angles, and to evaluate high achievements based on expertise.

The salary standard does not always link directly to satisfaction. When viewing the category score of 'annual income of previous year', there is no direct relationship between high salary and high satisfaction. The highest minus value is seen in the highest salary rank of '¥10 million or more' group. The next was the '¥5 million' and '¥6 million' groups, which also have minus category scores. On the other hand, the lowest salary rank '¥4 million or less' has a plus category score. These imply that the absolute standard of salary does not always prescribe the satisfaction level. Greater significance lies in the contribution factor and whether the given salary is good enough for current household expenses.

'Difference of salary' between peers who joined the company in the same year shows plus category scores for 'almost no difference', but minus scores for those with differences. The larger the difference, the lower the satisfaction (although the relationship between the 10 per cent group and the 20 per cent group is reversed). People who see large variations in salaries among peers are those who have less satisfaction. However, there is no information as to whether the person was higher or lower ranked. The trend shows that large differences in salary between peers have minus effects on satisfaction.

The effect of 'age' in satisfaction is very small, and no direct relationship can be observed. The age factor has minus effects on satisfaction in the young group of under 30, and the middle age group of late thirties and early forties. Needless to say, the age variable itself has no effect on satisfaction; the problem lies in the circumstances in specific age groups.

The career type also has less to do with satisfaction, but satisfaction is higher for 'specialist-orientated' people than for 'management-oriented' people; those who do not belong to either group fall in between.

Finally, the difference of 'company' also had little effect on the satisfaction level. The category score was minus in electronics company B, chemical company C and electric power company D, and plus in automotive company A and department store E, but the differences are not so large.

Career satisfaction is first decided by the current and future prospects for promotion (whether the person will climb up the corporate ladder fairly). Second, is whether the salary is well balanced with the worker's contribution. Third is that there is no large difference in salary between peers, and that the range is not too large; the smaller the difference in salary between peers, the greater the satisfaction. The combination of the first and third conditions can be described as equal promotion of peers while high expectations for promotion can result in high satisfaction. However, this is not easy.

A general trend of all the workers in Japan is that people have a strong desire for uniformity; nobody wants to be late in the competition to climb the corporate ladder. This desire has supported the morale of the employees. Such a trend is especially apparent with white-collar workers. However, it is clear that there are no career circumstances that can satisfy the expectations of all workers. There is always a gap between the number of available posts and expectations for promotion. This is how the dual personnel management by qualification and position as well as many other systems started. The personnel system for white-collar workers developed to solve this problem. But, this system has come to its limits, with the ageing of employees and fewer posts available. Then, would this mean that the Japanese career system with satisfaction largely depending on promotion has reached a turning-point?

10.4 WHY PROMOTION IS SOUGHT AFTER

The struggle to climb the corporate ladder in large enterprises is a competition to reach as high a position as possible compared to those joining the company in the same year. The difference is not so apparent in the early stage of a career; it becomes apparent in their thirties, when many are promoted to the post of manager. Only 1.2 per cent of the university graduate males reached the post of manager in their early thirties in this study, while 25.6 per cent became manager in their late thirties. Only 18.1 per cent maintain their general or section head posts in their forties, when 58.8 per cent are managers, and 23.1 per cent are senior or division managers. Now, how would the difference in promotion affect career satisfaction?

Figure 10.1 shows the satisfaction in each position in their late thirties and 40 and over. It is clear at first glance that the higher the position, the higher the satisfaction index in most items, but the meaning can be different according to the age group. In the 40 and over group, where most are already above the manager class, the satisfaction of those still below the section head class is noticeably low. The 40 and over group of the manager class has lower satisfaction compared to the late thirties group. As most people are already in a manager position in their forties, the satisfaction will not rise unless they reach the next target, senior or division manager.

The items where satisfaction is notably low for the general/section head class of the forties and over group, is first, 'higher salary', and then, 'higher post', 'training of subordinates' and 'leadership'. Low satisfaction is also observed with items related to the work itself, as 'work with more authority', 'apt work', 'result of work is evaluated' and 'discretion of work'. These items have close relationships to the work itself, and the manager class of the late thirties group and the senior manager class of the forties and over group, which are relatively high ranking in the competition up the corporate ladder, have higher rates of satisfaction. This indicates that promotion not only improves the position and salary, but also brings about some kind of fulfilment in work.

When asked what the attraction to being promoted to a manager post is, the first was 'can work at own discretion' ('very attractive' + 'attractive' 96.6 per cent). Next was 'higher income' (95.0 per cent), 'Can work with more authority' (91.3 per cent), but 'can control people' (70.5 per cent) was relatively not so attractive. The trend in which the feeling of fulfilment as a result of promotion is valued, and not the promotion itself is also pointed out in other studies (for example, Sano and Kawakita, 1993).

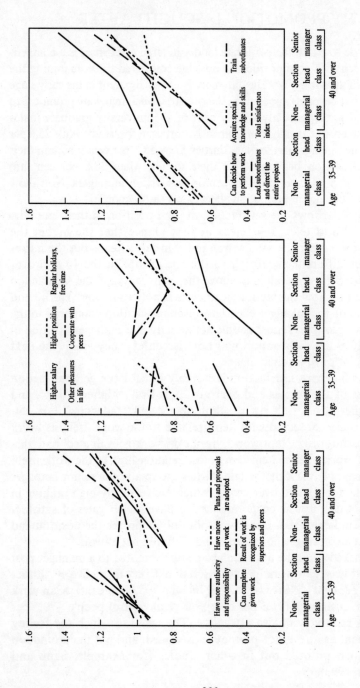

Note: The satisfaction index is calculated using 'very satisfied' = 2, 'satisfied' = 1, 'not satisfied' = 0.

Figure 10.1 Career satisfaction per age group, position group (university graduate males above 35)

If discretion and fulfilment in work are the target, there is no need to seek promotion in the corporate ladder. On this point, the white-collar workers are divided into three. About 40 per cent of the university graduate white-collar males answered that they wanted to 'work as line managers' (manager orientated), and 30 per cent wanted to 'work as specialists' (specialist orientated); others could not decide. The ratio of the three did not change by age, position, or other attributes. This means that the positions employees hold regarding promotion are polygenetic.

The comparison on the promotion of 'manager-orientated' and 'specialist-orientated' employees, as shown in Table 10.3, is roughly the same, except for

Table 10.3 Attractions and burdens of being promoted to a management post for each career type

Attraction of being promoted ('very attractive' + 'somewhat attractive')

	Management orientated	Specialist orientated
Have more authority and responsibility	95.1	95.3
Can control people	79.7	61.5
Can work at own discretion	98.2	95.4
Can work with more authority	94.7	87.2
Can participate directly in corporate management	93.2	81.6
Can be recognized for results and skills	88.9	83.9

Burden of being promoted ('very burdensome' + 'somewhat burdensome')

	Management orientated	Specialist orientated
Competition between peers becomes intense	56.9	60.7
Troublesome management of subordinates	52.4	78.2
Have to leave the union	14.0	29.2
More transfers of positions and workplace	57.7	77.9
Longer work hours	57.9	80.7
More responsibility	58.3	80.2

except for the fact that 'specialist-orientated' workers did not make much of being able to 'control people'. Both were more or less attracted to being promoted. The burden on being promoted to a manager position is remarkably heavy for the 'specialist-orientated' employees. Especially, 'troublesome management of subordinates', 'more transfers of positions and workplace', 'longer work hours' and 'more responsibility' were burdens to some 80 per cent. Of all university graduates, 84.3 per cent were not able to use up their paid holidays (92.5 per cent for manager class and up). Three-quarters answered that they had to work overtime without being paid.

Even though they were prepared to face such burdens, 40 per cent of the 'specialist-orientated' employees had prospects that they would be promoted to the manager class, while 20 per cent thought that they would be promoted to senior manager class. One-quarter had prospects that they would go to and beyond the director class. To perform their work 'making the best of their expertise', it is considered necessary to climb up the ladder to some extent, in the current career system. Once off the 'path', it may be difficult to obtain satisfaction in work.

10.5   NECESSITY OF MULTIPLE CAREER CHOICES

As studied above, underlying the promotion-seeking behaviour is the attitude of each person to his or her work. This attitude to work also varies. Table 10.4 shows the factor analysis results on satisfaction to work for 'specialist-orientated' and 'management-orientated' employees. The results show that the factors comprising satisfaction differ.

This study was conducted using three main factors that decide career satisfaction. For the management-orientated employees the most important factors were 'plans and proposals are adopted', 'result of work is evaluated' and 'leadership'. These can be seen as 'success at work as part of the organization'. The second important factors were 'higher position', and 'higher salary' which in turn can be seen as 'promotion of position and conditions'. The third factors are 'pleasures in life other than work' and 'holidays and free time', which are seen as a 'well-rounded life outside work'.

For those who are specialist orientated, the third factor group for the management-orientated people, 'well-rounded life outside work' was the most important factor for career satisfaction. The second factor group was 'higher position', which is the same as for management-orientated employees. The work-related factor is the third, but the contents are somewhat different. The factors in which those who are specialist orientated see satisfaction are 'plans and proposals are adopted', 'work at own discretion' and have 'more apt work', which can be considered as 'desired work'.

Management- and specialist-orientated employees balance their work and private lives differently. Even regarding work, the management-orientated people place emphasis on success at work as part of the organization, while those who are specialist orientated place emphasis on doing their desired work. Then, does the current career system support such diverse attitudes towards work?

The fact that Japanese white-collar workers comprise the professional specialist type as well as the power pursuing type has been noted for some time (for example, Okamoto, 1964). However, personnel systems have not been able to cope with such diversity in career, and have maintained the traditional single-line type career structure. There were, in fact, efforts to create promotion paths other than the traditional line, or to create specialist qualification systems, but these efforts did not lead to a new system that can accommodate all kinds of promotion needs. The voices of the white-collar employees heard in this study point out some important areas which enhance the motivation of those specialists: 'evaluate results and skills fairly' (77.2 per cent), 'increase the wages of the specialists' (61.7 per cent), 'clearly define the range of authority and responsibility' (48.6 per cent) and 'allow more delegation of authority' (45.4 per cent). There is still no established specialist system, which explains the reason why such specialist-orientated people also have to seek promotion.

According to a recent study (Japan Institute of Labour, 1994), which analysed careers within a large company using white-collar worker transfer data, the promotion pattern of Japanese university graduate white-collar workers has a multi-level structure of three stages. The 'simple seniority type' applies to the early stage of several years after joining the company; there is still not much difference at this stage. Then, the 'promotion speed competition' rule applies to the next intermediate stage where competition to rise up the corporate ladder starts. The highlight is the promotion to the position of manager. At this stage, most of the runners still hold the same qualification, and the latecomers still seem to have another chance. Finally, at the last stage of the career, those to be promoted to higher positions and those left behind will become apparent, in a 'tournament type competition' (the same fact was also found in this study, and examined in Chapters 5 and 6).

At this point, the more interesting fact is that this multi-level promotion race system can be considered as a system that allows the participation of many people, thus increasing incentives. On the other hand, even when the result of the competition is determined, it is not very clear. Thus, workers get bound up in the manager position. The actual result of the competition is decided for the most part at the second stage when being promoted from section head to manager (this result also coincides with the result of the study centring promotion to the post of manager examined in Chapter 4).

Table 10.4 Decisive factors in career satisfaction for manager- and specialist-orientated employees (result of analysis)

Manager orientated (university graduate, male, manager orientated, 490 samples)

	Common	Factor load		
		Factor 1	Factor 2	Factor 3
Plans and proposals are adopted	0.484	**0.684**	-0.059	0.113
Result of work is evaluated	0.434	**0.654**	0.080	0.019
Leadership at work	0.455	**0.603**	-0.090	0.288
Work with authority and responsibility	0.334	0.567	0.109	-0.022
Work at own discretion	0.370	0.556	-0.070	0.237
Train subordinates	0.443	0.546	-0.105	0.365
Have more apt work	0.295	0.538	-0.019	0.072
Can complete given work	0.242	0.473	-0.083	0.108
Cooperate with peers to complete work	0.272	0.454	0.079	0.244
Can acquire special knowledge and skills	0.286	0.451	0.024	0.286
Higher position	0.606	0.448	**0.633**	-0.066
Higher salary	0.483	0.313	**0.620**	-0.021
Pleasures in life other than work	0.461	-0.074	0.182	**0.650**
Holidays and free time	0.373	0.000	0.263	**0.551**

	Factor 1	Factor 2	Factor 3
Character of factor	Success at work as part of the organization	Promotions of position and conditions	Well-rounded life outside work
Rate of explained variance Error 0.0494	3.748	0.906	0.884

Specialist orientated (university graduate, male, manager orientated, 392 samples)

	Common	Factor load		
		Factor 1	Factor 2	Factor 3
Pleasure in life other than work	0.550	**0.741**	0.007	-0.022
Holidays and free time	0.315	**0.548**	0.118	-0.016
Cooperation with peers to complete work	0.331	0.425	0.139	0.362
Train subordinates	0.318	0.404	0.106	0.379
Higher position	0.561	0.157	**0.727**	0.092
Higher salary	0.506	0.161	**0.690**	-0.069
Plans and proposals are adopted	0.401	0.073	0.246	**0.579**
Discretion of work	0.372	0.203	0.132	**0.560**
Have more apt work	0.332	0.136	0.160	**0.536**
Result of work is evaluated	0.367	0.175	0.303	0.495
Work with authority and responsibility	0.380	-0.004	0.396	0.473
Can acquire special knowledge and skills	0.253	0.241	0.067	0.436
Leadership in work	0.342	0.367	0.219	0.399
Can complete given work	0.191	0.207	-0.021	0.384

	Factor 1	Factor 2	Factor 3
Character of factor	Well-rounded life outside work	Promotion of position and conditions	Desired work
Rate of explained variance	3.421	0.908	0.890

Error 0.0586

Note: Three axes are set for up to 100 per cent accumulated contribution after varimax rotation.

235

Not all university graduate white-collar workers are suited to leading subordinates and achieving business objectives, while undertaking responsibility. Moreover, not everyone desires to do so. So, if the actual result of the competition is decided at an early stage, why not prepare for another choice of career, besides the ordinary corporate ladder? This can be the main reason why the number of managers, including staff specialists, is increasing to reduce the range of the labour union, and thus magnifying the trend of white-collar labour union members to be just temporary members. It can be said that the issues surrounding the promotion of the white-collar workers and those of the organization of the labour union are, in fact, deeply linked.

10.6 COUNTERMEASURES OF LABOUR UNIONS TOWARDS THE WHITE-COLLAR LABOUR ISSUE

As the historical booming market faded out in the early 1990s, a 'cooling period' awaited the white-collar workers. The greatest feature of this business recession was that the white-collar workers, especially the middle-aged managers, became redundant, and thus became the target of restructuring. The short-term let-up in demand caused by the business cycle, as well as the issue of structural adjustment, caused enterprises to restructure their business, and desk-work and administration sections became the target of this restructuring. This can mean that the current white-collar crisis cannot be regarded as merely temporary.

As the candidates for the post of manager increased, mainly the baby-boom generation, the competition for promotion became intense, and fewer people were able to rise to the post of manager. According to the Statistics Bureau's 'Labour Force Survey', there were 110,000 fewer managers in 1993 compared to the previous year. The dissatisfaction of white-collar workers can no longer be alleviated by giving them a managing position, and this will certainly make their dissatisfaction in the workplace more and more apparent.

Needless to say, no careers are inherently easy. All professionals continue their work with some dissatisfaction. Mills argued that 'The union leader is a manager at discontent. He makes regular what otherwise might be disruptive . . . is a regulator of disgruntlement and ebullience . . . an agent in the institutional channelling of animosity' (Mills, 1948, p. 9).[4]

This 'constitutional channel' is inherited today in the theory of the labour union as the 'collective voice' (Freeman and Medoff, 1984). The function of the union is not only to maintain and improve labour conditions, and to take care of complaints, but also to take a positive initiative to maintain employee morale and improve output, as the 'voice' of the 'manager of discontent'.

However, labour unions have not always performed well in their role of 'manager of discontent' in the recent worsening of white-collar labour issues. Therefore, the following section will discuss several problems that should not be overlooked when considering the future.

First, is to reconsider the range of non-union members, and expand the range of the labour union organization. Automatic rejection of managers without subordinates and specialist-managers who cannot be regarded as 'representative of management' must be reconsidered. Unless the employment and labour conditions of such manager groups are stable and well, these are the people who are in the weakest position; they are at the 'bottom' of the managing organization and, not being union members, their 'voices' are not represented. Today, reconsidering the range of non-union members is becoming a contentious issue. For example, in the report issued by the JEIU (Japanese Electronics and Information Union), a proposal was made to reconsider the range of non-union members. Interpreting the conditional clause of article 2 of the Trade Union Law more strictly, it says 'it may be necessary to include employees regardless of their title or qualification as union members, except for "those who are in a position to decide labour conditions and other labour management positions and are a part of management"' (JEIU, 1994, pp. 15–16). The range of the union members is naturally the self-ruling option of the union itself, and should be decided independently by the union. The point of the Trade Union Law not recognizing the 'representatives of management' in the union, is to protect the autonomy of the union, and so reconsideration of the definition of 'representatives of management' according to the change of situation is only natural. However, reconsidering the range of union membership does not solve all the problems. There is always the issue of whether the workers want to maintain their status as managers without subordinates or specialist managers. Considering the special position of middle management, which stands between labour and management, there is also a debate on structuring a completely new voicing organization independent of both the management and the labour union (Inoki, 1993). The choice will be seen in the near future. While labour unions start reconsidering their range of membership, they will also have to study the needs of middle management, and will try to reorganize themselves into attractive organizations that can answer the needs of middle management.

Second, is to reinforce the voice not only of the union members, but of all employees. The fact that Japanese labour unions have close communication with management is well known. According to a recent survey

(Labour Issue Research Centre, 1993), targeting enterprise unions nation-wide, the most frequent answer to union–management communication activities was 'informal meetings' (64.0 per cent), followed by 'effective commitment to management strategy' (56.5 per cent), and 'virtual voicing of manager opinions' (42.2 per cent). Unions can strengthen their rela-tionships with white-collar workers by acting as a voice for the management, as representatives of all employees.

Third, is to reinforce the commitment of the union in forming careers, especially to establish a flexible personnel system that can create a whole range of choices for careers other than participating in the competition to climb the corporate ladder. Although we already have some movements to form heterogeneous career systems by establishing multi-layer person-nel systems and specialist systems, the new systems may gradually turn into another selection mechanism. So, it is the mission of the labour unions to curb the management to prevent this from happening. The key points will be, first, to structure a career system that can achieve profes-sional authority and challenge without promotion to a manager position. Second, to guarantee the right to choose from various courses the one that best fits the individual's aptitudes and wishes. The latter will become especially important during the early stages of career formation. Since most employees are members of unions at this stage, the labour union can expect its influence to widen the individual choice in the career courses selection.

Fourth, is to grasp the needs of specialists and to take necessary mea-sures. Engineers have a more apparent trend to 'specialist orientation' and are not always of the traditional promotion-type corporate order. This specialist technician group is expanding the fastest in the recent trend towards expansion of the white-collar group. It will thus be an important strategy for labour unions to provide a voice for their interests, and to encourage their positive involvement in union activities.[5]

Fifth, is to strengthen the efforts to allow enhancement of individual skills and self-improvement. In the recent trend to re-question the rela-tionship between individuals and the company, and the need to enhance skill and self-improvement efforts, many union members expect their union to take a positive part in assisting such needs (RIALS, 1994b). Responding to such needs can also contribute to enhancing the reliability of the labour union. One big factor that allowed success in organizing white-collar workers in Sweden was the training system, which was directly conducted by the union (Cole, 1965). In Sweden, the training system is more advanced in unions with higher skills. Participating in the training programme of the union can even influence promotion in some industries. It is understood that introducing such a Swedish training system is difficult in the Japanese corporate training system, but there are certainly lessons to be learned for unions to get positively involved in training sessions.

Finally, I would like to describe the strategic meaning of white-collar workers in the labour union movement. The role of white-collar workers was not minor in the Japanese post-war labour union movement. Many of them stood at the forefront of the labour union movement in the post-war expansion of the labour unions, and were instrumental in incorporating the social reform characteristics of the pre-war union movement, as well as forming collective agreement relationships with the management. In the process of Japan's rapid growth, when employment increased enormously, the white-collar workers in unions were relegated to a somewhat sympathetic bystander position. In recent years, the involvement of white-collar workers in the labour union movement has intensified. Today's labour unions have more and more white-collar workers and university graduates, with university graduate white-collar workers being a majority in the thirties age group (Japan Institute of Labour, 1992). These were the people who led the 'union identity' reconstruction movement that became active in the late 1980s.

Membership of both white- and blue-collar workers in a single labour union can also cause conflicts of interest between job descriptions. In fact, there have been cases of unions being disorganized into first and second unions, as a result of such conflicts. Japanese enterprise unions have since learned how to avoid such serious rifts caused by differences of interest. This was made possible by the abolishment of the old status system, which separated the white-collar workers from the blue-collar workers, in the process of post-war democratization. The sense of class has become weak, and the social distance between the two was no longer recognized. It is recommended that labour unions structure the wide-ranging solidarity of employees by taking advantage of this tradition.

White-collar workers can introduce a rational and deliberate programme into the labour union movement, with wider viewpoints and deeper insights. There is no need to emphasize the importance of integrating white-collar workers into the labour union movement, as permanent, not temporary members, making the most of their skills for the better future of the unions.

NOTES

1. This study was conducted by asking 'how important is each item for you to work with a challenge?' and selecting the answer from the following three: 'very important', 'important' and 'not important'. This degree of importance can also be used as the weight to calculate a general satisfaction index, but as it was difficult to find a non-arbitrary weight reference, the arithmetic average of satisfaction for each item was used.
2. TSI (Total Satisfaction Index) is estimated by the following model:

$$TSI_{ijklmnop} = U + S1_i + S2_j + S3_k + S4_l + S5_m + S6_n + S7_o + S8_p + E$$

   where U : constant term
   $S1_i$: category score for ith category of Variable 1 (Age)
   $S2_j$: category score for jth category of Variable 2 (Current position)
   $S3_k$: category score for kth category of Variable 3 (Future prospects)
   $S4_l$: category score for lth category of Variable 4 (Career orientation)
   $S5_m$: category score for mth category of Variable 5 (Difference of salary)
   $S6_n$: category score for nth category of Variable 6 (Contribution and salary)
   $S7_o$: category score for oth category of Variable 7 (Annual income)
   $S8_p$: category score for pth category of Variable 8 (Company type)
   E : error term

3. Marginal Sum of Squares is the proportion of variance by each explanatory variable when the entire variance of dependent variable is 100. For example, the MSS of the first variable (age) is calculated as follows:

$$MSS_1 = \frac{C_2 C_3 C_4 C_5 C_6 C_7 C_8 \cdot \sum_{j=1}^{C1} (S_{1j}^2)}{C_2 C_3 C_4 C_5 C_6 C_7 C_8 \cdot \sum_{j=1}^{C1} (S_{1j}^2) + C_1 C_3 C_4 C_5 C_6 C_7 C_8 \cdot \sum_{j=1}^{C2} (S_{2j}^2) + \cdots + C_1 C_2 C_3 C_4 C_5 C_6 C_7 \cdot \sum_{j=1}^{C8} (S_{8j}^2)}$$

   where C_i : The number of categories of each explanatory variable.
   S_{ij} : Category score corresponding to each category of explanatory variable.

4. Mills's argument does not always evaluate why the labour union exists as such (see Dahrendorf, 1956). It must also be noted that blue-collar workers are the subject here. However, his 'institutional channel' is a forerunner of the view of the labour union as a 'collective voice' organization.
5. According to a survey of engineers, conducted by Matsushita Electric Labour Union, R&D Branch, 60.5 per cent gave 'service' as a 'factor for challenge'. Only 6.3 per cent gave 'promotion' as a driving factor. The Branch proposed the improvement of the status of the specialist system and the creation of a multiple career system (Koichiro, 1994).

REFERENCES

Cole, Robert E. (1965), 'Organization of White-collar Workers in Sweden: The Cause of its Success', *Bulletin of the Japan Institute of Labour*, **7** (1), 50–53.

Dahrendorf Ralf (1956), *Industrie und Betriebssoziologie*, (The sociology of industry and occupation), Berlin: Walter de Gruyer.

Freeman, R. and J. Medoff (1984), *What Do Unions Do?*, New York: Basic Books.

Inoki, Takenori (1994), 'Chuukan Kanrishoku Wo Mamoru Soshiki Wo' (The need to create a voice mechanism for middle managers), *Nihon Keizai Shinbun*, 29 March.

Japan Institute of Labour (1992), *Yunion Rihda No Ishiki To Kyaria Keisei* (Career formation of the union leaders), Tokyo: Japan Institute of Labour.

Japan Institute of Labour (1994), *Soshikinai Kyaria No Bunseki: White Collar No Shoshin Kozo* (The analysis of organizational career: promotion structure of white-collar workers), Tokyo: Japan Institute of Labour.

JEIU (1994), 'Chuken Kumiai Ni Okeru Jimu Gijutsu Rodosha No Ido To Kyaria Keisei' (Career formation of white-collar workers), *JEIU Research Bulletin* No. 270, 15–16

Koichiro, Imano (ed.) and Matsushita Electric Labour Union R&D Branch (1994), *Yomigaere White Collar* (Towards the revitalization of white-collar workers), Tokyo: Kohgyo-chosaki.

Labour Issue Research Centre (1993), *Roudou Kumiai No Gendaiteki Yakuwari To Union Rihda* (The role of contemporary trade unionism and the union leaders), Tokyo: Labour Issues Research Centre.

Mills, C. Wright (1948), *The New Men of Power: America's Labour Leaders*, New York: Harcourt Brace & Company, p. 9.

Mills, C. Wright (1951), *White Collar: The American Middle Class*, Oxford: Oxford University Press.

Nihon Sesansei Honbu (1990), *Doitsu No Gijutsusha, Nihon No Gijutsusha* (German engineers, Japanese engineers), Tokyo: Nihon Seisansei Honbu.

Nihon Seisansei Honbu (1991), *Beikoku No Gijutsusha, Nihon No Gijutsusha* (American engineers, Japanese engineers), Tokyo: Nihon Seisansei Honbu.

Okamoto, Hideaki (1964), 'White Collar No Rodo Kumiai' (White-collar unions) and 'Nihon No White Collar' (Japanese white-collar workers), in Kitagawa Takayosi and Okamoto, Hideaki, *White Collar*, Tokyo: Kawade-Shobo, pp. 101–260.

RIALS (1994a), *Rodo Kumiai Ni Okeru Kumun No Han-i Ni Kansuru Chosakenkyuu* (Survey of union member coverage in the corporate structure), Tokyo: RIALS.

RIALS (1994b), *Chuukounennreisha No Jiko Keihatsu Ni Kannsuru Chousa Kenkyuu Houkokusho* (Educational needs of Japanese white-collar workers), Tokyo: RIALS.

Sano, Yoko and Takashi Kawakita (1993), *White Collar No Kyaria Kanri* (Career management of white-collar workers) Tokyo: Chuo-Keizaisha.

11. Conclusions

Toshiaki Tachibanaki

This book has analysed many issues associated with promotion in the firm, and adopted various methods to investigate them. It is risky, and almost impossible to attempt to write a summary based on these studies because we obtained so many results. Also, there remain some differences in several propositions and opinions among the writers of this book. It would be useful, nevertheless, to present a very brief summary for readers, by picking up several selected topics which are recognized to be important for understanding Japanese business. Towards the end of the introduction, we described six subjects, which have formed the basis for the investigation in this book, and a brief section will be devoted to each subject, respectively. This brief summary is based on the findings of all the chapters in this book. Thus, it reflects the propositions and opinions of respective authors, but it also includes some personal preferences of the editor.

11.1 WHO IS PROMOTED, AND WHAT IS THE MECHANISM OF PROMOTION?

It is necessary to distinguish between promotion to top executive positions (board members) and promotion to middle management positions (department heads). Chapter 1 (Tachibanaki), Chapter 2 (Noda), Chapter 3 (Itoh and Teruyama) and Chapter 8 (Ohashi), analysed the former, while Chapter 4 (Kobayashi), Chapter 5 (Itoh and Teruyama), Chapter 6 (Mitani) and Chapter 7 (Matsushige) investigated the latter.

The following results were obtained for top executives. First, Tachibanaki found that the most important factor was individual performance in business activity. Steady effort made by workers, encountering good managers, and luck were also important. At the same time, one's lifestyle must be devoted to company life almost exclusively, and a strong desire for promotion is required. Second, both Noda, and Itoh and Teruyama, obtained the result that the factors were different between top executives in larger firms and those in smaller firms. This arises from the fact that top executives in larger firms are normally appointed through internal promotion, while those in smaller firms are appointed through both internal promotion and external transfer from parent firms or financial institutions. In other words, the difference between internal experience and external experience matters. Third, the graduates of prestigious universities have a higher probability of achieving top executive positions than those of other universities, as Tachibanaki, Noda and Ohashi proposed.

The following observations were obtained regarding promotion to middle manager positions (department heads). First, Kobayashi found that the most important element was superior individual performance in business activity. The next element is age and tenure, and finally the influence of managers. The economic interpretation of the effect of age and tenure will be made later. The complicated and delicate element is the manager's influence. It may be because of the name of the appointee's university, favouritism, or truly superior performance and productivity of the employee. Although it is difficult to identify the essential and intrinsic item among the above three, the real story will be a mixture of the three items. Second, Matsushige found that the selection year (that is, the starting year) of promotion to section head was about 10 years after the entry to the firm, and that promotion to department head was about 13–14 years in large firms. During this period, differentiation in promotion possibility among employees who started their career in the firm in the same year does not appear. A more interesting observation is that most of these employees recognize who is outstanding and productive, and who is likely to be promoted to a higher position among colleagues during the first few years after entering the firm.

How can we interpret this? The observation implies that employees perceive future candidates for promotion among themselves very early, and that the firm does not recognize them. Some say that the firm is aware, but whether it is or not, a more crucial element is that during the early stages of an employee's career, the firm has not differentiated any promotion possibility among employees who started with the company in the same year.

First, the fact that employees can identify who is outstanding and therefore who is a future candidate for promotion after only a few years' experience implies that employees' intrinsic capability and training in university education, or only a few years' working history in the firm, are important to demonstrate their calibre. This is an astonishing result because there has been a belief in Japan that it is impossible to identify employees who are outstanding after only a few years' working history in the firm. Other firms wanted to observe individual performance in business activity for a considerably longer period.

Second, the principal motivation for putting off promotion (that is, late promotion) lies in the fear that employees who fail to be promoted would lose their incentive to work. Firms wanted to retain their employees' incentive by adopting a late promotion policy, because those people can hope for possible promotion in future. This is the situation in Japan. The United States adopted the opposite policy, namely, early promotion, to foster very high and strong work incentives in employees who have been selected for early promotion. US firms believe that these employees will make very significant contributions to the firm.

Third, it is possible to recommend a policy such that employees, who are found to be less promising during their early career, leave the firm as early as possible, so as to reduce the consequences of a possible mismatch. It would be feasible to find more suitable jobs and firms for them, if they make the change early in their professional life. Finally, it should be desirable to prepare a reconsideration system for those workers who have been found to be less promising. Unfortunately, this issue is not investigated here.

11.2 THE SENIORITY SYSTEM AND WORK-INCENTIVE THEORY: THEORETICAL AND EMPIRICAL DISCUSSIONS

Chapter 6 (Mitani) and Chapter 5 (Itoh and Teruyama) provided useful analyses in these subjects. According to Mitani, the following four factors affect the work-incentive of workers: (i) workers' risk-aversion parameter, (ii) the effect of worker performance on the firm's business performance, (iii) reliability and fairness of assessments of worker performance, and (iv) reaction to effort incentive. The elements that have some influence on these four factors are worker attributes (age, education, and so on), industry and a promotion system based on seniority or merit. It is concluded that Japanese firms have constructed a nearly ideal system, by combining the optimum contribution of each element. The important observation is that such a combination strategy differs not only from firm to firm but also from industry to industry.

Itoh and Teruyama also found that the system induced the highest work incentive in workers, although the method of their study is different from Mitani's because they were concerned with the difference in wage payments among workers. Itoh and Teruyama suggested the following three hypotheses to explain the economic rationality of the Japanese type of seniority principle: work incentive, human capital and insurance contract. They found that it was impossible to select the most plausible hypothesis among the three.

The overall finding based on both Mitani, and Itoh and Teruyama is that the Japanese system of promotion and wage determination is effective for raising the work incentive of workers. It is worthwhile to repeat that this was also verified in this study for white-collar workers, whose average labour productivity is supposed to be lower by international standards, although that of blue-collar workers is believed to be higher, because of their higher work incentive. It is necessary to investigate further to confirm this result because it includes some contradictions to popular belief. In particular, it would be necessary to compare the present result with the result for non-manufacturing industries, or for smaller firms which are understood to have inferior average labour productivity.

11.3 ARE CAREERS OF WHITE-COLLAR WORKERS BROADER, AND DO THEY CHANGE THEIR POSITION IN THE FIRM MORE FREQUENTLY THAN BELIEVED PREVIOUSLY? WHAT IS THE ROLE OF A PROFESSIONAL JOB?

Chapter 1 (Tachibanaki) analysed the career of top executives, while Chapter 7 (Matsushige) and Chapter 9 (Tomita) analysed it for white-collar workers, including middle managers (department heads), in general. It is vital to distinguish between these two levels in the following sense. First, the career pattern of top executives is the story only of successful workers. There are many employees among their contemporaries who have not been promoted to top executive. Second, the career pattern of middle managers has not finished yet. It will continue. It other words, it represents only the intermediary stage of the career.

Tachibanaki made the following observations. First, top executives experienced, relatively speaking, many different sections, departments and directorates. Second, jobs in sales, production and technology, and general administration (that is, indirect managerial jobs) at an early stage of one's career and in middle management, lead to a higher probability of being promoted to top executive in the future.

Matsushige, Tomita and others found that the career pattern was narrower (that is, a much smaller number of different job experiences) than believed. Also, Matsushige proposed that transfer among establishments, transfer among directorates or departments within one establishment, or temporary transfer to subsidiary firms should also be taken into account when a change in jobs in the firm is discussed.

Tomita found that white-collar workers who studied science and technology tend to prefer professional or specialized, to managerial or administrative, jobs. Thus, their career pattern is narrower than that of non-science graduates. It is suggested that treatment of workers who do not occupy managerial and administrative positions, willingly or unwillingly, is one of the most important policy reforms in the field of human resources management. The concluding section of this chapter will propose such a reform.

11.4 ROLE AND MANAGEMENT PRINCIPLES OF TOP EXECUTIVES AND CORPORATE GOVERNANCE

The role and management principles of top executives were examined in Chapter 1 (Tachibanaki), Chapter 2 (Noda), Chapter 3 (Itoh and Teruyama) and Chapter 8 (Ohashi). The consensus from these studies suggests the following. The top priority should be to keep employees in the firm. Second in importance is the growth of the firm, and strengthening the relative position of the firm in the industry. Finally, enjoying the confidence of shareholders and financial institutions is considered to be very marginally important.

It was found by Itoh and Teruyama that the role and management principles differ in relation to the size of firm, and also that opinions about management goals vary considerably among top executives such as the president, vice-president, managing executives, ordinary executives, and others. Auditors have special roles. The difference in responsibility even among top executives is an important reason for having such different management principles. Tachibanaki and Noda estimated the salary function for top executives, and found that salaries vary considerably according to the position of top executives, as do the ways in which salaries are determined.

The empirical results from the analysis of the role and management principles of top executives varied partly because the concerns and purposes, as well as the methods for investigation, differed among the chapters. Therefore, the findings and propositions are different, and the evaluation of Japanese business and corporate governance is slightly different among the authors. Also, it is important to point out that the difference in the size of firm cannot be ignored. Consequently, I avoid proposing any solid conclusion on this subject, and each chapter will have to be referred to separately. It is possible, nevertheless, to suggest that the Japanese firm can be represented by the notion of labour-managed firms, or firms which are managed by employees (that is, by the representatives of the employees who are, in fact, top executives and have been promoted internally). The last point is the editor's personal judgement.

11.5 PRESTIGIOUS VERSUS NON-PRESTIGIOUS UNIVERSITIES, AND SCIENCE VERSUS HUMANITIES GRADUATES.

Chapter 1 (Tachibanaki), Chapter 2 (Noda) and Chapter 8 (Ohashi) examined the effect of the difference between prestigious and other universities, while Chapter 9 (Tomita) focused on the difference between science and humanities graduates in university education.

All the studies in this book emphasized the advantages for graduates of prestigious universities on the promotion probability to top executive. Ohashi focused on this subject, and presented various investigations. He concluded that the economic rationality for this is explained by the screening hypothesis of education rather than by the human capital theory. Ohashi proposed some other factors such as social stratification, which is a reflection of the name of one's university, and a propensity to form groups on the basis of favouritism. Although the economic interpretation is quite straightforward, social stratification and propensity to form groups is related to human nature, which cannot be easily judged as fair or unfair.

Tomita found that it would be impossible to confirm that the probability of achieving the position of top executive is lower for science and technology graduates than for humanities and social science majors, in contrast to popular belief. More importantly, it was found that workers who studied science and technology prefer professionally orientated positions and become specialists rather than being managerially orientated people who seek promotion on the vertical hierarchy.

11.6 THE ROLE OF SPECIALISTS AND OF TRADE UNIONS

Chapter 9 (Tomita) and Chapter 10 (Suzuki) discussed this issue. These two authors proposed that there are two different classes of white-collar employees, those who prefer specialist jobs, and those who prefer managerial and administrative jobs. Broadly speaking, the majority of science graduates prefer the former, while the majority of humanities graduates prefer the latter. Obviously, there are a significant number of exceptions regarding the difference in preference between science and humanities majors.

Suzuki found that the degree of satisfaction regarding working life for white-collar workers would be higher if their career prospects were clearly anticipated, and if their desire for career patterns was fulfilled. Therefore, it should be desirable to have a human resource management policy such that white-collar employees who prefer specialist jobs should be engaged in that capacity, and those who prefer managerial and administrative jobs should be employed in those fields. It is true, however, that many white-collar employees wish to be promoted to at least middle management (department head), and prefer to be treated such that the discrepancy in wage differentials is not so large. These preferences are somewhat self-centred, and therefore it is not easy to prepare a human resource management policy which satisfies all white-collar employees. Also, such a policy may not be efficient from the point of the view of the firm.

What kind of human resource management programmes would be preferable? The following is my own personal opinion which did not receive any support from the other writers of this book. Competition for higher positions on the vertical line of promotion is fierce, so employees who prefer such a vertical line of hierarchy must work very hard, and therefore show strong determination. Successful employees can climb up the vertical hierarchical ladder to department head, director, and finally top executive. Related to this subject, Suzuki found that the degree of satisfaction for those white-collar employees was higher because they like jobs where they can take the initiative, and which are associated with leadership, planning and command. Simply, they achieved the prestigious position of strong leadership, and are satisfied with it. It is a success story. Therefore, since it is likely that they will receive considerable remuneration in the form of non-pecuniary payment, such as prestige, satisfaction and golf club membership, it is not necessary to increase their salary so significantly.

Those who were unsuccessful in the competition for promotion, and those who prefer specialist jobs, are expected to increase their degree of professional knowledge much further, and to become workers who are productive in the business activity of their field. Thus, considerably wide wage differentials between specialists who are very productive and those who are not, should be accepted as fair. In this case a fair assessment system, of course, must be prepared to justify such wide wage differentials. One reason for proposing the above policy comes from the fact that it is easier to assess performance in professional and specialist jobs than in managerial jobs. A typical example is research and development.

Those who were unsuccessful in professional and specialist or managerial and administrative job activities, have to accept relatively lower wage payments. Firms cannot pay higher wages to people who are not effective or productive. One justification for proposing the above policy is that the salary paid to those on a lower scale is still above the minimum subsistence level because there is a relatively high average wage level which reflects the strong Japanese economy. Another justification is that those employees do not complain about their relatively lower wages because it is understand that they work to ensure a decent standard of living, and do not want their private life to be dominated by their job.

Among many policy recommendations proposed above, the one which might receive criticism from the public is probably that which does not recommend a higher salary for the successful candidates in the promotion competition for managerial and administrative jobs. The reason for such a criticism is that it conflicts with the proposition of the tournament theory, which recommends considerably higher wages for the winners. My reasoning is that the winners will receive both non-pecuniary remuneration and pecuniary (that is, monetary) wages, and the sum total is already high. If the amount of non-pecuniary remuneration is high enough, it should not be necessary to increase monetary wages significantly. Of course, if the amount of non-pecuniary renumeration is low, the amount of monetary wage should be raised. Some people would not accept this proposition, and more discussion on the subject is desirable.

The role of trade unions is important. Suzuki, for example, proposed that the membership should be extended to include white-collar employees who have not been promoted, and promoted employees who do not have any subordinates. He emphasized the failure of the trade unions which ignored or, at least did not consider, the rights of promoted white-collar employees who cannot be regarded as representing the management point of view.

Finally, one overall conclusion in relation to the title of this book, namely 'who runs Japanese business?', and that is, Japanese firms are run by employees, and the winners (that is, top executives or board members) of the fierce competition for internal promotion, which has been examined in detail in this book, run Japanese business for their employees.

Index

Abraham, K.G. 148n, 153
academic background 89, 91, 112–20
  see also prestigious universities
accounting and finance occupations
  career patterns of top executives in
    2, 4, 5
  see also indirect managerial
    occupations
affiliates, transfers to/from xix, 2,
    4–10, 12, 59, 165, 169, 172,
    189, 243, 245
age
  and career satisfaction 224–6, 228–30
  function qualification system and
    83–7
  and promotion xxi, 38, 57–9,
    89–91, 93–5, 126–7, 132–7,
    138–9, 143–7, 150, 155, 157,
    158, 160, 168, 169, 173,
    204–5, 211–13, 243
  and remuneration xxi, 132, 134,
    201, 215–16
  of typical managers 80–83
  and work effort 138–9, 141–3,
    145–6, 244
agency theory 36, 44, 57
Aldrich–Nelson's measure 118
annual leave
  and job satisfaction 206–8, 223,
    230, 232–4
  unused 91, 92, 94, 232
    and work effort 127, 140,
    142–5, 147
annual salary systems 126
Aoki, M. 23, 42, 50, 54n, 56
aptitude tests 153
arbitration, by top management 42,
    50, 56
assessment systems
  as decisive factor for promotion 93–4
  external factors affecting 126,
    128–30

factors important for 114–15,
    126–7, 129–37, 147
  and hours worked 127, 140, 142–8
  and incentives for transfers 203–4
  measurement issues xxi, 127,
    128–31, 148
  objectivity of xxi, 100, 115, 127,
    130, 131, 134, 137, 138
  previous results of 123–4n
  satisfaction with 115, 117–19, 121,
    126–7, 134, 140, 147, 151, 244
  and satisfaction with salary
    216–17, 218
  self–assessment xxi–xxii
  in United States 153
auditors xvii, xix
  academic background of 179
  age of 57–9
  experience of 57–9
  goals and abilities of 69–74, 76, 246
  remuneration of 31–2
automotive companies
  careers and work attitudes of
    engineers in 196
  career satisfaction in 226, 228
  decisive factors necessary for
    promotion in 92–3
  employees' impressions about
    promotion in 87–90
  function qualification system of 83–7
  incentives in 98, 105–7, 109–15,
    117, 127, 132–6, 138, 141–3
  manager profile in 80–82
  seniority system reconsidered in 95
  survey of white–collar employees in
    xxv

backup by superiors 91–4, 123n, 124n,
    133, 135, 138–40, 143, 144–6,
    151, 188, 191–3, 243
Baker, G.P. 122n

251